L'Homme.
Europäische Zeitschrift für Feministische Geschichtswissenschaft

Herausgegeben von
Ingrid Bauer/Wien und Salzburg, Anna Becker/Aarhus, Bożena Chołuj/
Warschau, Maria Fritsche/Trondheim, Christa Hämmerle/Wien,
Gabriella Hauch/Wien, Almut Höfert/Oldenburg, Anelia Kassabova/Sofia,
Claudia Kraft/Wien, Ulrike Krampl/Tours, Christina Lutter/Wien,
Sandra Maß/Bochum, Claudia Opitz-Belakhal/Basel, Kristina Schulz/
Neuchâtel, Xenia von Tippelskirch/Frankfurt am Main,
Heidrun Zettelbauer/Graz

Initiiert und mitbegründet von Edith Saurer (1942–2011)

Wissenschaftlicher Beirat
Angiolina Arru/Rom, Sofia Boesch-Gajano/Rom, Susanna Burghartz/Basel,
Kathleen Canning/Ann Arbor, Jane Caplan/Oxford, Krassimira Daskalova/
Sofia, Barbara Duden/Hannover, Ayşe Durakbaşa/Istanbul, Ute Frevert/Berlin,
Ute Gerhard/Bremen, Francisca de Haan/Budapest, Hanna Hacker/Wien,
Karen Hagemann/Chapel Hill, Daniela Hammer-Tugendhat/Wien,
Karin Hausen/Berlin, Waltraud Heindl/Wien, Dagmar Herzog/New York,
Claudia Honegger/Bern, Isabel Hull/Ithaca, Marion Kaplan/New York,
Christiane Klapisch-Zuber/Paris, Gudrun-Axeli Knapp/Hannover,
Daniela Koleva/Sofia, Margareth Lanzinger/Wien, Brigitte Mazohl/Innsbruck,
Hans Medick/Göttingen, Herta Nagl-Docekal/Wien, Kirsti Niskanen/
Stockholm, Helga Nowotny/Wien, Karen Offen/Stanford, Michelle Perrot/
Paris, Gianna Pomata/Bologna, Helmut Puff/Ann Arbor, Florence Rochefort/
Paris, Lyndal Roper/Oxford, Raffaela Sarti/Urbino, Wolfgang Schmale/Wien,
Gabriela Signori/Konstanz, Brigitte Studer/Bern, Marja van Tilburg/
Groningen, Maria Todorova/Urbana-Champaign, Claudia Ulbrich/Berlin,
Kaat Wils/Leuven

L'Homme. Europäische Zeitschrift für
Feministische Geschichtswissenschaft
36. Jg., Heft 1 (2025)

Macht(ver)Handeln um 1500

Herausgegeben von
Christina Lutter und Julia Burkhardt

V&R unipress

Inhalt

Christina Lutter und Julia Burkhardt
Editorial 9

Beiträge

Isabella Lazzarini
"Two Bodies and One Soul". Power Games between Spouses in
Northern Italian Principalities (Fifteenth Century) 19

Julia Burkhardt
Power Couples in Central Europe around 1500 35

Elodie Lecuppre-Desjardin
Foreign Princesses in the Service of the Great Principality of Burgundy:
Delegations of Power in Favour of Duchesses in the Fifteenth Century 51

Christina Lutter and Christof Muigg
Gendered Power Politics in a Nascent Empire. The Case of Maximilian of
Habsburg (1459–1519) and Mary of Burgundy (1457–1482) 67

Oliver Auge und Laura Potzuweit
Geschlechtsspezifische Ehelosigkeit und Herrschaft: Drei Beispiele aus dem
spätmittelalterlichen Ostseeraum 85

Extra

Sabine Veits-Falk
Amtsärztinnen in Bosnien und Herzegowina (1892–1918). Politik, Medizin,
Kultur und Geschlecht 99

Forum

Julia Heinemann
Verwandtsein als politische Ressource für Mütter, Söhne und Schwestern.
Zur Relationalität von Herrschaft, Verwandtschaft und Geschlecht in der
französischen Monarchie im 16. Jahrhundert 115

Christina Antenhofer
Medieval and Early Modern Gendered Power Politics from the Perspective of
Material Culture 123

Aus den Archiven

Carina Siegl
Geschlecht und Herrschaftshandeln im Spiegel der Quellen der Hofstaaten
von Maria von Habsburg und Anna Jagiełło (1515–1520) 135

Ulrike Marlow
„Die gute Tante war der ganzen Familie ein so reger geistiger Mittelpunkt …"
Zur mangelnden Sichtbarkeit weiblicher adliger Lebensläufe am preußischen
Hof im 19. Jahrhundert 141

Rezensionen

Sandro Guzzi-Heeb
Andrea Griesebner u. Evdoxios Doxiadis (eds.), Gender and Divorce in
Europe: 1600–1900. A Praxeological Perspective 147

Vanina Kopp
Theresa Earenfight, Catherine of Aragon. Infanta of Spain, Queen of
England 150

Christof Muigg
Christina Antenhofer, Die Familienkiste. Mensch-Objekt-Beziehungen im
Mittelalter und in der Renaissance 153

Christof Rolker
Ruth Mazo Karras, Thou Art the Man. The Masculinity of David in the
Christian and Jewish Middle Ages 156

Frederieke Maria Schnack
Gabriela Signori u. Claudia Zey (Hg.), Regentinnen und andere
Stellvertreterfiguren. Vom 10. bis zum 15. Jahrhundert 159

Jörg Schwarz
Andrea Stieldorf, Linda Dohmen, Irina Dumitrescu u. Ludwig D. Morenz
(Hg.), Geschlecht macht Herrschaft – Interdisziplinäre Studien zu
vormoderner Macht und Herrschaft 162

Abstracts 167

Anschriften der Autor*innen 171

Editorial

Wie und wo wurde in Europa um 1500 Politik gemacht? Wer traf aus herrschaftlichen Positionen heraus Entscheidungen? Wer konnte solche Positionen einnehmen und welche Personen wurden in die Aushandlung und Kommunikation dieser Entscheidungen eingebunden? In welchen Kontexten und an welchen Orten wurden Herrschaftsansprüche geltend gemacht und repräsentiert? Kurz gesagt: Wie wurde Macht verhandelt und ausgeübt? Derartige Fragen haben die Geschichtswissenschaften seit langem beschäftigt; sie werden allerdings aus kulturwissenschaftlicher Perspektive seit einigen Jahrzehnten in veränderter Weise wahrgenommen. Diskutiert werden die vielfältigen Formen politischer Kommunikation, die Bedeutung von Kooperation und Konsens sowie die symbolischen Ausdrucksformen politischer Macht einschließlich der materiellen Dimensionen von Herrschaft.[1] Ein besonderer Stellenwert kommt dabei dem Blick auf die zahlreichen Akteure zu, die an jeglicher Herrschaftsausübung beteiligt waren, in Städten und Gemeinden ebenso wie in geistlichen und weltlichen Fürstentümern – oft prominent, viel häufiger aber durch Überlieferung und Forschung unsichtbar gemacht oder gehalten.[2]

Dementsprechend wurden die ‚großen' Figuren der traditionellen Geschichtswissenschaft zunehmend aus dem Zentrum der Betrachtung gerückt: zunächst die ‚großen Männer' der dynastischen Historiographie, später aber auch jene ‚Ausnahmefrauen', die zwar in der älteren Frauengeschichtsschreibung nach oft jahrhundertelanger Un-

---

1 Exemplarisch sei verwiesen auf Jeroen Duindam, Dynasties. A Global History of Power, 1300–1800, Cambridge 2015; sowie auf die Beiträge in Matthias Becher, Stephan Conermann u. Linda Dohmen (Hg.), Macht und Herrschaft transkulturell. Vormoderne Konfigurationen und Perspektiven der Forschung, Göttingen 2018 und in Matthias Becher u. Katharina Gahbler (Hg.), Herrscher und Eliten zwischen Symbiose und Antagonismus. Kommunizieren in vormodernen Herrschaftsstrukturen, Göttingen 2023.
2 Vgl. bereits Alf Lüdtke (Hg.), Herrschaft als soziale Praxis. Historische und sozial-anthropologische Studien, Stuttgart 1991. Exemplarisch sind Peter Blickle, Resistance, Representation, and Community, Oxford 1997; Wim Blockmans, Constructing a Sense of Community in Rapidly Growing European Cities in the Eleventh to Thirteenth Centuries, in: Historical Research, 83, 222 (2010), 575–587; Susan Reynolds, Kingdoms and Communities in Western Europe 900–1300, Oxford 1997.

sichtbarkeit verdienstvolle Berücksichtigung erfuhren, wodurch jedoch oft abermals ein doppelt binäres Bild entstand. Einzelne außergewöhnliche weibliche Herrscherpersönlichkeiten standen nun der Mehrheit ihrer männlichen Pendants gegenüber, die vielfach stillschweigend als die Norm politischer Entscheidungsträger verstanden wurden.³ In diesem bereits verzerrten Rahmen wurden individuelle Herrscher oder Herrscherinnen auf ihren politischen Erfolg, ihre ‚Herrschaftsstärke' oder ihren ‚Einflussreichtum' hin untersucht. Dabei blieben aber die langfristigen und vielschichtigen Traditionen und Muster, die solchen Zuschreibungen zugrunde liegen, und ihre immer auch geschlechtlichen Kodierungen tendenziell im Hintergrund, wurden ausgeblendet oder zumindest nicht systematisch als analytische Kategorien thematisiert.

Neue Perspektiven auf die Kategorie Geschlecht in ihren komplexen Bezügen zu anderen Kategorien der Zugehörigkeit und damit zu sozialen Ein- und Ausschlussprozessen fanden im Zuge der zuerst sozial-, dann kulturwissenschaftlichen Wende zunächst aus Perspektiven ‚von unten' auf bislang verborgen oder unbeachtet gebliebene Personen und Gruppen Berücksichtigung.⁴ Rezente Zugänge wie die Kulturgeschichte des Politischen oder die neue Institutionengeschichte haben dazu beigetragen, auch die Geschichte des Herrschens multidimensional unter konsequenter Einbeziehung der Kategorie Geschlecht, aber nicht mit ausschließlichem Fokus auf sie, zu erzählen.⁵

An diesem Punkt setzt das vorliegende Themenheft an und fragt in vergleichender Perspektive nach dem Zusammenwirken von Herrschaft und Geschlecht in Europa um 1500. Uns interessiert, mit welchen kulturellen und sozialen Erwartungshaltungen vormoderne Herrscherinnen und Herrscher konfrontiert waren, wie sie die ihnen zur Verfügung stehenden Handlungsspielräume nutzten oder ausbauten und wie sie dabei

---

3 Programmatisch etwa Theresa Earenfight, Without the Persona of the Prince: Kings, Queens and the Idea of Monarchy in Late Medieval Europe, in: Gender & History, 19, 1 (2007), 1–21; Heather J. Tanner (Hg.), Medieval Elite Women and the Exercise of Power, 1100–1400. Moving beyond the Exceptionalist Debate, Cham 2019. Für eine noch grundsätzlichere Kritik jenseits herrschaftlicher Eliten vgl. z. B. Gianna Pomata, Partikulargeschichte und Universalgeschichte – Bemerkungen zu einigen Handbüchern der Frauengeschichte, in: L'Homme. Zeitschrift für Feministische Geschichtswissenschaft (L'Homme. Z. F. G.), 2, 1 (1991), 5–44.
4 Pioniercharakter hat Natalie Zemon Davis, Gesellschaft und Geschlechter. Studien über Familie, Religion und die Wandlungsfähigkeit des sozialen Körpers, Berlin 1976, rev. ed., 1986. Der bahnbrechende konzeptuelle Entwurf stammt von Joan Wallach Scott, Gender: A Useful Category of Historical Analysis, in: American Historical Review, 91, 5 (1986), 1053–1075; für eine rezente Einführung vgl. Claudia Opitz-Belakhal, Geschlechtergeschichte, 2., aktualisierte und erweiterte Auflage, Frankfurt am Main 2018.
5 Vgl. Theresa Earenfight, A Lifetime of Power: Beyond Binaries of Gender, in: Tanner, Medieval Elite Women, wie Anm. 3, 271–293; Christina Lutter, Herrschaft und Geschlecht. Relationale Kategorien zur Erforschung fürstlicher Handlungsspielräume, in: Matthias Becher, Achim Fischelmanns u. Katharina Gahbler (Hg.), Vormoderne Herrschaft. Geschlechterdimensionen und Spannungsfelder, Göttingen 2021, 199–231; Gabriela Signori u. Claudia Zey (Hg.), Regentinnen und andere Stellvertreterfiguren. Vom 10. bis zum 15. Jahrhundert, Berlin 2023.

mit strukturellen und personellen Veränderungen in ihren Einflussbereichen umgingen. Für diese übergeordneten Fragen empfiehlt sich eine geographisch und chronologisch breite Herangehensweise ebenso wie eine systematisch vergleichende Perspektive.

In zahlreichen europäischen Königreichen oder fürstlichen Herrschaftsgebieten avancierten im Laufe des Mittelalters erb- und wahlrechtliche Argumente bei der Herrschaftserhebung ebenso wie deren längerfristige Behauptung zu den wichtigsten, bisweilen freilich mit anderen konkurrierenden Legitimationsmustern.[6] Gerade in strittigen Nachfolgesituationen oder politischen Krisenmomenten mussten unter Bezugnahme auf vielfältige Aspekte Herrschaftsansprüche geltend gemacht, begründet und ihre Anerkennung verhandelt werden. Politische Unterstützung – gegründet auf Verwandtschaft, Freundschaft und andere Allianzen – wurde durch persönliche Verbindungen immer wieder neu aktiviert und ausgehandelt.[7] Vormoderne Herrschaft kann schon deshalb niemals nur durch den Blick auf die vermeintlich ‚großen' Einzelfiguren verstanden werden. Vielmehr ist komplexes Herrschaftshandeln – unabhängig vom Geschlecht der Akteure – immer in mehrfach relationalen Dimensionen zu denken: Im kooperativen oder auch konfliktiven Miteinander wurde das gestaltet, was später als *die* Herrschaft einzelner Personen wahrgenommen wurde.[8]

Um zu eruieren, welche Rolle die Kategorie Geschlecht in der praktischen Dimension vormoderner Herrschaftsausübung spielte, sind deshalb stets die Beziehungsgeflechte einer größeren Anzahl Herrschaft mitgestaltender Akteure zu berücksichtigen: Es geht mithin nicht nur um einzelne Herrscherinnen und Herrscher, sondern stets auch um deren verwandtschaftliche Beziehungen, um generationelle und soziale Hierarchien, politische Allianzen und Konkurrenzen sowie um die Mitbestimmung politischer Eliten, die sich innerhalb dieser Beziehungskonstellationen be-

---

6 Vgl. Fredéricque Lachaud u. Michael Penman (Hg.), Making and Breaking the Rules: Succession in Medieval Europe, c. 1000 – c. 1600 / Établir et abolir les normes: la succession dans l'Europe médiévale, vers 1000 – vers 1600, Turnhout 2008; Matthias Becher (Hg.), Die mittelalterliche Thronfolge im europäischen Vergleich, Ostfildern 2017.

7 Zu den Klassikern in jeweils unterschiedlichen politischen Milieus zählen mit jeweils unterschiedlich stark ausgeprägter Berücksichtung der Kategorie Geschlecht: Gerd Althoff, Verwandte, Freunde und Getreue. Zum politischen Stellenwert der Gruppenbindungen im früheren Mittelalter, Darmstadt 1990; Klaus Oschema, Freundschaft und Nähe im spätmittelalterlichen Burgund. Studien zum Spannungsfeld von Emotion und Institution, Köln 2006; Simon Teuscher, Bekannte – Klienten – Verwandte. Sozialität und Politik in der Stadt Bern um 1500, Köln/Weimar/Wien 1998.

8 Zu diesem Argument anhand der Herrschaft Maximilians I. vgl. Christina Lutter, Gendering Late Medieval Habsburg Dynastic Politics: Maximilian I and His Social Networks, in: Austrian History Yearbook 2024, 1–16, unter: https://doi.org/10.1017/S0067237824000274; grundlegend sind Bernd Schneidmüller, Konsensuale Herrschaft. Ein Essay über Formen und Konzepte politischer Ordnung im Mittelalter, in: Paul-Joachim Heinig u. a. (Hg.), Reich, Regionen und Europa in Mittelalter und Neuzeit. Festschrift für Peter Moraw, Berlin 2000, 53–87; Julia Burkhardt, Frictions and Fictions of Community. Structures and Representations of Power in Central Europe, c. 1350–1500, in: The Medieval History Journal, 19, 2 (2016), 191–228.

sonders in Zeiten politischer Konflikte und der durch diese bedingten sozialen Dynamiken in unterschiedlichen Gremien formierten.⁹ Die so geschaffenen sozialen Bezugssysteme konnten einander bestätigen, überlappen oder auch gegenläufig wirken. So wurde zuletzt immer wieder erörtert, ob dynastische Bezugssysteme fürstlicher Familien in Europa eine größere Bindekraft zu entfalten vermochten als alternative kollektive Ordnungsmuster.¹⁰

Diese Frage gewinnt mit Blick auf die territoriale Entwicklung in Europa um 1500 an Bedeutung: Infolge von dynastischen Eheschließungen oder Erbfällen einerseits, andererseits aber auch durch zunehmend intensivierte herrschaftliche Organisation und dynamisierende, oft gewaltförmig ausgetragene Konflikte und kriegerische Expansion wurde die Zusammensetzung und Ausübung von Herrschaft komplexer. Konkurrierende Ansprüche führten in erweiterten zeitlichen und räumlichen Dimensionen expandierender Territorien zu neuen Formen geteilter und gemeinsamer Herrschaft. Langzeitkonflikte wie der ‚Hundertjährige Krieg' zwischen England und Frankreich und die ‚Italienischen Kriege' des 15. Jahrhunderts, Regentschaften und stellvertretende Herrschaften in vielen kleineren und größeren europäischen Fürstentümern, die Expansionsbestrebungen des Osmanischen Reiches seit dem 14. Jahrhundert oder der Familien der Valois, Habsburger oder Jagiellonen (um nur einige zu nennen) seit dem 15. Jahrhundert erforderten den Einsatz von mehr Personal, oftmals beiderlei Geschlechts, an der politischen Spitze von Herrschaftsgebieten.¹¹

Denn in der Regel bildeten diese Herrschaften keine zentrale Organisation aus, sondern mussten situationsabhängig die je spezifischen Machtverhältnisse in den unterschiedlichen Territorien aushandeln oder bestätigen. Das zeigen in dieser „L'Homme"-Ausgabe die fünf Haupt- und zwei Forumsbeiträge sowie einer der Archivbeiträge für unterschiedliche geographische Räume Europas exemplarisch, aber

---

9 Vgl. etwa Duncan Hardy, Associative Political Culture in the Holy Roman Empire. Upper Germany, 1346–1521, Oxford 2018; Julia Burkhardt, Assemblies in the Holy Roman Empire and the East Central European Kingdoms: A Comparative Essay on Political Participation and Representation, in: Grischa Vercamer u. Dušan Zupka (Hg.), Rulership in Medieval East Central Europe. Power, Rituals and Legitimacy in Bohemia, Hungary and Poland, Leiden/Boston 2022, 198–214; Christina Lutter u. Jonathan Lyon, (Hg.), Central Europe in the Fifteenth Century. Patterns of Conflict and Negotiation, Austrian History Yearbook, Thematic Journal Issue, 55 (2024); Julia Burkhardt u. András Vadás (Hg.), Meaning of Diversity in the Middle Ages, Hungarian Historical Review, Special Issue, 13, 2 (2024).
10 Vgl. Duindam, Dynasties, wie Anm. 1; idem u. Sabine Dabringhaus (Hg.), The Dynastic Centre and the Provinces. Agents and Interactions, Leiden 2014; Jean-Marie Moeglin, „Dynastische Ordnung" und Nation im Spätmittelalter, in: Michael Stolz (Hg.), Randgänge der Mediävistik 7. Mit Beiträgen von Pierre Monnet und Jean-Marie Moeglin, Bern 2017, 29–53.
11 Vgl. John Watts, The Making of Polities. Europe, 1300–1500, Cambridge 2009; idem, Power, Government, and Political Life, in: Isabella Lazzarini (Hg.), The Short Oxford History of Europe 5: The Later Middle Ages, Oxford 2021, 19–41; John H. Elliott, A Europe of Composite Monarchies, in: Past & Present, 137 (1992), 48–71; Charlotte Backerra, Personal Union, Composite Monarchy, and ‚Multiple Rule', in: Elena Woodacre u. a. (Hg.), The Routledge History of Monarchy, London 2019, 89–111.

gleichzeitig repräsentativ für große Teile des Kontinents. Geo- und machtpolitische Veränderungen um 1500 hatten unmittelbare Effekte auf die praktischen Handlungsspielräume, persönlichen Netzwerke und Anforderungen an Herrscher und Herrscherinnen. Ebenso bewirkten sie intensivierte konzeptuelle Diskussionen über die Grundlagen der Legitimation von Herrschaftsausübung und die Kriterien für den Zugang zu oder Ausschluss von Machtausübung. Geschlecht als dynastische ebenso wie als soziale Kategorie war ein zentrales Kriterium in diesem argumentativen Instrumentarium.[12]

Um solche Dynamiken und die damit einhergehenden Herausforderungen für fürstliche Herrschaft in vergleichender Perspektive untersuchen zu können, orientieren sich die in diesem Heft versammelten fünf Hauptbeiträge an drei zentralen Fragen:
(1) Welche einschränkenden, aber auch welche ermöglichenden Einflüsse hatten Wahrnehmungen, Rollenmodelle, Bilder und Repräsentationen von Herrschaft und Geschlecht auf die Handlungsspielräume der betroffenen Personen?
(2) Wie gestaltete sich gemeinsames Herrschaftshandeln der Schlüsselfiguren in unterschiedlichen Konstellationen?
(3) Wie handelten Herrscherinnen und Herrscher geleitet und begleitet von, mit und teilweise auch gegen Personal unterschiedlicher Herkunft, unterschiedlichen Standes, Alters und Geschlechts?

Diese Schwerpunktthemen werden in differenzerter Gewichtung in geographisch repräsentativ verorteten Fallstudien aus dem Norden Europas ebenso wie aus dessen Süden, Osten und Westen behandelt. Durch die Orientierung an einem für alle Beiträge entwickelten gemeinsamen Frageraster wird eine systematisch vergleichende europäische Perspektive gewährleistet. Eine weitere inhaltliche Verdichtung leisten die thematischen Rezensionen, welche dieses „L'Homme"-Themenheft abrunden. Um der spezifischen Dynamik europäischer Herrschaftsentwicklung um 1500 gerecht zu werden und bewusst vermeintlich klare Epochengrenzen durch die Analyse politischer Kontinuitäten wie auch Umbrüche hinterfragen zu können ebenso wie aufgrund der laufend besseren Überlieferungslage, erstreckt sich der Untersuchungszeitraum in den Beiträgen vom 14. bis zum 16. Jahrhundert.

Am Beispiel norditalienischer Fürstentümer sowie der Königreiche von Polen und Ungarn im 15. Jahrhundert gehen Isabella Lazzarini und Julia Burkhardt in ihren jeweiligen Beiträgen der Frage nach, wie Herrschaft, die stets sowohl personell markiert als auch dynastisch legitimiert war, von fürstlichen Ehepaaren ausgestaltet wurde. Lazzarini und Burkhardt zeigen einerseits, dass Fürstinnen und Königinnen abhängig von den jeweiligen rechtlichen und politischen Rahmenbedingungen eigene Formen der Herrschaftsausübung entwickelten. Andererseits ergänzten einander geschlechts-

---

12 Vgl. Heide Wunder (Hg.), Dynastie und Herrschaftssicherung in der Frühen Neuzeit. Geschlechter und Geschlecht, Berlin 2002.

spezifische Handlungsmuster und individuell entsprechend situativer Herausforderungen wahrgenommene Handlungsspielräume durch das Zusammenwirken der jeweiligen Paare. Dadurch eröffneten sich neue Partizipationsformen und Instrumentarien für die Aushandlung von Konflikten. Besonders die offenen Konstellationen der politischen Landschaft Oberitaliens in der zweiten Hälfte des 15. Jahrhunderts, die Lazzarini vergleichend diskutiert, und das Fehlen fester Muster von Herrschaftsübernahme und -ausübung ermöglichten neue Wege herrschaftlichen Handelns: Fürsten und Fürstinnen teilten Aufgaben ebenso wie sie gemeinsam agierten. Wie sie das taten, hing von einem Set von Ressourcen ab, die gleichzeitig als herrschaftsrelevante analytische Kategorien nutzbar gemacht werden können: Neben dem Geschlecht waren dies vor allem Verwandtschaftsverbindungen, die Position in der Geschwisterfolge, Lebensalter und Stand zum Zeitpunkt der Herrschaftsübernahme, Reichtum und Ausbildung und nicht zuletzt Herrschafts- und Lebensdauer.

Die Offenheit der kombinierten Nutzung dieser Ressourcen unterschied die italienischen *Signorie* des 15. Jahrhunderts im Beitrag Lazzarinis von den deutlich älteren europäischen Monarchien Ungarns und Polens, an deren Spitze die namengebenden „Power Couples" des Beitrags von Burkhardt standen. Dennoch war auch deren Herrschaftshandeln von einer großen Bandbreite von Optionen charakterisiert. Das effektive, mit dem Begriff „Power Couples" markierte gemeinschaftliche Herrschaftshandeln der von Burkhardt diskutierten zentraleuropäischen Königspaare dokumentiert einen strategischen Umgang mit geschlechtlich konnotierten Zuschreibungen und Rollenerwartungen, die zeitgenössische Beobachter in oft deutlich stärker stereotypisierter Form wiedergeben.

Die analytische Relevanz sozialer Ressourcen als mehrfach relationale Kategorien (explizit so bezeichnet im Beitrag von Lutter/Muigg und im Forumsbeitrag von Heinemann) offenbart sich auch anhand der Fragestellungen von Elodie Lecuppre-Desjardin sowie Christina Lutter und Christof Muigg, die sich den geschlechtlichen Repräsentationen von Herrschaft und deren Wirkmacht in den burgundischen Territorien im langen 15. Jahrhundert widmen. Mit Blick auf die politische und kulturelle Vielfalt dieser komplex zusammengesetzten Herrschaft untersucht Elodie Lecuppre-Desjardin über drei Generationen die Handlungsspielräume ‚auswärtiger' Ehefrauen der Herzöge von Burgund. Nehmen Lazzarini und Burkhardt das komplementäre Herrschaftshandeln von weiblichen und männlichen Akteuren auf derselben zeitlichen Ebene vergleichend in den Blick, fokussiert Lecuppre-Desjardin in diachroner Perspektive Handlungsfelder burgundischer Herzoginnen. Dabei lassen sich wiederkehrende Muster erkennen, die geschlechtsspezifische Rollenbilder bestätigen, etwa die Übernahme von Aufgaben der Vermittlung und Friedensstiftung, Patronage und ostentativer Frömmigkeit. Wenn nötig, konnte die Autorität der burgundischen Herzoginnen aber über diese Handlungsfelder hinaus wirksam werden, etwa wenn sie als Strateginnen in kriegerischen Auseinandersetzungen tätig wurden, auch wenn sie nicht selbst in den Kampf zogen.

Den Wechselwirkungen und Widersprüchen von geschlechtsspezifischen Rollenbildern und praktischen Prioritätensetzungen widmet sich der Beitrag von Christina Lutter und Christof Muigg am Beispiel der politischen Handlungsmöglichkeiten der burgundischen Erbtochter Maria und ihres nun seinerseits ‚auswärtigen' Ehemannes, Erzherzog Maximilian I., zwischen deren Eheschließung 1477 und Marias frühem Tod 1482. Anhand des direkten Vergleichs des Herrschaftshandelns zweier Personen unterschiedlichen Geschlechts wird einerseits deutlich, dass zeitgenössische Rollenerwartungen Männer ebenso wie Frauen betrafen. Männliche Herrscher waren also keineswegs die ‚unmarkierte' neutrale Norm. Ihre Ausgangspositionen und ihr Herrschaftshandeln waren ebenso wie jene von Frauen zahlreichen Erwartungen unterworfen und wurden permanent bewertet. Maximilian kam nicht als Kaiser nach Burgund, sondern als jugendlicher Erzherzog mit wenig Erfahrung. Seine Braut Maria vereinigte als Erbtochter mit beachtlichem ökonomischen Hintergrund einige Ressourcen, die zu jenen Maximilians sowohl komplementär als auch konkurrierend wahrgenommen wurden. Diese Kategorien wurden aber nicht nur in Hinblick auf Herrscherin und Herrscher verhandelt. Vielmehr zeigt der Beitrag von Lutter und Muigg den Einfluss weiterer, besonders korporativer Akteure – Ratgebergremien und Vertretungen von Territorien und Städten –, die gerade in Zeiten politischer und dynastischer Krise in *composite polities* wie den habsburgischen Niederlanden Teil einer komplexen Machtbalance wurden und ihrerseits mit teils geschlechtlich kodierten Zuschreibungen operierten.

Einen fokussierten Blick auf die Bedeutung familiärer Zusammenhänge als Ressource für die Ausgestaltung der Herrschaft von Frauen und Männern bieten der Beitrag von Oliver Auge und Laura Potzuweit sowie der Forumsbeitrag von Julia Heinemann. Beide Texte setzen sich mit zeitgenössischen Konstruktionen und Zuschreibungen von Verwandtschaft und Ehe sowie deren Verhandlung zum Erhalt von Herrschaftskontinuität auseinander. Wie grundlegend Verwandtschaft und Geschlecht als mehrfach relationale Kategorien für den Erhalt und die Weitergabe dynastischer Herrschaft interagierten, demonstriert Julia Heinemann am Beispiel der französischen Königsfamilie im 16. Jahrhundert. Sie historisiert beide Kategorien, um zu zeigen, wie Verwandt*sein* kontextabhängig für Herrschaft aktiviert und ausgestaltet werden konnte. So hatte die Durchsetzung des Prinzips der Primogenitur in der französischen Monarchie den Effekt, dass sowohl Töchter als auch alle nicht erstgeborenen Söhne rechtlich von der Herrschaftsnachfolge ausgeschlossen waren. Mütter konnten allerdings sehr wohl für ihre Söhne die Regentschaft übernehmen. Blickt man also nicht binär auf ‚Frauen' und ‚Männer', sondern auf die relationalen Kategorien Verwandtschaft und Geschlecht, so wird eine deutlich größere tatsächliche Bandbreite von Möglichkeiten praktischen Herrschaftshandelns für individuelle Personen sichtbar.

In ähnlicher Weise untersuchen Auge/Potzuweit an ausgewählten Fallbeispielen des 14. bis 16. Jahrhunderts, wieso im Ostseeraum Herrschende beiderlei Geschlechts zur

Stabilisierung der Macht ihrer Familien auf Eheverbindungen verzichteten und wie diese ‚weltliche Ehelosigkeit' von zeitgenössischen Beobachtern bewertet wurde. Abhängig von der individuellen Situation musste bewusst gewählte Ehelosigkeit nicht – wie idealtypisch zeitgenössischen, aber auch später konstruierten Wahrnehmungsmustern entsprechend – als Mangel gelesen werden, sondern sie konnte ihrerseits neue Handlungsspielräume eröffnen. Insbesondere wenn die ‚dynastischen Hausaufgaben' bereits erledigt waren und die Herrschaftsnachfolge durch Nachkommenschaft gesichert war, nutzten Frauen wie Männer den ehelosen Lebensentwurf, um ihre politischen Gestaltungsmöglichkeiten zu erweitern.

Anhand von Quellen zum höfischen Umfeld norditalienischer sowie habsburgischer Fürstinnen des 15. und 16. Jahrhunderts demonstrieren schließlich Christina Antenhofer und Carina Siegl das Potential objekt- und sozialgeschichtlicher Perspektiven auf das Thema Geschlecht und Herrschaft. Christina Antenhofer analysiert zunächst die finanzielle und materielle Ausstattung fürstlicher Bräute aus der Familie der Visconti und untersucht dann die Bedeutung von Objekten als Geschenke in unterschiedlichen politischen und sozialen Kontexten. Gezielt setzten die Visconti-Fürstinnen die ihnen zur Verfügung stehenden materiellen Ressourcen ein, um überregionale personale Netzwerke zu schaffen oder zu bestätigen, die sie politisch nutzbar machten. Wie umfassend die Quellen um 1500 auch über die höfische Umgebung von Fürstinnen Auskunft geben, ist dem Archivbericht von Carina Siegl zu entnehmen: Die von ihr untersuchten Hofstaaten der beiden jugendlichen Fürstinnen Maria von Habsburg und Anna Jagiełło lassen sich aus Hofordnungen, Hofamtslisten, Hofverwaltung und Korrespondenzen rekonstruieren. Das Material ermöglicht detaillierte Einblicke in die vielschichtigen Beziehungsgeflechte vormoderner Herrscherinnen, die – wie in Antenhofers Beispielen – oft durch Geschenke und den Umgang mit Objekten akzentuiert wurden. Damit öffnet sich der Blick auf jene Personen beiderlei Geschlechts im herrschaftlichen Umfeld, denen oft wenig Beachtung geschenkt wurde.

Gleichzeitig zeigen sich vielversprechende epochenübergreifende Parallelen zwischen dem Beitrag von Carina Siegl und jenem von Ulrike Marlow, die Lebenswege von Frauen am preußischen Hof des 19. Jahrhunderts untersucht. Sie kann zeigen, in welchem Ausmaß in der einschlägigen Forschung der „Gender-Data-Gap" durch an männlichen Lebensläufen modellierte Datenerhebungsstrukturen erzeugt und durch die Anwendung digitaler Methoden teilweise noch verstärkt wurde. Sowohl Marlow als auch Siegl machen deutlich, dass konzeptuell offenere Erhebungen und Auswertungen der umfangreichen prosopographischen Quellen aus höfischen Kontexten ebenso wie netzwerkorientierte Forschungsansätze besondere Möglichkeiten bieten, bestehende Datenlücken zu schließen. So können sowohl Karrieren von Frauen unterschiedlicher sozialer Zugehörigkeit systematischer untersucht als auch in Bezug zu Fragen der Herrschaftspraxis gesetzt werden.

Schließlich widmet sich der „L'Homme Extra"-Beitrag von Sabine Veits-Falk ebenfalls dem späten 19. Jahrhundert und skizziert Frauenkarrieren am Beispiel von Amtsärztinnen in Bosnien und Herzegowina – Gebiete, die ab 1878 unter der Verwaltung der österreichisch-ungarischen Monarchie standen. Diese Frauen gehörten zu den ersten, die in der Habsburgermonarchie als Ärztinnen praktizieren durften. Vor dem konzeptuellen Hintergrund einer innereuropäischen Kolonialgeschichte zeigt die subtile Analyse, wie die österreichisch-ungarische Monarchie situativ einen vergleichsweise offenen Umgang mit der Kategorie Geschlecht nutzte, um imperialistisch definierte zivilisatorische Zwecke in den als rückständig erachteten Gebieten durchzusetzen. Gleichzeitig beförderten diese machtpolitischen Ziele in ambivalenter Weise die individuellen Karrieren der betroffenen Frauen ebenso wie neue Berufsrollenbilder.

Wie die Beiträge zum engeren Thema dieses Heftes bieten also auch die Texte von Veits-Falk und Marlow eine Erweiterung der Perspektive über den binären analytischen Rahmen von herrschenden Frauen und Männern beziehungsweise über eindimensional hierarchisch gedachte Machtverhältnisse hinaus. Vielmehr ermöglicht auch hier das Ernstnehmen mehrfach relationaler sozialer und zugleich analytischer Kategorien ein deutlich komplexeres Bild der Ambivalenzen und auch Widersprüche, denen Repräsentationen und Praktiken von – immer auch, aber nie ausschließlich – geschlechtlich kodierter Herrschaft um 1500 ebenso wie in der Neuzeit unterworfen waren.

Christina Lutter und Julia Burkhardt

Isabella Lazzarini

"Two Bodies and One Soul". Power Games between Spouses in Northern Italian Principalities (Fifteenth Century)

In March 1459, Francesco Sforza, duke of Milan, wrote a letter in his own hand to Marquis Ludovico Gonzaga, the father of Francesco's future daughter-in-law Dorotea and the duke's captain general. Francesco Sforza only wrote in his own hand when it was absolutely necessary: in this case, the reason was that he wanted the marquis to have some very important political information. Francesco advised Ludovico not to tell anyone what the duke wrote to him. However, as if struck by an afterthought, Sforza added that he did not include Barbara, Ludovico's wife, in the veto, because when he wrote "you", he meant both Ludovico and Barbara. He knew that they were two bodies and one soul.[1]

Among the princely dynasties of fifteenth-century Italy, close collaboration within the ruling couple was not limited to the two marquises of Mantua, although their marriage, blessed with many children and not too many infidelities, was particularly successful. The idea of a union of intent was both a reality and an ideal: it depended on many factors, and its multi-layered nature is the focus of this paper.

1. Context and case studies

The Italian peninsula in the late Middle Ages was composed of a wide range of different political entities; the result was a quite distinctive environment, considered as a whole, in which several principalities, mainly born from communal cities, played a crucial role.[2] Troubled by conflicts of various kinds between the end of the fourteenth century and the mid-fifteenth century, the peninsular system remained difficult despite the legal framework introduced by the Italic League of 1455, and the survival of each power was the result of a complex combination of internal and external elements. The

---

1 Cf. Francesco Sforza to Ludovico Gonzaga, Milan, 8 March 1459, in Archivio di Stato di Mantova, Archivio Gonzaga, b. 1607, l. 65. On power couples and their perception by contemporaries, see the remarks in Julia Burkhardt's contribution in this issue.
2 Cf. Andrea Gamberini and Isabella Lazzarini (eds.), The Italian Renaissance State, 1350–1520, Cambridge 2010.

principalities, in particular, were new, composite in territory, fragile in legitimacy and precarious; women played a crucial role in the struggle to consolidate dynastic power. The control of vast wealth, the definition and hereditary transfer of seigneurial authority, the construction, consolidation and use of the power to decide, judge and order, and finally the ability to translate this empowered authority into the day-to-day governance of complex and territorial political societies were all built on the initiative of both men and women, in different but equally crucial ways.[3]

An initial overview of the role of the princesses in late medieval Italy reveals the features of what was born as a shared authority, due to its only partially legitimate origin (these dynasties had no legitimate title to rule over the cities from which they emerged) and its inchoate nature (these political systems were far from the potential solidity and awareness of monarchical or imperial polities).[4] In such a fluid context, the spouses of fifteenth-century princes had no model to adapt to, but instead defined their own roles and built up their own retinues, as the complementary role of their respective consorts grew and increasingly defined its own characteristics. However, while the sharing of power between prince and princess was the norm, the success of princely couples depended on a number of factors: the origin and rank of the brides, the lifespan of both spouses, their fertility and the number and sex-ratio of their children, the balance between male and female members of the adopted and the natural family (over more than one generation), the interchange and cooperation in governing both in emergencies and in everyday life, the military and diplomatic trends that conditioned old and new dynastic networks.[5]

Because of this flexibility, the paper focuses on several case studies, covering the fifteenth century over three generations and considering the principalities of the Po plain and their allies, from Milan to Savoy, from Mantua or Ferrara to Pesaro and Urbino. Culture, power, devotion, wealth, age, luck or misfortune all played a role in the shared life and success of the couples we will examine. The choice of cases is based on three factors: a chronological range covering almost a century; exemplary use of specific tools and methods; and, finally and inevitably, the availability of eloquent

---

3 Cf. Letizia Arcangeli and Susanna Peyronnel (eds.), Donne di potere nel Rinascimento, Rome 2008. While there is a lack of synthetic works in the Italian context and little collective research, the historiographical debate on these issues has reached a very high level at the European scale: cf. Anne J. Duggan, (ed.), Queens and Queenship in Medieval Europe, Woodbridge 1997; Jeroen Duindam, Dynasties. A Global History of Power, 1300–1800, Cambridge 2016; Martha Howell, The Problem of Women's Agency in Late Medieval and Early Modern Europe, in: Sarah Joan Moran and Amanda Pipkin, Women and Gender in the Early Modern Low Countries, Leiden 2019, 21–31.
4 On the 'necessity' of delegations of power for particular conditions of the different principalities, see the observations of Elodie Lecuppre-Desjardin on the case of the duchesses of Burgundy between the fourteenth and fifteenth centuries in this issue.
5 Cf. Serena Ferente, Women and the State, in: Gamberini/Lazzarini, The Italian Renaissance State, see note 2, 345–367; eadem, Women, Lifecycles, and Social Mobility in Late Medieval Italy, in: Sandro Carocci and Isabella Lazzarini (eds.), Social Mobility in Medieval Italy, 1100–1500, Rome 2018, 217–229.

sources and reliable studies. The aim is not to provide a catalogue of anecdotes or a list of 'exceptional' princesses,[6] but rather a matrix model in which each case reveals a facet of the whole picture in its complexity and interconnectedness: the ultimate objective is to trace some common features among all these possibilities, if there were any, in a comparative and cross-generational perspective.

2. Paola Malatesta (1393–1453) and Gian Francesco Gonzaga (1395–1444)

When she married Gian Francesco Gonzaga, Paola Malatesta was seventeen years old: the daughter of Malatesta dei Sonetti, lord of Pesaro, and Elisabetta da Varano, lady of Camerino, she brought with her a dowry that was never fully paid, and the burden of three brothers, who were losing their grip on the lordship of Pesaro for the benefit of more aggressive, newer lords such as Alessandro Sforza, brother of Francesco, the future duke of Milan.[7] The Gonzaga, lords of a small domain in the Po plain, often married in the fourteenth century into the many branches of the Malatesta family, rooted in the papal lands of Romagna and the Marca Anconitana. Gian Francesco himself was the son of another Malatesta, Margherita, in turn a cousin of Paola's father, and Paola's uncle Carlo, Margherita's brother and lord of Rimini, married Gian Francesco's aunt, Elisabetta. Despite her acclaimed wisdom, Paola is best remembered for the spinal deformity she is said to have brought into the Gonzaga family. But Paola did much more and is interesting here because of her unique combination of rigorous spirituality and attention to education. The more than three decades that she ruled in Mantua were crucial for the city and the dynasty. Gian Francesco spent his life at war, in the heat of the endless conflicts between Milan and Venice: she stayed in Mantua and ruled the lordship on his behalf.[8] While doing so, Paola was comforted by her wholehearted adherence to the Observant reform. In mid-May 1418, the General Chapter of the Friars Minor was celebrated in Mantua: it was on this occasion that Paola met Ber-

---

6 Cf. Heather J. Tanner (ed.), Medieval Elite Women and the Exercise of Power, 1100–1400, Moving Beyond the Exceptionalist Debate, Cambridge 2019.
7 Cf. Isabella Lazzarini, Paola Malatesta Gonzaga, in: Dizionario Biografico degli Italiani 81, Rome 2014, at: https://www.treccani.it/enciclopedia/paola-malatesta-gonzaga-prima-marchesa-di-mantova_%28Dizionario-Biografico%29/, access: 27 Sept. 2024; Philip Jones, The Malatesta of Rimini and the Papal State, Cambridge 1974; Isabella Lazzarini, Fra un principe e altri stati. Relazioni di potere e forme di servizio a Mantova nell'età di Ludovico Gonzaga, Roma 1996.
8 On the events, see Francesco Cognasso, Il Ducato visconteo da Gian Galeazzo a Filippo Maria, in: Storia di Milano, vol. 6, Il Ducato visconteo e la Repubblica ambrosiana, ed. by Francesco Cognasso, Milan 1958, 1–383; Michael Mallett, La conquista della Terraferma, in: Storia di Venezia dalle origini alla caduta della Serenissima, vol. 4, Il Rinascimento. Politica e cultura, ed. by Alberto Tenenti Rome 1996, at: https://www.treccani.it/enciclopedia/la-conquista-della-terraferma_(Storia-di-Venezia)/, access: 27 Sept. 2024.

nardino of Siena, to whose influence she owed her decision to install the Poor Clares in the women's convent of *Corpus Domini*. During Martin V's stay in Mantua (between November 1418 and February 1419), Paola obtained six bulls from the pope, probably concerning the introduction of the Poor Clares: in these years (1416–1419), next to the *Corpus Domini*, Paola built a church dedicated to Santa Paola Romana, under whose name the convent itself was later identified. In 1420, at Paola's request, Bernardino of Siena returned to Mantua to preach during Lent. According to tradition, the saint's words and the excitement felt by the entire city community were to be credited with eight other papal bulls obtained by Paola for the foundation of three convents of Poor Clares and four of Observants in the dioceses of Mantua, Milan, Piacenza or elsewhere as she wished, and for the conversion of some other urban and suburban Mantuan monasteries to Franciscan observance.[9] The city rallied around the marchioness, whose intense spirituality, unprecedented before (and since), was passed on to her sons and daughters (her daughter Cecilia refused marriage and took the veil at the *Corpus Domini*, the first in an unusually long list of Gonzaga princesses). Another initiative that echoed Paola's attention to sincere spirituality was the opening in Mantua of the Ca' Zoiosa, the 'school' founded in 1423 by the humanist educator Vittorino Rambaldoni da Feltre, who was persuaded by the seigneurial couple to move to Mantua to take care of the education of the lords' children, their daughters-in-law and the many other aristocrats and citizens – both boys and girls – who gathered around him.[10]

Coming from a declining seigneurial lineage and suffering from fragile health, Paola managed to strengthen the nascent and vulnerable marquisate (the title was given to Gian Francesco in 1433), not only by ruling in her husband's absence but also by promoting an avant-garde religiosity and contributing to a completely innovative educational experiment aimed at both princes and civil society.

---

9 Cf. Cesare Cenci, Antonio da Pereto, ministro generale O. F. M. e i capitoli di Roma (1411) e di Mantova (1418), in: Archivum Franciscanum Historicum, 55 (1962), 468–500; idem, I Gonzaga e i frati minori dal 1365 al 1430, in: Archivum Franciscanum Historicum, 58 (1965), 3–47, 201–279. On the tendency of princesses to favour the Observance and the Poor Clares, see the example of the duchesses of Burgundy in Elodie Lecuppre-Desjardin's contribution in this issue.

10 Cf. Nella Giannetto (ed.), Vittorino da Feltre e la sua scuola. Umanesimo, pedagogia, arti, Florence 1981; Monica Ferrari, Matteo Morandi and Federico Piseri (eds.), Maestri e pratiche educative in età umanistica: contributi per una storia della didattica, Brescia 2019; Isabella Lazzarini and Raffaele Tamalio (eds.), Alfabetizzazione, formazione e cultura tra medioevo e prima età moderna. Ricordando la Ca' Giocosa di Vittorino da Feltre (1423–2023), forthcoming.

3. Anne of Lusignan (1419–1462) and Ludovico of Savoy (1413–1465)

Piedmont, Monferrato and Saluzzo were located in a region – the western part of the Po plain between the Alps and the Ligurian mountains – open to Angevin influences: with cities less populated and less wealthy than the rest of the sub-alpine area and ruled by a number of feudal lineages of marquises, earls and dukes of ancient legitimacy (Savoy, Savoy-Acaia, Paleologoi, Saluzzo), these lands were more closely linked to the transalpine coordination of the French and imperial principalities than to the Italian principalities to the east. Moreover, thanks to this long-standing connection with the French-Angevin powers, the local dynasties developed, from the twelfth century onwards, a political and dynastic 'familiarity' with the Christian Levant and the *Outremer*.[11] The marriage in 1433 between Ludovico, son of Duke Amedeo VIII of Savoy (later Pope Felix V) and Duchess Mary of Burgundy, and Anne, daughter of Janus of Lusignan and of Charlotte of Bourbon, of the royal lineage of Cyprus, had a certain peculiarity.[12] Anne was the first 'Levantine' princess to come to Savoy and Piedmont to marry one of their princes (almost all the other marriages between the fourteenth and fifteenth centuries involved western princesses going east), and her arrival encouraged another Cypriot marriage, that between her son Ludovico and Princess Charlotte – the last living and legitimate heir of King John II of Lusignan, Anne's brother – even though the effect of this second union was that Ludovico moved to Cyprus as king.[13] Anne was accompanied by a group of Cypriots – men and women – who stayed with her in Savoy, serving her and being appointed to offices and functions by both the duke and the duchess.

She was given authority over territorial offices (*castellanie*) in Piedmont and Savoy, and was entrusted with public revenues, such as those relating to public waters in Piedmont; she controlled land and men to the point of choosing the officers of 'her' *castellanie,* and, finally, at a time of endless financial crisis in the duchy, she was rich enough to be able to lend money to the duke whenever he needed it. The nature of the Sabaudian records – that is, the unusual abundance of surviving registers of accounts – reveals an important facet of a princess's agency, control over both landed property and

---

11 Cf. Florian Chamorel, Un destin méditerranéen. Les princes de la Maison de Savoie en Méditerranée orientale (XIVe–XVe siècle), Paris 2023; Francesco De Caria and Donatella Taverna (eds.), Anna di Cipro e Ludovico di Savoia e i rapporti con l'Oriente, Turin 1997.
12 Cf. Chiara Barbero, Anna di Cipro, duchessa di Savoia. Forme di potere femminile alla corte sabauda (1433–1462), PhD thesis in History, tutor Maria Nadia Covini, a. a. 2021–2022, on which I hugely rely here; Laura Gaffuri, Lo 'statum reginale' tra distinzione ed eccezione: il caso sabaudo (XV secolo), in: Jean-Pierre Genet and Ennio Igor Mineo (eds.), Marquer la prééminence sociale, Paris/Rome 2014, 129–156.
13 Cf. Eva Pibiri, Histoire de femme, histoire d'État. Stratégie matrimoniale à la cour de Savoie pour la couronne de Chypre, 1455–1457, in: Bollettino storico-bibliografico subalpino, 102 (2004), 443–472.

jurisdiction over people. However, her foreigners and her influence over the duke, bolstered by her fertility and resilience, have been stigmatised by chroniclers and later scholars alike. A princess of royal blood was nothing new in Savoy or Piedmont – the counts of Savoy married Valois princesses, they and the marquises of Monferrato gave daughters to the Byzantine emperors – but Anne's otherness and her Cypriot heritage made her somehow different and built her negative reputation, despite her undeniable success as a mother, spouse and possibly ruler. This makes it easier to underestimate both the difficulty of the transition from Amedeo VIII to Ludovico I and the impact of the transformation of the mainly French-oriented principality into a mainly Italian-oriented one at a time of radical change in Italy and in Europe.[14]

4. Barbara of Hohenzollern (1422–1481) and Ludovico Gonzaga (1412–1478)

The habit of seeking spouses from different cultures and countries outside the inner circle of the major and minor Italian dynasties was not exactly new in the fifteenth century: the last decades of the Trecento had seen a flourishing of French, English and even Scottish options for the Visconti and the counts and marquises of the west, and many husbands from the German-speaking imperial commonwealth for the daughters of the lords of the Marca Trevigiana in the east.[15] However, for Gian Francesco Gonzaga and Paola Malatesta the choice of a German bride for their first-born son Ludovico was clearly an important step towards a new rank. The opportunity arose during the Council of Basel, where Gian Francesco's agents were working to secure the Gonzaga's investiture as marquis of his domain, and developed during Sigismund of Luxemburg's journey to Rome to be crowned emperor in 1432–1433.[16] A very young Barbara, daughter of John III the Alchemist, margrave of Brandenburg, and Barbara of Saxony, and therefore of Habsburg blood, arrived in Mantua in November 1433: she grew up in the city and was educated by Vittorino da Feltre at the Ca' Zoiosa, where she learned to read and write in Italian to the point that her written German faded away.[17]

---

14 Cf. Guido Castelnuovo, Ufficiali e gentiluomini. La società politica sabauda nel tardo medioevo, Milan 1994; Alessandro Barbero, Il ducato di Savoia. Amministrazione e corte di uno stato franco-italiano, Roma/Bari 2002.
15 Cf. Andrea Gamberini, Visconti, Bernabò, in: Dizionario biografico degli Italiani, 99, Rome 2020, at: https://www.treccani.it/enciclopedia/bernabo-visconti_%28Dizionario-Biografico%29/, access: 27 Sept. 2024.
16 Cf. Isabella Lazzarini, Gianfrancesco Gonzaga, in: Dizionario biografico degli italiani, 54, Rome 2000, at: https://www.treccani.it/enciclopedia/gianfrancesco-i-gonzaga-marchese-di-mantova_%28Dizionario-Biografico%29/, access: 27 Sept. 2024. The letters of the Mantuan agents are in the Archivio di Stato di Mantova, Archivio Gonzaga, bb. 723 and 2185 (Simone da Crema).
17 Cf. Ingeborg Walter, Barbara di Hohenzollern, in: Dizionario Biografico degli Italiani, 6, Rome 1964, at: https://www.treccani.it/enciclopedia/barbara-di-hohenzollern-marchesa-di-mantova_%

Barbara gave to Ludovico five sons and five daughters, whose friendly personal relationships – in particular between the elder brothers, Marquis Federico and Cardinal Francesco – testify to their mother's attention to them: she is said to have destroyed Ludovico's will (which would have left the entire marquisate to the first-born son, Federico) after the marquis's sudden death from the plague in 1478 and instead decided to create smaller domains within the marquisate for the cadets in order to keep peace between her sons.[18] Her role in the joint government of the marquisate is attested not only by Francesco Sforza's words, from which we have started, but also by countless letters and records.[19]

Moreover, the young princess's foreignness was significant but at the same time so familiar to her husband's political culture that it allowed her to play an increasingly prominent diplomatic role.[20] She was instrumental in the choice of Mantua as the seat of the diet convened by Pope Pius II to launch the crusade against the Ottoman Sultan Mehmed the Conqueror in 1459–1460, and in the elevation of the second son of the marquises, Francesco, to the purple in 1461. In the 1450s and 1460s, she acted as a spokesperson for the interests of the princes of the Po plain (the Gonzaga, but also the Sforza, to whom the Mantuans were linked by a promised marriage that never happened) in the imperial circles, facilitating contacts and protection. The political moment was not easy. While the situation in Italy was troubled by the war in the Kingdom of Naples following the death of Alfonso the Magnanimous in 1458, the imperial context was also riven by various lines of division: between princes (Ludwig of Bavaria and Albert of Brandenburg, or the emperor's brothers, Sigmund and Albert of Habsburg) and between the emperor and the various rulers of the eastern European kingdoms (George Podiebrady in Bohemia as well as John Hunyadi and Matthias Corvinus of Hungary). The popes themselves were pursuing a policy that was both anti-Hussite and anti-Ottoman.[21] The marchioness therefore had to tread carefully,

---

28Dizionario-Biografico%29/, access: 27 Sept. 2024; Ebba Severidt, Familie und Politik: Barbara von Brandenburg, Markgräfin von Mantua (30 Sept. 1422–7 Nov. 1481), in: Innsbrucker Historische Studien, 16 (1997), 213–238.

18 A different maternal decision (Bianca Maria's potential desire to leave Cremona not to her first-born son and Duke Galeazzo Maria, but to another son, Sforza Maria) could be at the root of many troubles: Lorenzo de' Medici, Lettere, I, (1460–1474), ed. by Riccardo Fubini, Florence 1977, 104.

19 Cf. Isabella Lazzarini, Fra un principe e altri stati. Relazioni di potere e forme di servizio a Mantova nell'età di Ludovico Gonzaga, Rome 1996.

20 On the diplomatic functions performed by late medieval princesses by virtue of their 'foreign' status, see again the contribution in this issue by Elodie Lecuppre-Desjardin, in particular on Isabella of Portugal.

21 On the Italian situation and the Neapolitan war, see Riccardo Fubini, Italia quattrocentesca. Politica e diplomazia nell'età di Lorenzo de Medici, Milan 1994; Francesco Senatore, "Uno mundo de carta". Forme e strutture della diplomazia sforzesca, Naples 1998; on the Empire, see Cristopher Allmand (ed.), The New Cambridge Medieval History, vol. VII, c. 1415–c.1500, Cambridge 1998, in particular the chapters by Tom Scott (Germany and the Empire, 337–366), John Klassen (Hus, the Hussites and Bohemia, 367–391) János Bak (Hungary: crown and estates, 707–726) and

attempting to manage both the immediate interests of the marquisate and those of her allies, navigating a difficult and sometimes contradictory political landscape. The Mantuan correspondence reveals that Barbara was at the centre of a complex network of lay imperial correspondents (her extensive family network) and a lesser-known network of German clerks and courtiers who acted as her agents in Rome and wherever they were needed in Germany. At the same time, before and after the diet in Mantua, she kept the entire curial network open and oiled by writing to cardinals and protonotaries, sending gifts, promising protection to their clients and asking the same for hers.[22]

5. Bianca Maria Visconti (1425–1468) and Francesco Sforza (1401–1466)

Bianca Maria, the illegitimate daughter of Filippo Maria, third duke of the house Visconti, and Agnese del Maino, from an ancient and influential Milanese family, legitimised in 1430 by Sigismund of Luxemburg, was the exception that proved the rule: a native princess for a sovereign couple in which not only was the husband a foreigner (as he was in the absence of male heirs) but also someone whose personal rank and status were far less important than hers.[23] Bianca Maria "was the key to Francesco Sforza's rise to domination over Milan and Lombardy": their marriage on 25 October 1441 not only gave to the renowned military captain of semi-obscure origins control over the cities of Cremona (her dowry) and Pontremoli, but also the most certain path to succeeding his reluctant father-in-law, Duke Filippo Maria.[24] After Filippo Maria's death on 13 August 1447, and despite the birth of three children (Galeazzo Maria, 1444; Ippolita Maria, 1445; Filippo Maria, 1447), Francesco and Bianca Maria had to

---

Aleksander Gieysztor (The Kingdom of Poland and the Grand Duchy of Lithuania, 1370–1506, 727–747).

22 Cf. Isabella Lazzarini, La nomination d'un cardinal de famille entre l'Empire et la Papauté. Les pratiques de négotiation de Bartolomeo Bonatti, orateur de Ludovico Gonzaga (Rome, 1460–1461), in: Stefano Andretta, Stéphane Péquignot, Marie-Karine Schaub, Jean-Claude Waquet and Christian Windler (eds.), Paroles de négociateurs: l'entretien dans la pratique diplomatique de la fin du Moyen Âge à la fin du XIXe siècle, Rome 2009, 51–69; eadem, La marchesa e il papa. Rapporti diplomatici tra Barbara di Hohenzollern e la curia romana tra la dieta di Mantova e la nomina di Francesco Gonzaga a cardinale (1459–1461), in: Isabella Lazzarini, Patricia Rochwert-Zuili and Juan Manuel Nieto Soria (eds.), Correspondences des femmes et diplomatie (Espagne, France, Italie, IXe–XVe siècle), Paris 2021, at: https://books.openedition.org/esb/3992, access: 27 Sept. 2024.

23 Cf. Franco Catalano, Bianca Maria Visconti, in: Dizionario biografico degli italiani, 10, Roma 1968, at: https://www.treccani.it/enciclopedia/bianca-maria-visconti-duchessa-di-milano_%28Dizionario-Biografico%29/, access: 27 Sept. 2024. On the importance of being *la princesse naturelle*, see the case of Mary of Burgundy, discussed by Christina Lutter and Christof Muigg in this issue.

24 Maria Nadia Covini, Donne, emozioni e potere alla corte degli Sforza. Da Bianca Maria a Cecilia Gallerani, Milan 2012, 11–36, 11.

wait three more years of ruthless politics and harsh warfare before they could enter Milan as duke and duchess. Bianca Maria was crucial to her husband's success: not only was she the sole heir of the previous dukes but she also controlled an extensive and deeply rooted network of Milanese Ghibelline families and the many branches of the Visconti lineage in Milan and the region. Bianca Maria's networks were crucial to internal consensus and to balancing the impact on the Milanese political society of the group of trusted Sforza men, all from outside the duchy, who had arrived with Francesco. On the one hand, the Sforza military *compagnia* became "the duke's army", slowly integrating itself into the pre-existing political and military structure of the duchy.[25] On the other hand, the duchess's party, not only in Milan but also in other key cities of the domain such as Cremona and Pavia, became a laboratory for building internal support for the ducal couple. Bianca Maria carefully avoided personal rule, except for the short periods when Francesco was absent from Milan (for instance, during the last war against Venice in 1452–1454) or when he was seriously ill (in the autumn-winter of 1462–1463): in other words, she took a step back, and did not exercise the everyday power characteristic of the other princesses we have seen.[26] This decision was probably motivated by a desire not to hinder or overshadow in any way the authority and reputation of the 'new' duke. Even in Cremona, 'her' city, she did not exercise direct governmental authority until the death of the duke in 1466. Rather than share Francesco's power, she maintained a wide sphere of 'soft power' through the careful distribution of favours, offices, resources and even ecclesiastical benefices.[27] She also had to 'invent' her behaviour and role: the previous duchesses, Beatrice Cane, executed by Filippo Maria for adultery, and Maria of Savoy, married for purely political reasons and sadly neglected by the duke, did not offer the young Visconti a useful model.[28] In this sense, the government of Bianca Maria and Francesco was completely new and the two of them – together – had to recover resources, transform customs and

---

25 Maria Nadia Covini, L'esercito del duca. Organizzazione militare e istituzioni al tempo degli Sforza (1450–1480), Rome 1998.
26 Cf. Paolo Margaroli, Diplomazia e stati rinascimentali. Le ambascerie sforzesche fino alla conclusione della Lega italica (1450–1455), Florence 1992; on Francesco's illness, see Giorgio Cosmacini, La malattia del duca Francesco, in: Isabella Lazzarini (ed.), Carteggio degli oratori mantovani alla corte sforzesca, III (1462), Rome 2000, 23–26.
27 Cf. Covini, Donne, emozioni e potere, see note 24, 14–24. On Cremona, see Paolo Margaroli, Bianca Maria e Galeazzo Maria Sforza nelle ultime lettere di Antonio da Trezzo (1466–1469), in: Archivio storico lombardo, 113 (1985), 327–377; on ecclesiastical benefices, see Michele Ansani, La provvista dei benefici. Strumenti e limiti dell'intervento ducale (1450–1466), in: Giorgio Chittolini (ed.), Gli Sforza, la Chiesa lombarda, la corte di Roma. Strutture e pratiche beneficiarie nel ducato di Milano (1450–1535), Naples 1989, 1–113.
28 Cf. Covini, Donne, emozioni e potere, see note 24, 11–12; Jean-Claude Maire Vigueur and Elisabeth Crouzet Pavan, Decapitées. Trois femmes dans l'Italie de la Renaissance, Paris 2018.

build both the internal consensus and a new dynasty while seeking external recognition.²⁹

6. Battista Sforza (1442–1472) and Federico da Montefeltro (1422–1482)

Federico da Montefeltro, duke of Urbino, has gone down in history as one of the icons of the early Italian Renaissance: a great captain who came to rule the small dominion of Montefeltro through a combination of circumstances to which his personal 'virtue' was not incidental. Educated at Vittorino da Feltre's Ca' Zoiosa, he was a great patron of the arts and architecture and the creator of the ducal palace in Urbino, which has since become the symbol of the city. Widowed in 1457 by his first wife, Gentile Brancaleoni of Massa Trabaria, Federico remarried in 1460 to Battista, daughter of Alessandro Sforza of Pesaro (brother of Francesco, duke of Milan, who in 1444 took over Pesaro from Galeazzo Malatesta, brother of Paola Malatesta Gonzaga) and Costanza da Varano.³⁰ Young Battista was the first born of the couple and took her name from her great-grandmother, Battista da Montefeltro Malatesta, the cultured and spiritual sister-in-law of Paola Malatesta Gonzaga, who corresponded for a long time with the marchioness of Mantua. It is not an exercise in erudition to point out the existence of these dynastic threads over several generations: the world of Italian lordships and principalities was interwoven and sustained thanks to this dense dynastic network, which involved major and minor powers and was a powerful factor of mutual legitimation and reinforcement.

Orphaned by her mother in 1447, her father Alessandro sent her to Milan in 1450, where she grew up at the court of Francesco Sforza and Bianca Maria Visconti. In 1458 she returned to Pesaro, where she continued her education: she was a keen student, learning Latin and Greek and enjoying composing sonnets and epigrams.³¹ In 1460 she married Federico and moved to Urbino, where she spent most of her life: after six daughters, in 1472 she gave to her husband the longed-for son, Guidobaldo. That summer she died suddenly of pulmonary disease: her funeral oration written by Gio-

---

29 In the process of creating a new dynasty, it is worth mentioning the attention that Bianca Maria and Francesco paid to the education of their children, cf. Monica Ferrari, Per non manchare il tuto del debito mio. L'educazione dei bambini Sforza nel Quattrocento, Milan 2000.
30 Cf. Gino Benzoni, Federico da Montefeltro, in: Dizionario Biografico degli Italiani, 45, Rome 1995, at: https://www.treccani.it/enciclopedia/federico-da-montefeltro-duca-di-urbino_%28Dizionario-Biografico%29/; access: 24 Sept. 2024; Giorgio Cerioni Baiardi, Giorgio Chittolini and Piero Floriani (eds.), Federico da Montefeltro. Lo stato, le arti, la cultura, 3 vols., Rome 1986.
31 On the importance of a high level of education in government, in addition to the case of Eleanor of Aragon, discussed below, see also the examples of the duchesses of Burgundy, in particular Isabella of Portugal, in the contribution by Elodie Lecuppre-Desjardin in this issue.

vanni Antonio Campano, bishop of Teramo – a true biography – was printed in Cagli as early as 1476.[32]

During her twelve years in Urbino, Battista did what was expected of her. Apart from giving children to her house, she ruled with greater continuity and consistency the further away Federico was, fighting all over in Italy. She played the Sforza card against Sigismondo Malatesta of Rimini and acted as sovereign, mediating in internal conflicts and securing peace agreements between the cities of the domain. Her political skills were such that even Sigismondo Malatesta had to acknowledge that she was proven and wise enough to rule the Kingdom of France.[33] The additional piece of the puzzle we are putting together, however, is the quality of her personal artistic and literary commitment to the image of magnificence and splendour of her duchy and dynasty. Urbino was a small domain: the counts, then dukes, of Montefeltro had ruled it with alternating fortunes from the thirteenth century onwards, finally receiving the ducal title from the pope in 1474. Apart from Urbino, their domain included some towns, villages and castles (Gubbio, Fossombrone, San Leo, Cagli) scattered along rivers and valleys, but no large cities, in the middle of a region contested by Florence and the Papacy, and disputed by many other aggressive lineages such as the various branches of the Malatesta, the Ubaldini, the di Carpegna and the Brancaleoni.[34]

Federico and Battista had the task of making a principality out of this composite and fragmented domain: they needed his military reputation and expertise as well as a brilliant cultural programme of patronage. Many buildings in the various towns were renovated or newly built as part of the extensive military and civil architectural programme, culminating in the renovation of the ducal palace in Urbino by Luciano Laurana and Francesco di Giorgio Martini.[35] While Battista seems to have been closely involved in the construction of buildings, which she did not decide on alone, her personal initiatives were more evident in the fields of visual arts and literature. Here her patronage, tastes and choices were more explicit, and the tributes that she received during her life and after her death from humanists such as Tideo Acciarini, Sabatino degli Arienti, Pandolfo Collenuccio, Martino Filetico, Porcellio Pandoni and Giovanni

---

32 Cf. Edoardo Rossetti, Battista da Montefeltro, in: Dizionario Biografico degli Italiani, 92, Rome 2018, at: https://www.treccani.it/enciclopedia/battista-sforza_%28Dizionario-Biografico%29/, access: 27 Sept. 2024; Marinella Bonvini Mazzanti, Battista Sforza da Montefeltro. Una "principessa" nel Rinascimento italiano, Urbino 1993.
33 Cf. Riccardo De Rosa, I rapporti politico-diplomatici tra Francesco Sforza e Federico da Montefeltro dal 1444 alla pace di Lodi (1454), in: Studi montefeltrani, 21 (2001), 73–92; Walter Tommasoli, Momenti e figure della politica dell'equilibrio (Federico da Montefeltro e l'impresa di Rimini), Urbino 1968; Giovanni Sabatino de li Arienti, Gynevra de le clare donne, ed. by Corrado Ricci and Alberto Bacchi della Lega, Bologna 1888, 288–312, 294.
34 Cf. Giorgio Chittolini, Su alcuni aspetti dello stato di Federico, in: Cerioni Baiardi/Chittolini/Floriani, Federico da Montefeltro, see note 30, vol. I, 61–102.
35 Cf. Francesco Paolo Fiore (ed.), Francesco di Giorgio alla corte di Federico da Montefeltro, 2 vols., Florence 2001; Alessandro Angelini, Gabriele Fattorini and Giovanni Russo (eds.), Federico da Montefeltro e Francesco di Giorgio: Urbino, crocevia delle arti, Venice 2023.

Santi bear witness to her taste.³⁶ If her political role is still partly unknown, also due to the dispersion of the Urbino archives in the early modern period, her personal interpretation of the programme of cultural splendour inaugurated by Federico is only beginning to be understood and gives reason, if any, for her splendid portrait in the famous diptych by Piero della Francesca.³⁷

7. Eleonora of Aragon (1450–1493) and Ercole d'Este (1431–1505)

If the royal blood of Anne of Lusignan brought to Savoy a title and a Cypriot entourage, and earned her a bad reputation, that of Eleonora of Aragon brought to Ferrara, and more generally to the northern principalities, a new political culture and an adult princess who was educated to use it. Ercole, the only legitimate son of Marquis Niccolò III of Este and Ricciarda of the marquises of Saluzzo, became duke after two illegitimate half-brothers, Leonello and Borso. His succession had overtaken the legitimate son of his half-brother Leonello and Margherita Gonzaga, Niccolò (who would soon conspire against his uncle): therefore Ercole, although of legitimate and undisputed birth, needed a high-profile bride. The Neapolitan wedding raised Ferrara's European connections to a whole new level: Eleonora was not only the daughter of Ferrante, king of Naples, but also the granddaughter of Alfonso the Magnanimous, the niece of John II, king of Aragon, and the sister of Beatrice, wife of the king of Hungary, Mattias Corvinus.³⁸ Educated at a court renowned for its attention to culture, which made humanism an instrument of royal government and a framework for its ideological justification,³⁹ she was the dedicatee of Diomede Carafa's third *Memoriale*, devoted to *I doveri del principe*, written before 1477 and translated into Latin by Battista Guarino

---

36 Cf. Marinella Bonvini Mazzanti, La politica culturale di Battista Sforza, in: Bonita Cleri (ed.), Bartolomeo Corradini (Fra Carnevale) nella cultura urbinate del XV secolo, Urbino 2002, 45–68.
37 Cf. Lina Bolzoni, Il cuore di cristallo. Ragionamenti d'amore, poesia e ritratto nel Rinascimento, Turin 2010, 236, 238–240.
38 On her, see Pietro Messina, Eleonora d'Aragona, in: Dizionario Biografico degli Italiani 42, Rome 1995, at: https://www.treccani.it/enciclopedia/eleonora-d-aragona-duchessa-di-ferrara_%28Dizionario-Biografico%29/, access: 27 Sept. 2024; Valentina Prisco, Eleonora d'Aragona. Pratiche di potere e modelli culturali nell'Italia del Rinascimento, Rome 2022; on Eleonora's relationship with her sister Beatrice, see Jessica O'Leary, Elite Women and Diplomatic Agents in Italy and Hungary, 1470–1510: Kinship and the Aragonese Dynastic Networks, Leeds 2022. On Eleonora's sister, Beatrice of Hungary, and on the refined education received by both princesses, see the contribution by Julia Burkhardt in this issue.
39 Cf. Fulvio Delle Donne, Alfonso il Magnanimo e l'invenzione dell'umanesimo monarchico: ideologia e strategie di legittimazione alla corte aragonese di Napoli, Rome 2015; Francesco Storti, 'El buen marinero'. Psicologia politica e ideologia monarchica al tempo di Ferdinando I d'Aragona re di Napoli, Rome 2014; Bianca de Divitiis (ed.), A Companion to the Renaissance in Southern Italy (1350–1600), Leiden 2023.

at her request.⁴⁰ When she arrived in Ferrara in 1473, Eleonora was 23 years old: she was well prepared for her role. Eleonora brought with her an awareness of the sovereign nature of her power that had few equals among her fellow princesses of the Po plain. This awareness is evident in her letters and became a lesson for her daughters. In 1482, during the first months of the war against Venice, in which she held the duchy in Ferrara while Ercole was on the battlefield, she spoke of "her" duchy, "her" dominion, in a letter to her father Ferrante, in rather strong tones ("the Venetians have come to wage a surprise war against *me* […]. *My* affairs are going terribly wrong").⁴¹ In 1491, a year after Isabella's wedding with Francesco Gonzaga, Eleonora wrote to her daughter to give her a proper education on how to be a wife and mother, having been born a princess: Isabella should do all that was necessary in Mantua with a light heart, knowing that "she who has a husband and a state must also have the labour, reminding you that you will also have children and must devote yourself to their support, to the preservation of their property and state, and to doing what is necessary for your subjects and citizens according to circumstances".⁴²

Eleonora introduced several innovations to the Ferrarese chancery (including the use of her own signature as a sign of sovereignty, as her grandfather Alfonso had done in Naples), which spread to the other northern courts thanks to her daughters Isabella, marchioness of Mantua, and Beatrice, duchess of Milan. She managed international affairs and the day-to-day administration of the duchy, kept weekly accounts of the finances and was present at the courts of justice, secured military supplies and resisted in times of conspiracy, maintained a Renaissance court and was a 'political' mother, although she was devoted to her children.⁴³ She was an entirely political sovereign: first, and for a long time, as an 'agent' of her father, with whom she maintained a constant

---

40 Cf. Diomede Carafa, I memoriali, ed. by Franca Petrucci Nardelli, Rome 1988; Enrica Guerra, Eleonora d'Aragona e i 'doveri del principe' di Diomede Carafa tra realtà e precettistica, in: Angela Giallongo (ed.), Donne di palazzo nelle corti europee. Tracce e forme di potere dall'età moderna, Milan 2005, 113–119; Jessica O'Leary, Politics, Pedagogy, and Praise: Three Literary Texts Dedicated to Eleonora d'Aragona, Duchess of Ferrara, in: Itatti Studies, 19 (2016), 285–308; Prisco, Eleonora, see note 38, 230–237.

41 Eleonora to Ferrante of Aragon, Ferrara, 24 May [1482], in: Archivio di Stato di Modena, Carteggi con principi esteri, b. 1511, l. 30, cit. following Prisco, Eleonora, see note 38, 192–193.

42 Eleonora to Isabella d'Este, Ferrara, 15 April 1491, in: Archivio di Stato di Mantova, Archivio Gonzaga, b. 1185; cf. Monica Ferrari, Un'educazione sentimentale per lettera: il caso di Isabella d'Este (1490–1493), in: Isabella Lazzarini (ed.), I confini della lettera. Pratiche epistolari e reti di comunicazione nell'Italia tardomedievale, in: Reti Medievali Rivista, 10 (2009) 351–371, at: http://www.serena.unina.it/index.php/rm/article/view/urn%3Anbn%3Ait%3Aunina-3104, access: 27 Sept. 2024.

43 Cf. Isabella Lazzarini, 'Lessico familiare': linguaggi dinastici, reti politiche e autografia nella comunicazione epistolare delle élites (Italia, XV sec.), in: Antonio Castillo Gomez and Veronica Blas (eds.), Cartas – Lettres – Lettere. Discursos, praticas y representaciones epistolares (siglos XIV–XX), Alcalà de Henares 2014, 163–179; Prisco, Eleonora, see note 38, 81–236; Marco Folin, La corte della duchessa: Eleonora d'Aragona a Ferrara, in: Arcangeli/Peyronnel, Donne di potere, see note 3, 481–512.

and vital relationship, and then, increasingly, as duchess of Ferrara. Her royal birth and upbringing, and her awareness of a long-standing tradition – both Neapolitan and Aragonese – of reigning queens, allowed Eleonora to express more openly than others the power and authority that these princesses exercised daily in one way or another.[44]

8. A concluding note

This essay could continue at length: the six examples above certainly do not exhaust a group that included dozens of powerful women at the top of fifteenth-century Italian political society alone, not to mention the middle and lower ranks of this princely world and its cadet branches. They were chosen on the basis of diversity and representativeness, but others could also have been chosen. In the volatile Italian political scene, diversity was the only constant: the resources available to the princely couples were many, as were the political languages at their disposal, and the combination of the two. In the process of stabilising a few principalities of questionable legitimacy among the many seigneurial governments that tried their luck in the fourteenth century, the princesses were often able to develop both individual and gender-specific strategies to help strengthen their respective domains (and their personal roles). Such strategies were characterised by a wide range of options – culture, spirituality, economic resources, networks, diplomacy, education – enforced through multiple relational dimensions and at different levels of formality. Often constrained by legal traditions, they were in fact freer than their male relatives to adapt different political models and patterns to their day-by-day rule, as the case of Eleonora of Aragon and her ability to mould regal models into a seigneurial domain very different from her own homeland shows.

However, given all the variables and patterns, and the volatility of the peninsular political scenario, at least three elements emerge from this selection of case studies. The first is the reality of a core of shared power that women educated to live at the top of political society routinely exercised alongside their husbands from a very young age. There were no exceptions to this: if many of them have attracted less scholarly attention than others, it is because they have not been (or cannot be) specifically studied, or because of their early deaths (think of Isabella and Beatrice d'Este: the former died in 1539 at the age of 65, the latter in 1497 at the age of 22). This power was not limited to what is known as 'regency': it was exercised daily, wherever and whenever it was advantageous. It was born of necessity and convenience: it had no formal legal basis (which would have been difficult to imagine) and had no precise profile.

---

44 Cf. Serena Ferente, Joanna of Anjou-Durazzo. The Glorious Queen, in: Machtelt Israel and Louis A. Waldman (eds.), Renaissance Studies in Honor of Joseph Connors, 2 vols., Florence 2013, I, 24–30.

Therefore, female power had to invent its own rituals and forms, borrowing them from the various political cultures that circulated (including, of course, humanism). In this sense, each princess, with her own personal and family history, and depending on her lifespan, fertility and other conjunctural factors, gave her reign a particular flavour.

Finally, a definition – both formal and ideal, concrete and ritualised – of female princely power was long in the making, and was not achieved until the sixteenth century, after endless wars and the dramatic reduction in the number of Italian principalities in the late Middle Ages. The wealth of possibilities and cases makes it superfluous and probably wrong to look for a single dominant model: the variety of case studies considered is but one example of the multiplicity of opportunities and solutions that characterised the princely age in fifteenth-century Italy.

Julia Burkhardt

Power Couples in Central Europe around 1500[*]

In 1490 the Austrian physician Johann Tichtel reflected on the complicated political situation of the time in his diary, a collection of entries covering political, family and business matters from 1477 to 1494.[1] A few weeks earlier, Matthias "Corvinus" Hunyadi (1443–1490), the Hungarian king who had claimed the title of Duke of Austria after conquering Vienna, Wiener Neustadt and other parts of the country in the 1480s, had died. His widow, Queen Beatrice of Aragon (1457–1508), immediately sought allies to assert her own claim to rule, disregarding any rights that Matthias's only son (and her stepson) John Corvinus (1473–1504) might have had.[2] When the Bohemian king Vladislav II (1456–1516) was elected king of Hungary just a few months later, Beatrice allied herself with him, thus gaining the support of several influential Hungarian noblemen. The widow even agreed to marry her late husband's successor, but their marriage was soon criticised on legal grounds as Vladislav II was already married to Barbara of Brandenburg.[3]

---

[*] This article is an abridged translation of my article *Gemischtes Doppel. Herrscherpaare im spätmittelalterlichen Polen und Ungarn zwischen Fragilität und Stabilität*, which is currently being prepared for print in: Martin Kintzinger and Klara Hübner (eds.), Fragile Fürstenherrschaft im mittelalterlichen Zentraleuropa (12.–15. Jahrhundert). I would like to thank Paul Schweitzer-Martin (Munich) and the peer reviewers for their helpful comments.

[1] Cf. Theodor Georg von Karajan (ed.), Johannes Tichtel's Tagebuch: MCCCCLXXVII bis MCCCCXCV (Fontes rerum Austriacarum. Scriptores 1), Wien 1855. On Tichtel, see Harald Tersch, Österreichische Selbstzeugnisse des Spätmittelalters und der Frühen Neuzeit (1400–1650). Eine Darstellung in Einzelbeiträgen, Wien/Köln/Weimar 1998, 99–110.

[2] Cf. Áron Petneki, Exequiae Regis. Die Begräbniszeremonie des Königs Matthias Corvinus vor ihrem ungarischen Hintergrund, in: Lothar Kolmer (ed.), Der Tod des Mächtigen. Kult und Kultur des Todes spätmittelalterlicher Herrscher, Paderborn 1997, 113–123; Jessica O'Leary, Elite Women as Diplomatic Agents in Italy and Hungary, 147–1510: Kinship and the Aragonese Dynastic Network, Leeds 2022.

[3] This eventually led to an investigation and a papal ruling in 1500 declaring the marriage invalid, cf. O'Leary, Elite Women, see note 2, 63–64 and David D'Avray, Papacy, Monarchy, and Marriage, 860–1600, Cambridge 2015, 161–169. On Vladislav's election and coronation, see András Kubinyi, Die Wahlkapitulationen Wladislaws II. von Ungarn (1490), in: Rudolf Vierhaus (ed.), Herrschaftsverträge, Wahlkapitulationen, Fundamentalgesetze, Göttingen 1977, 140–162.

For Tichtel, this was proof enough: the woman was to blame for the difficult situation! "As is almost always the case", he summarised, "great disturbances in the world usually arise because of a woman".[4] Of course, there would have been other arguments to explain the complex succession situation in Hungary: the ambition of the Habsburg representatives Emperor Fredrick III and his son, King Maximilian I, the dynastic entanglements with Poland and Bohemia, or the interference of papal legates,[5] but Tichtel perceived things differently. Although his discrediting remark about Beatrice is at least partly related to the queen's influence, it is also paradigmatic of critical views of female rulers, often expressed in rumours or misogynistic remarks.[6]

Although Tichtel presumably favoured the Habsburg line of succession, the Hungarian queen could also have been viewed from other angles, such as her and her husband's joint patronage of artists and writers, or her repeated mediation in political conflicts.[7] At the politically crucial moment of 1490, however, the focus seemed to be on the individual and her specific interests rather than on the couple and their legacy. In addition, political actions of the ruler (in this case the queen) were tied to contemporary gender roles and expectations. This observation is an interesting starting point for thinking about the meanings and perceptions of ruling couples. How did contemporary observers assess royal couples and their actions? Did it make a difference whether the king and queen acted alone or together? Or did marital interaction enable forms of participation that complemented individual strategies or provided new instruments for conflict resolution?

---

[4] Von Karajan, Johannes Tichtel's Tagebuch, see note 1, 50: "Sic fere semper magna mundi disturbia per feminam oriri solent."

[5] Cf. Bence Péterfi, Multiple Loyalties in Habsburg-Hungarian Relations at the Turn of the Fifteenth and Sixteenth Century, in: Hungarian Historical Review, 10, 4 (2021), 621–652.

[6] Cf. Tracy Adams, Powerful Women and Misogynistic Subplots: Some Comments on the Necessity of Checking the Primary Sources, in: Medieval Feminist Forum, 51 (2016) 2, 69–81, at: https://scholarworks.wmich.edu/mff/vol51/iss2/8/, access: 25 September 2024; for a critical discussion of the term misogyny, see Paula M. Rieder, The Uses and Misuses of Misogyny: A Critical Historiography of the Language of Medieval Women's Oppression, in: Historical Reflections / Réflexions Historiques, 38 (2012), 1–18.

[7] More recently, numerous cultural and gender historical studies have been published on Beatrice's life and education at the Neapolitan court, her family networks and her patronage of the arts at the royal court in Buda, for instance. Cf. the following studies (selection): Patrik Paštrnák, Travelling Grooms. A Royal Progress or A Wedding Journey, in: Anthony Musson and J.P.D. Cooper (eds.), Royal Journeys in Early Modern Europe. Progresses, Palaces and Panache, London/New York 2023, 113–126; Jessica O'Leary, Wife, Widow, Exiled Queen: Beatrice d'Aragona (1457–1508) and Kinship in Early Modern Europe, in: Lisa Hopkins and Aidan Norrie (eds.), Women on the Edge in Early Modern Europe, Amsterdam 2019, 139–158; Péter Farbaky, Patrons and Patterns: The Connection between the Aragon Dynasty of Naples and the Hungarian Court of Matthias Corvinus, in: Radovi Instituta za Povijest Umjetnosti, 41 (2017), 23–31; Gabriella Balla and Zsombor Jékely (eds.), The Dowry of Beatrice. Italian Maiolica Art and the Court of King Matthias. Exhibition catalogue, Budapest 2008.

Against this background, this article discusses the scope and significance of "power couples" in premodern Central Europe, focusing on two examples: the Polish royal couple Elizabeth of Habsburg (1436–1505) and Casimir IV (1427–1492) and, in Hungary, Beatrice of Aragon and Matthias Hunyadi.[8] The term "power couples" is understood as a reference to the shared nature of political power of premodern princes of both sexes, but also along the lines of the style adopted – and the public image generated – by modern power couples.[9] I will discuss forms of joint as well as individual and competitive rule against the background of contemporary reflections and representations of both royal couples.

1. Research outline and comparative approach

Research on the forms and dimensions of premodern princely rule has significantly benefited from considerations of cooperation and consensus. In most cases, the focus lay on individual male or female rulers, their personal networks and gendered roles;[10] far less often, however, have princely couples and their role in government been studied.[11] Several studies on princes and princesses have focused on marriage policy, dynastic strategies or patronage for the benefit of their family *memoria*,[12] often applying

---

8 For a biographical overview, see Almut Bues, Die Jagiellonen. Herrscher zwischen Ostsee und Adria, Stuttgart 2010, 80–103; Marian Biskup and Karol Górski (eds.), Kazimierz Jagiellończyk: Zbiór studiów o Polsce drugiej połowy XV wieku [Casimir Jagiellonian: A collection of studies on Poland of the second half of the 15th century], Warszawa 1987; see also the recently published volume Darius von Güttner-Sporzyński (ed.), The Jagiellon Dynasty, 1386–1596. Politics, Culture, Diplomacy, Turnhout 2024; András Kubinyi, Matthias Corvinus. Die Regierung eines Königreichs in Ostmitteleuropa 1458–1490, Herne 1999; Jörg K. Hoensch, Matthias Corvinus. Diplomat, Feldherr und Mäzen, Graz/Wien/Köln 1998.
9 Cf. Anne Bielman Sánchez (ed.), Power Couples in Antiquity. Transversal Perspectives, London/New York, NY 2019. For power couples in the principalities in Northern Italy, see also the case studies discussed by Isabella Lazzarini in this issue.
10 Cf. Claudia Opitz-Belakhal, Macht und Geschlecht in der Vormoderne. Forschungsergebnisse und -desiderate einer Geschlechtergeschichte des Politischen, in: Matthias Becher, Achim Fischelmanns and Katharina Gahbler (eds.), Vormoderne Macht und Herrschaft. Geschlechterdimensionen und Spannungsfelder, Göttingen 2021, 13–32; Theresa Earenfight, A Lifetime of Power: Beyond Binaries of Gender, in: Heather J. Tanner (ed.), Medieval Elite Women and the Exercise of Power, 1100–1400: Moving beyond the Exceptionalist Debate, Cham 2019, 271–293.
11 For an exception, see Theresa Earenfight, Two Bodies, One Spirit: Isabel and Fernand's Construction of Monarchical Partnership, in: Barbara Weissberger (ed.), Queen Isabel I of Castile. Power, Patronage, Persona, Woodbridge 2008, 3–18.
12 Again, exceptions confirm the rule, e. g. Michel Pauly (ed.), Die Erbtochter, der fremde Fürst und das Land. Die Ehe Johanns des Blinden und Elisabeths von Böhmen in vergleichender europäischer Perspektive = L'heritière, le prince étranger et le pays. Le mariage de Jean l'Aveugle et d'Elisabeth de Boheme dans une perspective comparative européenne, Luxembourg 2013; Julia Burkhardt and Christina Lutter, Ich, Helene Kottannerin. Die Kammerfrau, die Ungarns Krone stahl, Darmstadt 2023.

a strict gender dichotomy to princely rule. However, more recent studies have discussed how "gendered differences" and their perception became an important factor in social hierarchies.[13] In this perspective, gender appears as a "social category" and ruling couples can thus be recognised as the dynastic, political or representative unit that they were conceived of at the time.[14] Using the marriage of Isabella of Castile (1451–1504) and Ferdinand of Aragon (1452–1516) as an example, Theresa Earenfight showed how a couple deliberately staged a "distinctive marital monarchical partnership".[15] Isabella and Ferdinand purposefully drew on contemporary models of queenship and kingship from their respective regions of origin in order to create an overarching 'institution' with a corporate character and new and diversified opportunities for participation.[16]

Based on these recent approaches and findings, I will compare the Polish and Hungarian rulers of the second half of the fifteenth century from two perspectives: forms of joint or competing rule, and contemporary representations and reflections. The example of these two couples is particularly suitable for comparison: both the reigns of Casimir IV and Matthias Hunyadi were relatively long, due to the longevity of both rulers. Their marriage constellations, however, show striking differences: while Casimir and the nine years younger Habsburg princess Elizabeth, granddaughter of Emperor Sigismund of Luxembourg and daughter of his heiress Elizabeth and King

---

13 Christina Lutter, Zur Repräsentation von Geschlechterverhältnissen im höfischen Umfeld Maximilians I., in: Johannes Helmrath, Ursula Kocher and Andrea Sieber (eds.), Maximilians Welt. Kaiser Maximilian I. im Spannungsfeld zwischen Innovation und Tradition, Göttingen 2018, 41–60, quote at 45. On gendered representations of premodern rule, see the contribution by Christina Lutter and Christoph Muigg in this issue.

14 With regard to examples from the Iberian peninsula, Raphaela Averkorn even spoke of "working couples as a norm": Raphaela Averkorn, Das Arbeitspaar als Regelfall. Hochadlige Frauen in den Außenbeziehungen iberischer Frontier-Gesellschaften des Spätmittelalters, in: Corina Bastian, Eva Kathrin Dade, Hillard von Thiessen and Christian Windler (eds.), Das Geschlecht der Diplomatie. Geschlechterrollen in den Außenbeziehungen vom Spätmittelalter bis zum 20. Jahrhundert, Köln/Weimar/Wien 2014, 15–32. For the exact opposite case (self-chosen unmarried state), see the article by Oliver Auge and Laura Potzuweit in this issue. A pioneering study is Heide Wunder, Überlegungen zum Wandel in den Geschlechterbeziehungen im 15. und 16. Jahrhundert aus sozialgeschichtlicher Sicht, in: Heide Wunder and Christina Vanja (eds.), Wandel der Geschlechterbeziehungen zu Beginn der Neuzeit, Frankfurt am Main 1991, 12–26. On premodern "working couples" see also the recent work by Eva-Maria Cersovksy, Geschlechterverhältnisse in der Krankenfürsorge. Straßburg im 15. und 16. Jahrhundert, Ostfildern 2023, esp. 166–179.

15 Earenfight, Two Bodies, see note 11, quote at 4. Cf. also Theresa Earenfight, Absent Kings: Queens as Political Partners in the Medieval Crown of Aragon, in: eadem (ed.), Queenship and Political Power in Medieval and Early Modern Spain, Aldershot 2005, 32–52. On other (earlier) examples from the Iberian pensincula, see Averkorn, Arbeitspaar, see note 14. On the discussion of the monarchy as a "cooperative and complementary institution", see Sebastian Roebert, Die Königin im Zentrum der Macht. Reginale Herrschaft in der Krone Aragón am Beispiel Eleonores von Sizilien (1349–1375), Berlin 2020, 17–23.

16 Cf. Earenfight, Two Bodies, see note 11, 18: "Royal authority was not isolated in one or the other, but it admitted a range of power-sharing options."

Albert of Habsburg, were married for 38 years until Casimir's death in 1492[17], the marriage between Matthias and Beatrice, who was fourteen years younger than her husband when they married in 1476, was considerably shorter at 14 years.[18] In dynastic terms, both cases were 'extreme': Matthias and Beatrice remained childless. The personal and political dimension of this circumstance is remarkable, but the situation was made socially more piquant and legally more complex by the fact that Matthias had a son (John Corvinus) from an extramarital relationship, whom the king tried to establish as heir to the throne even after marrying Beatrice. After Matthias's death, this stepmother-stepson constellation gave rise to a complex set of family loyalties and individual favouritism.[19]

By contrast, Casimir IV and Elizabeth had 13 children between 1456 and 1482, 11 of whom reached adulthood; four of their sons became kings, one a cardinal, while their daughters married high-ranking princes.[20] In addition to the political potential of these connections, this observation is also important for the question of accessibility and publicity: after all, Elizabeth was pregnant almost continuously until the 1470s.[21] Contemporary observers cultivated the distinct dynastic value of the couple and their progeny, among them the chronicler Jan Długosz (1415–1480), who completed his *Annals of Polish History* (*Annales seu Chronicae incliti Regni Poloniae*) around 1480. In

---

17 Cf. Julia Burkhardt, Das Erbe der Frauen: Elisabeth von Luxemburg und Elisabeth von Habsburg, in: Martin Bauch, Julia Burkhardt, Tomáš Gaudek and Václav Žůrek (eds.), Heilige, Helden, Wüteriche. Herrschaftsstile der Luxemburger (1308–1437), Köln/Weimar/Wien 2017, 261–284; Urszula Borkowska, Małżeństwa jagiellońskie, in: Paweł Kras and Martin Nodl (eds.), Manželství v pozdním středověku: Rituály a obyceje [Marriage in the Late Middle Ages: Rituals and Customs], Praha 2014, 153–165; Urszula Borkowska, Marital contracts of the House of Jagiellon, in: Majestas, 13 (2005), 75–93.

18 Cf. Orsolya Réthelyi, King Matthias on the Marriage Market, in: Péter Farbaky, Enikő Spekner, Katalin Szende and András Végh (eds.), Matthias Corvinus, the King. Tradition and Renewal in the Hungarian Royal Court 1458–1490. Exhibition catalogue, Budapest 2008, 247–250; Árpád Mikó, Queen Beatrix of Aragon, in: idem, 251–265; Volker Honemann, The Marriage of Matthias Corvinus to Beatrice of Aragón (1476), in: Martin Gosman, Alasdair A. MacDonald and Arjo J. Vanderjagt (eds.), Princes and Princely Culture, Vol. 2, Leiden 2005, 213–226.

19 Cf. Péter Farbaky, The Sterile Queen and the Illegitimate Son: Beatrice of Aragon and John Corvinus's Rivalry at Matthias Corvinus's Court, in: Helena Dánová, Klára Mezihoráková and Dalibor Prix (eds.), Artem ad vitam. Kniha k pocte Ivo Hlobila [Book in Honour of Ivo Hlobil], Praha 2012, 419–428. On dynastic resources and the importance of princely fertility, see also the contributions by Lutter/Muigg and Lazzarini in this issue.

20 Probably the most prominent example is the so called "Landshut Wedding" between Hedwig of Poland and George of Bavaria-Landshut in 1475. Cf. Roman Deutinger and Christof Paulus, Das Reich zu Gast in Landshut. Die erzählenden Texte zur Fürstenhochzeit des Jahres 1475, Ostfildern 2017. On the Jagiellonians' dynastic politics, see Urszula Borkowska, Dynastia Jagiellonów w Polsce [The Jagiellonian Dynasty in Poland], Warszawa 2011.

21 Cf. Beata Możejko, O okolicznościach narodzin królewskich dzieci w świetle itinerarium Kazimierza Jagiellończyka i Elżbiety Rakuskiej [On the Circumstances of the Birth of Royal Children in the Light of the Itinerary of Casimir Jagiellon and Elizabeth of Habsburg], in: Studia z Dziejów Średniowiecza, 24 (2020), 126–158.

his report about a dispute in 1461 between Casimir IV and Duke Erich II of Pomerania-Wolgast, which was finally resolved through the mediation of Erich's wife, Sophia, Długosz laid down that the duchess's clever actions made Casimir regret that he had not married Sophia himself: beauty and wealth led the king into temptation.[22] In the end, remembering the personal qualities and dynastic value of Queen Elizabeth helped Casimir resist temptation.[23]

2. Stronger together? Forms of joint and competitive rule

This interpretation reveals a typical staging of Elizabeth as the bearer of a dual imperial-royal heritage, supported by her use of titles or coats of arms, often referring to her grandfather, Emperor Sigismund of Luxembourg.[24] Bolesław Sobczyk emphasised that following the marriage of Elizabeth and Casimir and the resulting claims to Bohemia and Hungary, special efforts were made to reinforce the 'appearance of legitimacy' and the autonomy of royal rule.[25] A seal from 1459 could also fit in with this reading: it shows the coats of arms of Poland and Lithuania as well as the inscription "Seal of Casimir, by the Grace of God King of Poland, Grand Duke of Lithuania, etc." Between the coats of arms are the letters "K : E", which probably refer to Casimir and Elizabeth and were possibly intended to express the political significance of the royal couple just a few years after their marriage.[26]

---

22 Cf. Anna Obara-Pawłowska, Polish Monarchs' Sexuality in the Light of the "Annals" by Jan Długosz, in: Res Historica, 51 (2021), 103–143. DOI:10.17951/rh.2021.51.103-143.
23 Cf. Krzysztof Baczkowski et al. (eds.), Joannis Dlugossii Annales seu Cronicae incliti regni Poloniae. Liber Duodecimus 1445–1461, Cracoviae 2003, quote 363: "Eam tamen penitudinem, quociens animum regium subibat caritas et modestia sponse sue Elisabeth, ex alto sanguine cesarum sate et prole quinarian iam suscepta, regnorum quoque et terrarium iusta et legitima devolucio ad illum ad natos suos Divinitate propicia perventura, dispellebat."
24 Cf. Andrea Langer, Frauen – Kunst – Kulturtransfer. Forschungsstand und Perspektiven zur Rolle der weiblichen Mitglieder der jagiellonischen Dynastie im 15. und 16. Jh., in: Dietmar Popp and Robert Suckale (eds.), Die Jagiellonen. Kunst und Kultur einer europäischen Dynastie an der Wende zur Neuzeit, Nürnberg 2002, 85–94. Langer attributes this to Elizabeth's intentions of emphasising the "equation of the Polish monarchy with the imperial house as well as the dynastic claim of the Jagiellonians to the succession in Bohemia and Hungary", own translation of original German quote at 89.
25 Cf. Bolesław Sobczyk, Rex imperator in regno suo. Suwerenność króla polskiego w końcu XV wieku w miniaturach "Graduału Jana Olbrachta" [Sovereignty of the Polish King at the End of the 15th Century in the Miniatures of "Gradual of Jan Olbracht"], in: Folia Historiae Artium, 10 (1974), 81–104.
26 Cf. Paweł Stróżyk, Sygle na pieczęci podkanclerskiej Kazimierza Jagiellończyka. Przyczynek do źródłoznawczej lektury inskrypcji napieczętnych [Sigla on the Subchancellor Seal of Casimir Jagiellonian. A Contribution to the Method of Reading Seal Inscriptions], in: Roczniki Historyczne LXXXVII (2021), 57–78.

An obvious and plausible starting point for the analysis of joint rule is the *itineraria* and places of residence. Taken together, the evidence for Casimir IV's and Elizabeth's itineraries provides the following picture.[27] Casimir and Elizabeth spent most of the year together travelling through the vast territory of Poland-Lithuania, even when the king went into battle, as he did during the war against the Teutonic Order (1454–1466). This even applies to the years when Elizabeth was pregnant; the queen only withdrew to give birth (usually to Kraków).[28] At the same time, an interesting pattern emerges: when Casimir IV travelled to meetings of the Sejm (the central political assembly of the realm) or to provincial diets, the couple often parted ways for short periods; Elizabeth, for example, travelled to another city or went to a nearby monastery for a few days.[29] At first glance, this would seem to indicate a separation of responsibilities. Generally, however, Elizabeth rejoined her husband immediately after the parliamentary meetings. Apparently, Casimir and Elizabeth were at the disposal of different groups of people with different authority and responsibilities, which nevertheless overlapped to some extent: instead of a clear separation of responsibility, the couple seemed to practise the principle of shared responsibilities in times of physical separation.[30] The fact that Elizabeth was by no means excluded from public debates[31] is demonstrated by numerous assemblies where the couple jointly answered to demands

---

27 Cf. for Casimir IV Grażyna Rutkowska, Itinerarium króla Kazimierza Jagiellończyka 1440–1492 [The Itinerary of King Casimir the Jagiellonien 1440–1492], Warszawa 2014 and for Elizabeth Tomasz Rombek, Otoczenie królowej Elżbiety Rakuszanki (1454–1505) [The Entourage of Queen Elisabeth of Habsburg (1454–1505)], Katowice 2012: Aneks Nr. 4 "Itinerarium królowej Elżbiety Rakuszanki (1454–1505)", 265–299. Many thanks to Beata Możejko (Gdańsk) for providing me with a copy of Rombek's (still unpublished) work.
28 Cf. Możejko, O okolicznościach, see note 21, esp. 155–156 with a table on Elizabeth's residence places before the respective births.
29 There is evidence of this, for example, in 1472, when Elizabeth (who had given birth to her daughter Elizabeth in Kraków earlier that year) stayed in the Cistercian monastery of Sulejów during the Sejm held in Piotrków in November. Cf. Rombek, Itinerarium, see note 27, 278; Rutkowska, Itinerarium, see note 27; Krzysztof Baczkowski et al. (eds.), Joannis Dlugossii Annales seu Cronicae incliti regni Poloniae. Liber Duodecimus 1462–1480, Cracoviae 2005, 295. For further examples, see Burkhardt, Gemischtes Doppel, see note *.
30 Cf. also Tomasz Rombek, Centrum a peryferia. Wieloprowieniencyjność terytorialna dworzan Elżbiety Rakuszanki [Center vs. Periphery. The Territorial Multiprovenience of the Courtiers of Elizabeth of Habsburg], in: Bożena Czwojdrak, Jerzy Sperka and Piotr Węcowski (eds.), Jagiellonowie i ich świat. Dynastia królewska w drugiej połowie XV i w XVI wieku [The Jagiellonians and Their World. The Royal Dynasty in the Second Half of the Fifteenth and into the Sixteenth Century], Kraków 2018, 39–51 on Elizabeth's court, which was characterised by the integration of people from very different areas of the realm into reliable networks throughout the country. On contemporary approaches to territorial fragmentation and integration, see the contributions by Elodie Lecuppre-Desjardin and Lutter/Muigg in this issue.
31 This was suggested by Karol Górski, Rządy wewnętrzne Kazimierza Jagiellończyka w Koronie [Domestic rule of Casimir Jagiellon in the Polish Crown], in: Biskup/Górski, Kazimierz Jagiellończyk, see note 8, 82–128, 126.

or led tax debates, or, of course, by Elizabeth's prominent role in negotiating their children's marriages.

Of particular interest are the periods when Casimir and Elizabeth were physically separated but acted in a complementary manner. For example, Elizabeth repeatedly acted as a mediator and judge when her husband was absent, as in the dispute between the voivode Andreas Tęczyński (1412/13–1461) and a Kraków armourer named Klemens. A conflict in July 1461 was apparently triggered by Tęczyński's criticism of the quality of Klemens's work. Although the case was initially brought before the city council and then before Queen Elizabeth (who was about to give birth to a son), protests followed, culminating in Tęczyński's murder by an angry mob.[32] Between the first dispute, the murder and (one year later) the final trial, Elizabeth imposed fines, initiated a moratorium until the king could make a final judgment and acted as a mediator. She also kept her husband and the involved parties informed about the events and her decisions. At first glance, Elizabeth appears to play the typical role of an intervener, with actions ranging from attempts to overturn royal decisions to independent influence on pending decisions.[33] Moreover, the Kraków example shows that Elizabeth acted on behalf of and in close consultation with her husband. Nevertheless, some of Elizabeth's interventions in comparable situations were perceived as disruptive and even weakening Casimir's position: on at least two occasions, the king publicly expressed his dismay at Elizabeth' decisions and then tried to reverse them.[34] Depending on the situation and perspective, the royal couple's actions seemed to oscillate between cooperation and competition.[35]

---

32 Cf. Burkhardt, Das Erbe der Frauen, see note 17; Baczkowski et al., Joannis Dlugossi Annales. Liber Duodecimus 1445–1461, see note 23, 357–358. Cf. also Anna Kochan, Spóźniona groźba. "Wiersz o zabiciu Andrzeja Tęczyńskiego" w świetle poetyki tzw. listu odpowiedniego [A Belated threat. "The Poem about the Killing of Andrzej Tęczynski" in the Light of the Poetics of the So-called 'Adequate Letter'], in: Pamiętnik Literacki, 99 (2008), 161–172.

33 Cf. Burkhardt, Das Erbe der Frauen, see note 17, 281 (note 53). For a comparative perspective on women ruling for their absent partners, see the examples discussed by Lecuppre-Desjardin in this issue.

34 Cf. Tomasz Rombek, Elżbieta Rakuska wobec otoczenia Kazimierza IV Jagiellonczyka (1454–1492) [Elizabeth of Habsburg and Casimir IV Jagiellonian's Entourage (1454–1492)], in: Leszek Paweł Słupecki (ed.), Materiały V Kongresu Mediewistów Polskich [Documents of the 5th Congress of Polish Medievalists], Rzeszów 2017, 311–324, esp. 314f.; Tomasz Rombek, Rola polityczna królowej Elżbiety Rakuszanki (1454–1505) [The Political Role of Queen Elizabeth of Habsburg (1454–1505)], in: Bożena Czwojdrak and Agata A. Kluczek (eds.), Kobieta i władza w czasach dawnych [Women and Power in History], Katowice 2015, 280–288, 284.

35 Political negotiations and conflict management include a case from 1478, when the queen intervened in negotiations with King Matthias of Hungary about a peace treaty (apparently also due to her language skills). Apparently, Elizabeth acted as an interpreter for her husband on various occasions. Cf. Baczkowski et al., Joannis Dlugossii Annales, Liber Duodecimus 1462–1480, see note 29, 407–408, 412. On the political context, see Bogusław Czechowicz, Traktat Ołomuniecki z 1479 roku [The Treaty of Olomouc 1479], in: Sobótka, 2 (2015), 17–32.

Issues of princely prestige and foreign policy considerations also played an important role in the marriage of Beatrice and Matthias. In 1476 the Hungarian monarch and his diplomats succeeded in arranging the marriage of Beatrice of Aragon, daughter of King Ferdinand I of Naples and Isabella of Clermont.[36] Together with her older sister Eleonora, Beatrice had been educated at the Neapolitan court;[37] both princesses received treatises from their teacher, Diomede Carafa, instructing them for their lives as queen and duchess.[38] Carafa told the future queen how to create goodwill on her arrival in Hungary: hire Hungarian court staff, learn the Hungarian language and distribute gifts.[39] Despite the careful preparation of the bride, the lavish staging of the wedding and the subsequent expansion of courtly representation in festivities, architecture, art and literature (largely due to Beatrice), the marriage was unsuccessful by contemporary standards in one essential respect: the couple remained childless throughout their marriage. Officially, the Hungarian-Neapolitan marriage put an end to another relationship: from around 1470, Matthias Hunyadi had been in a relationship with Barbara Edelpöck, who in 1473 gave birth to his desired heir (and only child) John.[40] Numerous sources attest that Matthias provided for his former partner's financial security; although Barbara was forced to retire to Austria after Matthias and Beatrice's wedding, she continuously received endowments. Matthias initially had his son John raised by his own mother, and brought him to the court of Buda about two years after his marriage. It is possible that by this time he had given up hope of having more children, for John was soon described as the "sole heir" and received the education of a royal son.[41] Father and son kept in touch with Barbara, and it soon became apparent

---

36 Cf. Honemann, The Marriage, see note 18; Patrik Paštrnák, Mechanics of Royal Generosity: The Gifts from the Wedding of King Matthias Corvinus and Beatrice of Aragon (1476), in: Speculum, 98 (2023), 802–825.
37 Cf. Mark K. Anson and Robert Gary Babcock, The Education of a Princess: Beatrice of Aragon and her Manuscript of Cicero's De Senectute, in: Codices manuscripti & impressi, 112/113 (2018), 1–12. On Eleonora, see the contribution by Lazzarini in this issue.
38 Cf. Valentina Prisco, Eleonora d'Aragona: pratiche di potere e modelli culturali nell'Italia del Rinascimento, Roma 2022, 230–236; edition for Beatrice's treatise "De institutione vivendi": Diomede Carafa, De institutione vivendi. Tanítás az életvezetés szabályairól. Emlékeztető Magyarország felséges királynéjának [Teaching about the Rules of Life. Commemorating the Queen of Hungary], ed. by Péter Ekler, Budapest 2006.
39 Cf. Diomede Carafa, De institutione vivendi, see note 38, 36 (Quid erga delegatos a marito viros et mulieres), 41–42 (De lingua pannonica edocenda) and 42–43 (De muneribus dono datis). Cf. Paštrnák, Mechanics of Royal Generosity, see note 36. On gendered instructions or even corrections of premodern princes and princesses, see the examples discussed by Lutter/Muig in this issue.
40 Cf. Vinzenz Oskar Ludwig and Franz Maschek, Matthias Corvinus und Barbara Edelpöck, in: Jahrbuch für Landeskunde von Niederösterreich, Ser. NF 32 (1955/56), 74–93; Péter Farbaky, The Heir: The Role of John Corvinus in the Political Representation of Matthias Corvinus, and as Patron of the Arts, in: Livia Varga (ed.), Bonum ut pulchrum: Essays in Art History in Honour of Ernő Marosi on his Seventieth Birthday, Budapest 2010, 413–432.
41 Enikő Spekner, "… to be judged worthy of your illustrious father and to rule over the Hungarians …". Matthias' struggle for John Corvinus' succession, in: Farbaky/Spekner/Szende/Végh (eds.), Matthias Corvinus, the King, see note 18, 513–515.

how delicate this constellation was. In 1489, Queen Beatrice asked Barbara Edelpöck to meet her at the royal court. She claimed that Barbara was a witch and had used magic to make Beatrice infertile. The queen was supported by her nephew Ippolito d'Este (1479–1520), Archbishop of Esztergom. Ippolito and Beltramo Costabili, the Ferrarese ambassador and regent of the then minor Ippolito, reported Barbara's alleged offences to the papal legate in Hungary with the view to having Barbara excommunicated.[42] It is impossible to say whether this incident was the reason why King Matthias repeatedly complained to his father-in-law, Ferdinand of Aragon, about his unpopular wife's alleged incapability to rule.[43]

Although the dispute seems to have been bitter, it is unlikely that the royal couple were permanently estranged; on the contrary, there is evidence that Beatrice made appearances with Matthias on several occasions. According to their itineraries, Beatrice and Matthias often travelled together during their marriage,[44] especially in the 1480s, when the decades-long conflict between Matthias Hunyadi and Emperor Frederick III intensified and Beatrice repeatedly intervened or was asked to mediate.[45]

---

42 Cf. Farbaky, The Sterile Queen, see note 19. On Beatrice's relation to her nephew, see Jessica O'Leary, Motherhood and Epistolary Exchange in the Letters of Ippolito d'Este with Eleonora and Beatrice d'Aragona, in: Monica Ferrari, Matteo Morandi and Federico Piseri (eds.), Scriver dei figli: lettere 'eccellenti' tra Medioevo ed età moderna (XIV–XVIII secolo), Milano 2021, 195–204. On family networks as resources for foreign politics, see also the examples discussed by Lecuppre-Desjardin in this issue.

43 Cf. O'Leary, Wife, Widow, Exiled Queen, see note 7, 143, note 18: "la quale aspira, se non palesemente, per lo meno in segreto, a una cosa che non è nelle nostre facoltà di fare. La Regina desidera dopo la nostra morte, nel caso muoia prima di lei, succederci al trono e prendere nelle sue mani le redini del governo, ciò che non potremmo concedere anche volendo e che non possiamo neppure proporre ai nostri sudditi, se non vogliamo eccitare in questi un perpetuo odio contro di Noi e contro la Regina." However, I was unable to find the passage in the source cited by O'Leary (Acta vitam Beatricis reginae Hungariae illustrantia. Aragoniai Beatrix magyar királné életére vonatkozó okiratok, ed. by Albert von Berzeviczy, Budapest 1914, 98–99).

44 Cf. Richárd Horváth, Itineraria regis Matthiae Corvini et reginae Beatricis de Aragonia (1458–[1476]–1490), Budapest 2011.

45 Cf. Enrica Guerra, Niuna cosa violenta pò essere perpetua. I conflitti europei del secolo XV nella vita di Beatrice d'Aragona, regina d'Ungheria, in: Enrica Guerra (ed.), Voci di donne. La guerra nelle testimonianze femminili, Roma 2009, 37–60; on Croatian case studies see Borislav Grgin, Kraljica Beatrica Aragonska i ugarsko-hrvatsko-napuljski odnosi u posljednjoj cetvrtini 15. stoljeca [Queen Beatrice of Aragon and Hungarian-Croatian-Neapolitan Relations in the Last Quarter of the Fifteenth Century], in: Radovi. Zavod za Hrvatsku Povijest, 52, 3 (2020), 189–201, at: https://hrcak.srce.hr/255133, access: 25 September 2024.

3. Representations and contemporary reflections of power couples

The military and diplomatic conflict with the Habsburgs, Friedrich III and Maximilian I, shaped the politics of the Hungarian couple in the following years, culminating in Matthias's conquest of Vienna in 1485.[46] In addition to correspondence, treaties and documents, the many artistic manifestations reflect the multi-dimensional nature of the disputes and thus also the contemporary perceptions of the ruling couple. A prime example is a sumptuously designed edition of the work of the Greek scholar Flavius Philostratus, which was part of the famous book collection initiated by Matthias Hunyadi (also known as *Bibliotheca Corviniana*).[47] The manuscript was created after the conquest of Wiener Neustadt in August 1487. Its images are related to King Matthias's Austrian conquests, showing Matthias and most likely his young son (depicted riding on a triumphal chariot).[48] The framing text on fols. 2r-10r offers a summary of contemporary events by the chronicler Antonio Bonfini (1427–1502), and then moves on to Philostratus and his translation. The dedication is not only addressed to Matthias Hunyadi but also to Queen Beatrice, who arrived in Vienna a few days after her husband, and to John Corvinus.[49] The diary of the Viennese physician Tichtel, mentioned above, is another source that shows how the royal family presented itself in Vienna and positioned itself against its political rivals.[50] Until his death in 1490, Matthias spent most of his time in Vienna, Wiener Neustadt and the surrounding area,

---

46 Cf. Ferdinand Opll, Wienna caput Austrie ad Vngaros pervenit. Matthias Corvinus und Wien, in: Wiener Geschichtsblätter, 65 (2010), 1–20; Katalin Szende, "Proud Vienna suffered sore …". Matthias Corvinus and Vienna, 1457–1490, in: Farbaky/Spekner/Szende/Végh (eds.), Matthias Corvinus, the King, see note 18, 381–391; Richard Perger, Die ungarische Herrschaft über Wien 1485–1490 und ihre Vorgeschichte, in: Wiener Geschichtsblätter, 45 (1990), 53–87; Albert von Berzeviczy, König Matthias Corvinus und Königin Beatrix in Wien und Österreich, in: Ungarische Jahrbücher, 12 (1932), 205–214.
47 Cf. Philostratus, Codex Heroica. Budapest, Országos Széchényi Könyvtár, 3299 Cod. Lat. 417, fol. 2r, at: https://corvina.hu/kepnezegeto/index.php?corvina=codlat417&lang=en&img=7#7, access: 25 Sept. 2024. The codex contains various texts by Philostratus, which Antonio Bonfini had translated into Latin on behalf of the king; his text was subsequently copied and illuminated in Florence. Cf. the manuscript description by Árpád Mikó (Works of the Greek rhetor Philostratus, translated by Antonio Bonfini, in: Farbaky/Spekner/Szende/Végh, Matthias Corvinus, the King, see note 18, 474). Cf. also Csaba Csapodi, The Corvinian Library. History and Stock, Budapest 1973.
48 Description based on Mikó, Works of the Greek rhetor, see note 47.
49 Cf. Horváth, Itineraria, see note 44, 134. For the dedication, see Philostratus, Codex Heroica. Budapest, Országos Széchényi Könyvtár, 3299 Cod. Lat. 417, fol. 2r, see note 47: "Compluraque uolumina Maiestati tue ac Diue Beatrici filioque Ioanni fauste indolis adolescenti dedicassemus".
50 On the royal *adventus* to Vienna, see Von Karajan, Johannes Tichtel's Tagebuch, see note 1, 34. See also Otto Mazal, Notizen des Dr. Johannes Tichtl zur Geschichte der Auseinandersetzung Friedrichs III. mit Matthias Corvinus (1477–1485), in: Mitteilungen des Instituts für Österreichische Geschichtsforschung, 69 (1961), 97–99.

where John Corvinus and Beatrice were also regularly present.[51] Although Beatrice spent most of her time in Hungary, she apparently attached some importance to their joint representation in Vienna,[52] where the couple demonstratively presented themselves as the legitimate rulers of Austria: Matthias visited the relic treasure of St. Stephen's, paid university scholars for their teaching, awarded knighthoods and privileges, and organised tournaments and festivities with Beatrice.[53]

In both Hungary and Austria, Beatrice and Matthias sought the support of artists, scholars and writers from many different countries.[54] The demonstration of artistic knowledge and scholarship became a powerful means of presenting their royal image, and the couple were evidently willing to accept what the artists they sponsored had to offer. This included not only texts but also images of the royal family – a genre increasingly used in the fifteenth century to depict families and couples.[55] For example, after their marriage, two marble reliefs were made for the royal court in Buda. They show Beatrice and Matthias in the same size (55 x 38.5 cm), each in profile and looking at each other. According to Livia Varga, the similarity in size, format, material and style suggests that the reliefs were conceived as complementary parts of an ensemble. However, the context for which they were intended is unclear (for example wall mounting or display in representative rooms, although smaller rooms such as a *studiolo* seem more likely).[56] Beatrice and Matthias are portrayed in antique form as a virtuous and educated couple, befitting a power couple who developed their court into a centre of contemporary Renaissance culture.

In Poland, Elizabeth and Casimir managed to create and maintain an immensely harmonious image. This was largely due to the ostentatious piety of the couple and the

---

51 Cf. Horváth, Itineraria, see note 44, 119–131 (Matthias) and 134–137 (Beatrice).
52 This is underscored by a story told by Antonio Bonfini in his *Decades of Hungarian History* (*Rerum Ungaricarum Decades*): In 1487, Beatrice travelled to Vienna despite a severe fever, even though an infectious disease had claimed many victims there. Cf. Antonius de Bonfinis, Rerum Ungaricarum Decades, Bd. 4: Decades IV et dimidia V, Liber VIII, ed. by József Fógel, Béla Iványi and László Juhász, Leipzig 1941, 55.
53 Cf. Von Karajan, Johannes Tichtel's Tagebuch, see note 1, 37 or ibid., 44. A seal of Matthias Hunyadi as Hungarian King and Austrian Duke can be found on a letter of arms for the brothers Leopold, Peter, Ludwig and Hanns Feer and their cousin Heinrich (8 Dec. 1488). Cf. Staatsarchiv Luzern, URK 503/8984, at: https://query-staatsarchiv.lu.ch/detail.aspx?ID=1116090, access: 25 Sept. 2024.
54 From the abundant work on royal patronage, see e.g. Valery Rees, Buda as a Center of Renaissance and Humanism, in: Balázs Nagy, Martyn Rady, Katalin Szende and András Vadás (eds.), Medieval Buda in Context, Leiden/Boston 2016, 472–493; Jolán Balogh, A művészet Mátyás király udvarában [Art at the Court of King Matthias], 2 vols., Budapest 1966; Farbaky/Spekner/Szende/Végh, Matthias Corvinus, the King, see note 18.
55 Cf. Marianne Bournet-Bacot, Le portrait de couple en Allemagne à la Renaissance: D'un genre au genre, Rennes 2014.
56 Cf. Livia Varga, The Reconsideration of the Portrait Reliefs of King Matthias Corvinus (1458–1490), and Queen Beatrix of Aragon (1476–1508), in: Bulletin du Musée Hongrois des Beaux-Arts, 90/91 (1999), 53–72, 175–188, 56.

entire family, which scholars have aptly described as *pietas Jagiellonica*.[57] This is evidenced by the numerous donations of money and goods made by the king or queen to ecclesiastical and monastic institutions.[58] In particular, Elizabeth was responsible for the donation of numerous works of art (for example books, textiles or blacksmithing), thus promoting the furnishing of sacred spaces.[59] In 1472, the royal couple and their children were even received into the brotherhood of the local Pauline Fathers on the "Luminous Mount" in Częstochowa (without a prior personal visit, however, as is known from other royal pilgrimages).[60]

The close cooperation between Elizabeth and Casimir finally manifested itself in 1470, when they founded the Chapel of the Holy Cross in the Wawel Cathedral in Kraków. The chapel, consecrated in the tradition of Jagiellonian-Luxembourg's devotion to the Holy Cross, was located opposite a chapel donated by Casimir's mother and designed to serve as a joint burial chapel.[61] The walls and vaults were decorated with paintings in the Byzantine-Russian style. On the northern wall, an inscription in West Russian referred to the founders, thus presenting Casimir and Elizabeth through their claims to power and their dynastic traditions.[62] Keystones in the vault with the coats of

---

57 Cf. the correspondingly titled chapter in Borkowska, Dynastia Jagiellonów, see note 20, 390–471; cf. also eadem, La culture religieuse des Jagellons polonais, in: L'Eglise et le peuple chrétien dans les pays de l'Europe du Centre-Est et du Nord (XIVe–XVe siècles), Roma 1990, 249–265, at: https://www.persee.fr/doc/efr_0000-0000_1990_act_128_1_3765, access: 25 Sept. 2024.
58 Cf. Urszula Borkowska, The Jagiellonians as Founders of Ecclesiastical Institutions in the Grand Duchy of Lithuania and Poland, in: Popp/Suckale, Die Jagiellonen, see note 24, 123–130.
59 For a short overview, see Andrea Langer, "Ex longa stirpe Imperatorum". Zum Einfluß Elisabeths von Habsburg (1436/37–1505) auf die Kunst- und Repräsentationstraditionen am jagiellonischen Hof, in: Andrea Langer and Georg Michels (eds.), Metropolen und Kulturtransfer im 15./16. Jahrhundert. Prag – Krakau – Danzig – Wien, Stuttgart 2001, 121–140, esp. 126–137; more examples in: Burkhardt, Gemischtes Doppel, see note *. A central source is the queen's will of June 1505. Józef Garbacik, Testament królowej Elżbiety Rakuszanki żony Kazimierza Jagiellończyka [Testament of Queen Elizabeth of Austria, Wife of Casimir Jagiellon] (27 VI 1505), in: Zofia Budkowska, Jan Dabrowski and Kazimierz Lepszy (eds.), Prace z dziejów Polski feudalnej ofiarowane Romanowi Grodeckiemu w 70 rocznicę urodzin [Papers on the History of Feudal Poland Offered to Roman Grodecki on His 70th Birthday], Warszawa 1960, 309–319.
60 Cf. Jacek Szpak, Kontakty polskich królowych z sanktuarium i klasztorem paulinów na Jasnej Górze w Częstochowie [The Contacts of Polish Queens with the Sanctuary and the Pauline Monastery at Jasna Góra in Częstochowa], in: Rocznik Filozoficzny Ignatianum, 27, 2 (2021), 141–159; Aleksandra Witkowska, The Cult of the Jasna Góra Sanctuary in the Form of Pilgrimages till the Middle of the 17th Century, in: Acta Poloniae Historica, 61 (1990), 63–90. On royal pilgrimages, see Urszula Borkowska, Polskie pielgrzymki Jagiellonów [Polish pilgrimages of the Jagiellonians], in: Halina Manikowska and Hanna Zaremska (eds.), Peregrinationes. Pilgrzymki w kulturze dawnej Europy [Peregrinationes. Pilgrimages in the Culture of Ancient Europe], Warszawa 1995, 358–375.
61 Cf. Urszula Borkowska, Pobożność rodziny Kazimierza Jagiellończyka [Piety of the Family of Casimir Jagiellonian], in: Analecta Cracoviensia, 16 (1984), 23–41.
62 "By the benevolence and wisdom of the Almighty, this chapel was painted by order of the great illustrious King Casimir, by the grace of God King of Poland, Grand Duke of Lithuania, Lord of Ruthenia, Samogitia and Prussia, ruler of many other lands, and by his beautiful royal wife Elizabeth, of Austrian descent, granddaughter of the greatest Emperor Sigismund, Lord of Austria, and the

arms of Poland, Lithuania and Hungary (Elizabeth's heritage) symbolically confirm this impression. In 1484, their son Casimir was buried in the Chapel of the Holy Cross, followed by King Casimir himself in 1492; Elizabeth and her two daughters of the same name, who both died in infancy, were also buried here.[63] They established a new tradition, as Polish kings had previously been buried in the nave of the cathedral. Elizabeth and Casimir, however, met in death in a separate room whose inscriptions and symbols expressed the territorial and dynastic claims of the royal couple and their family.

This marital and dynastic unity is also reflected in the presentation of the Jagiellon family tree, which in 1506 was included in a comprehensive collection of legal statutes (the so-called *Statut Łaski*)[64]. The woodcut shows Elizabeth and Casimir as the ancestors of the dynasty: both are depicted as crowned figures sitting on a throne at the bottom right and left of the image, with the root of the tree growing upwards from their chests. The branches of the tree divide the picture into four sections, each containing three or four figures, whose scrolls, insignia and clothing identify them as the children of the royal couple, each in a different social position. The overall composition of the couple and their children, almost all of whom have achieved high political or ecclesiastical offices or social positions, is impressive both in terms of the number of children and their rank and dignity. This is certainly one of the reasons why many contemporary observers echoed the image of concentrated family power.[65] Of course, the woodcut was only made in 1506, when Casimir IV had been dead for 14 years and Elizabeth had just died. In that year, their son Alexander, then king, ordered the first comprehensive collection of laws in Poland, distributed in several hundred copies. With the woodcut included in this collection, he created a tribute to his parents as joint rulers, thus contributing to their posthumous influential image as a true power couple.[66]

Bohemian and Hungarian lands in 1470." Translation from the German version provided by Langer, Zum Einfluß, see note 59, 127. Cf. also Anna Różycka-Bryzek, Bizantyńsko-ruskie malowidła ścienne w kaplicy Świętokrzyskiej na Wawelu [Byzantine-Ruthenian wall paintings in the Holy Cross Chapel at Wawel Castle], in: Studia do dziejów Wawelu, 3 (1968), 175–293.

63 Cf. Tadeusz Lalik, Kaplica królewska i publiczne praktyki religijne rodziny Kazimierza Jagiellończyka [The Royal Chapel and Public Religious Practices of the Family of Casimir Jagiellonian], in: Kwartalnik Historyczny, 88 (1981), 391–415.

64 Elizabeth of Habsburg and Casimir IV of Poland and their children. Genealogical tree of the Jagiellonians in the so-called *Statut Łaski*. Commune incliti Poloniae Regni priuilegium …, Kraków 1506, fol. 85r. Warszawa, Biblioteka Narodowa, Sign. SD XVI.F.88 adl. Source: public domain, online accessible at: https://polona.pl/item-view/f89d11f3-7e47-48a8-98de-7a4996d8182b?page=207.

65 Cf. Burkhardt, Das Erbe der Frauen, see note 17, 277; Bues, Die Jagiellonen, see note 8, 90.

66 On the context, see Julia Dücker, Ein Bild des spätmittelalterlichen Königreichs Polen, in: Claus Ambos, Petra Roesch, Bernd Schneidmüller and Stefan Weinfurter (eds.), Bild und Ritual. Visuelle Kulturen in historischer Perspektive, Darmstadt 2010, 197–209; Julia Dücker, Pro communi reipublicae bono. König und Reich im jagiellonischen Polen um 1500, in: Florin Nicolae Ardelean, Christopher Nicholson and Johannes Preiser-Kapeller (eds.), Between Worlds. The Age of the Jagiellonians, Frankfurt am Main 2013, 61–78.

Fig. 1: Elizabeth of Habsburg and Casimir IV of Poland and their children. Genealogical tree of the Jagiellonians in the so-called *Statut Łaski*. Commune incliti Poloniae Regni priuilegium ..., Kraków 1506, fol. 85r. Warszawa, Biblioteka Narodowa, Sign. SD XVI.F.88 adl. Source: public domain (for detailed picture credits see footnote 64).

4. Conclusion

This article has discussed the political significance of, and the social reflections on, Central European royal couples around 1500. Previous studies have examined individual kings and queens separately, without considering the logics and benefits of joint rule. In order to avoid the construction of political gender dichotomies and to stimulate further discussions on the dynamics of gender and power in premodern

Europe, the article explored the significance and perception of joint royal rule, the emergence of new forms of participation or models of conflict resolution, and contemporary assessments of royal couples. The term "power couples" was used to highlight the shared nature of the political power of monarchs, princes and nobles of both sexes.

The contribution offered a systematic analysis and comparison of Elisabeth of Habsburg (1436–1505) and Casimir IV in Poland (1427–1492) and, in Hungary, Beatrice of Aragon (1457–1508) and Matthias "Corvinus" Hunyadi (1443–1490). As the examples of the Polish and the Hungarian royal couples show, power couples had an immense political and cultural impact in premodern Europe. They deliberately presented themselves as a marital or dynastic unit, always torn between biological contingency, dynastic representation and the awareness of being rulers.

Joint decisions were made in accordance with situational requirements and in recognition of the political conditions. This meant that the views and influences of contemporary observers were just as important as individual interests and dispositions. Although the partners sometimes not only complemented but also competed with each other, such marital dynamics were almost never perceived as destabilising the monarchs' power or even as a threat to the monarchy as a whole. Rather, power couples were usually able to exert outstanding political, social and / or cultural influence, and at the same time actively exploit the mutual influences between the pragmatic possibilities of joint rule and premodern concepts of gender and gendered role models.

Elodie Lecuppre-Desjardin

Foreign Princesses in the Service of the Great Principality of Burgundy: Delegations of Power in Favour of Duchesses in the Fifteenth Century

When, on 22 February 1472, Margaret of York spoke to the mayor and aldermen of Dijon, demanding that the *procureur syndic*, Jean Rabustel, be replaced by Guillaume Billocart, her tone was comminative:

> "We, who have not yet made a request since we became lady of this place, write to you to ask and demand that you respond favourably to this request, if it is reasonable, and it is. And you must not resist and take care to satisfy us by appointing from now on the said Guillaume Billocart to the said office, as my most revered lord has written to you and requested."[1]

The duchess demanded this. In her opinion, it was all the more legitimate since it was the first time that she had made a claim since her marriage to Duke Charles the Bold in 1468. However, the archives prove that this request was in fact not the first one, as Margaret of York had already applied to the Dijon authorities on 15 April 1470 on behalf of a certain Master Denis Baudot to obtain the position of chaplain in the Church of Notre-Dame.[2] In both cases, we are struck not only by the intransigence of the wording but also by the fact that the letter confirms an order already given by the prince. Hence, Margaret acted as an executor, using her privilege as the 'new lady' to reinforce and speed up the execution of her husband's demand. Regardless of the failure

---

1 Joseph Garnier (ed.), Correspondance de la mairie de Dijon, Dijon 1868, 1, nr. 77, 124–125 : "Nous qui encoires ne vous avons fait requeste dont nous avons souvenance depuis que nous somes venues à seignorie, escripvons présentement devers vous et vous prions et requérons si acertes que povons, que à ceste notre première requeste laquelle, posé qu'elle ne feust raisonnable, ce que elle est, ne nous devez résister, vous veuillez à nostre contemplacion commectre et instituer dès maintenant ledit Guillaume Billocart audit office de procuration, ainsi que mondit très redoubté seigneur le vous escript et mande [...]." There is a letter from Charles the Bold to the city of Dijon dated 16 Feb. 1472 (Dijon, AM, B451, fol. 19). The *procureur syndic* is a judicial officer.
2 Cf. Garnier, Correspondance, see note 1, nr. 68, 110–111: "Et pour ce [...] que, avons y cellui maistre Denis en singulière et espéciale recommandation et désirons sa promocion en sainte église [...], veuillez avoir ledit maistre Denis pour espécialement recommandé, attendu que c'est la première requeste que vous avons faite..." (And for this reason [...] that we have given this Maistre Denis a singular and special recommendation and desire his promotion in the holy Church [...], please have the said Maistre Denis specially recommended, since this is the first request we have made to you [...]).

of Margaret's request of 1472, this specific exchange has the merit of raising a key question of great concern to historians specialising in women's power. Did Margaret of York, like other princesses of her time, have any real room for manoeuvre in political decision-making? Or, on the contrary, was she merely a sort of extension of the prince, approving through her proximity to him the orders decided in council by other eminent male figures, such as the chancellors and other officers of the court? Research in the Burgundian-Habsburg area has tended to consider the lieutenancies of Charles V's aunt (Margaret of Austria) and sister (Mary of Hungary) as the first periods of strong personal political involvement by women and a recognised delegated authority in these territories. It is true that the regency (1507–1515), then the governance of the Netherlands (1519–1530), successively assumed by Margaret during Charles's minority and his departure for Castile, and the governance assumed by Mary after the death of her aunt, which lasted until 1555, provided ample evidence of full decision-making capacity of these powerful women. And even though Mary of Hungary believed that a woman "is never feared or respected like a man", it is clear from the number of their actions that these princesses made full use of the powers entrusted to them, with great political and financial acumen.[3]

However, this delegation of power was not unprecedented, and this way of governing is illustrated in the earlier examples discussed in this study. In the fifteenth century, the dukes of Burgundy compensated for the fragmentation of their territory by entrusting many responsibilities to their wives. Whether they were on the battlefield, engaged in civil war with the Armagnacs, embroiled in the turmoil of the Hundred Years' War or pursuing their ambitions to conquer the Empire, they all entrusted the affairs of part of their country to their wives for varying lengths of time. And the chronological cursor could be moved back much further, if we think in particular of the delegations of power inherited by the countesses of Flanders, especially during the crusading episodes in

---

3 Exact quote: "Et en mon endroit, il m'en a faillu plus faire par pure nécessité, pour le bien des affaires, que je désirois, oultre que la femme n'est jamais respectée et craincte comme l'homme, de quelle qualité qu'elle soit." Memoirs in Charles Weiss (ed.), Papiers d'État du cardinal de Granvelle, Paris 1843, IV, 474 (I thank Jules Dejonckheere for the precise reference to this confession). Marie de Hongrie had greater responsibilities than her aunt. Cf. Jean-Marie Cauchies, Marguerite d'Autriche, gouvernante et diplomate, in: Agostino Paravicini-Bagliani, Éva Pibiri and Denis Reynard (eds.), L'itinérance des seigneurs (XIVe–XVIe siècles), Lausanne 2003, 353–376; Waiting for Jules Dejonckheere's thesis to be defended at UCLouvain: idem., Marie de Hongrie, sentinelle des Pays-Bas (1531–1555); Bertrand Federinov and Gilles Docquier (eds.), Marie de Hongrie: politique et culture sous la Renaissance aux Pays-Bas, International Exhibitions, Morlanwelz 2009; Laetitia V. G. Gorter van Royen and Jean-Paul Hoyois (eds.), Correspondance de Marie de Hongrie avec Charles Quint et Nicolas de Granvelle, 1 (1532 et années antérieures), Turnhout 2009 and 2 (1533), Turnhout 2018; eadem, Maria van Hongarije, regentes der Nederlanden. Een politieke analysis op basis van den regentschap ordonnanties en haar correspondentie met Karel V, Hilversum 1995; eadem, De regentessen van Karel V in de Nederlanden. Beeld en Werkelijkheid, in: Tijdschrift voor geschiedenis, 110 (1997), 169–197.

which their husbands were involved in the twelfth century.[4] The list of princesses with decision-making powers in the absence of their husbands is therefore long, and only confirms the idea of a phenomenon that was, on the whole, very widely spread. The question, therefore, is not whether the delegation of power to a woman existed. Because it did. Rather, the article asks about the nature of this power and how it was exercised in practice. In other words, were the princesses, in this case the duchesses of Burgundy by marriage and not *suo jure*, merely puppets in the hands of the men in the council or did they conduct their own policies?[5] Did their arrival from more or less distant lands and their education in different curial cultures constitute an obstacle to the recognition of their authority? Or might it even have worked to their advantage? And in both cases, can we speak of a female exercise of power? In the end, this is the big question that recent studies on the *agency* of queens and princesses have been trying to answer.[6] As Martha Howell points out, *agency* has become a key word in studies of women's power, with the aim of assessing the extent to which women's political action was able to change patriarchal norms. Such an approach must be distinguished from that which guides other studies in which women act only as partners to their husbands, fathers, sons, nephews, etc.[7] If we take a broad definition of political *agency* as 'the ability or capacity to act or exert power', then the duchesses of Burgundy certainly demonstrated recognised *agency*. But if the definition is narrowed down to a challenge to male domination, then it must be said that the duchesses did not assume such a role. Did they have the means to oppose this male domination and, moreover, did they want to? By studying their origins and their integration into the court, and then their actions and investments in the matrimonial and religious affairs of their time, we will be able to respond to Martha Howell's call, in the tradition of Gabrielle Spiegel, to integrate

---

[4] Cf. in particular, Thérèse De Hemptinne, De gravinnen van Vlaanderen in de 12de eeuw, in: Spiegel historiael, 15 (1980), 450–456 and eadem, Women as Mediators between the Powers of Comitatus and Sacredotium. Two Countesses of Flanders in the Eleventh and Twelfth Centuries, in: Martin Gosman, Arjo Vanderjagt and Jan Veenstra (eds.), The Propagation of Power in the Medieval West, in: Mediaevalia Groningana, 23 (1997), 287–299; Pénélope Adair, Countess Clemence: Her power and its foundation, in: Theresa M. Van (ed.), Queens, Regents and Potentates, Dallas 1993, 63–72.
[5] The brief overview provided here does not include Margaret of Male, wife of Duke Philip the Bold, who was the legitimate heiress to the counties of Flanders, Artois and Burgundy.
[6] The bibliography is immense. See the essential points of these questions in Anne J. Duggan, Introduction, in: eadem (ed.), Queens and Queenship in Medieval Europe, Woodbridge 1997, XV–XXII. See also studies by Elena Woodacre, including Queens and Queenship, York 2021; Medieval Feminist Forum. A Journal of Gender and Sexuality, 51, 2 (2016): Beyond Women and Power: Looking Backward and Moving Forward, ed. by Kathy M. Krause.
[7] Cf. Martha Howell, The Problem of Women's Agency in Late Medieval and Early Modern Europe, in: Sarah Joan Moran and Amanda Pipkin, Women and Gender in the Early Modern Low Countries, Leiden 2019, 21–31, 22: "In what sense then can a woman sufficiently free herself of the patriarchal regime that is 'given and transmitted from the past' in order to claim agency."

agency into the structures and norms of their time, and to reveal a more subtle but nonetheless firm assertion of authority by the Burgundian princesses.[8]

1. Women ready to rule

The three princesses of Burgundy, who will provide us with some answers to these questions, are Margaret of Bavaria (1372–1424), wife of John the Fearless (1371–1419), Isabella of Portugal (1397–1471), third wife of Philip the Good (1396–1467), and Margaret of York (1446–1503), third wife of Charles the Bold (1433–1477).[9] Very little is known about the education of these princesses, who undoubtedly received the kind of training that could be found in the princely courts of Europe at the time, giving rise to the idea of an "international curial habitus", similar to what has been said about chivalric codes.[10] Margaret of Bavaria, daughter of Albert, duke of Bavaria, regent and later count of Hainaut, Holland and Zeeland, was 13 at the time of her wedding at Cambrai in 1385. It would appear that she had received a literate education equivalent to that which guided the first steps of the men in the family, minus the military training. Albert's court in The Hague was renowned for its bibliophily, and religious works – many of which have disappeared – were a staple of the princess's studies, as can be seen from her devotion to Colette de Corbie.[11] Isabella of Portugal left the court of

---

8 Cf. Howell, The Problem, see note 7. In this article, Howell draws on Gabrielle Spiegel's reflections on the intentionality of historical actors' deeds and adapts it to the issue of women's agency. Cf. Gabrielle M. Spiegel, Practicing History: New Directions in Historical – Writing after the Linguistic Turn, Baltimore 2005.
9 There are no major studies on Margaret of Bavaria. For the first reference, see Émile Varenbergh, Marguerite de Bavière, duchesse de Bourgogne, in: Annales de l'Académie Royale de Belgique, série 2, t. 8, 1872, 323–347, partly repeated in: Alain Marchandisse, Le pouvoir de Marguerite de Bavière, duchesse de Bourgogne, une esquisse, in: Éric Bousmar, Jonathan Dumont, Alain Marchandisse and Bertrand Schnerb (eds.), Femmes de pouvoir, femmes politiques durant les derniers siècles du Moyen Âge et au cours de la première Renaissance, Bruxelles 2012, 493–506. It should be noted, however, that the date of this princess's birth was re-established by Ludovic Nys, who, thanks to the messenger accounts, was able to establish that Marguerite was born in December 1372, ten years later than the date usually used. Cf. Ludovic Nys, Les Bavière-Straubing de basse-Bavière, Hainaut, Hollande, Zélande et Frise. Essai de chrono-généalogie, in: Revue du Nord, Special Issue, 33 (2023), 27–74, 59. For more information on Isabella of Portugal, consult the monograph by Monique Sommé, Isabelle de Portugal, duchesse de Bourgogne. Une femme au pouvoir au XVe siècle, Villeneuve-d'Ascq 1998; On Margaret of York, see Christine Weightman, Margaret of York, duchess of Burgundy (1446–1503), New York 1989 and the catalogue to the exhibition: Women of Distinction. Margaret of York & Margaret of Austria, Leuven 2005.
10 Werner Paravicini, Préface. La fin du mythe bourguignon?, in: idem (ed.), La cour de Bourgogne et l'Europe, Ostfildern 2013, 9–17. The education of princesses, is better documented in the following period. Cf. Tupu Ylä-Antilla, Habsburg Female Regents in the Early 16th Century, Doctoral dissertation, Helsinki 2019.
11 On court culture in Holland under the Bavarians, see Frits P. Van Ostroom, Court and Culture. Dutch Literature, 1350–1450, Berkeley/Los Angeles/Oxford 1992.

the Avis at the age of 33, and her education was not only carefully nurtured but also put to the test in practice, since at the age of 18, following the death of her mother Philippa of Lancaster, she was the only woman of authority at court, alongside her father and her five brothers.[12] The care Isabella took with her own son's education is further evidence of the particular attention she paid to books and their edifying content. By entrusting a number of translations to Vasque de Lucène and paying for the services of Antoine Haneron, a tutor who championed humanism in the northern lands, the princess showed the extent to which the customs of the Burgundian library became an integral part of the intellectual life of the Avis-Lancasters.[13] As for Margaret of York (1446–1503), the sixth of twelve children born to Cecile Neville and Richard Plantagenet, sister of Kings Edward IV and Richard III, her bibliophily, her devotional commitment and the presence of references in her own handwriting suggest that she too received a classical education that enabled her to read and write in her native language and in French, while her transfer to the court of Burgundy was an opportunity to learn some rudimentary Dutch.[14]

Despite the scarcity of sources, there is every reason to believe that the integration of these princesses from neighbouring or foreign houses was fairly smoothly. When Isabella of Portugal arrived at the Burgundian court, which was not characterised by the presence of a dowager duchess, her husband made the transition as pleasant as possible by welcoming part of the Portuguese retinue for several months.[15] A number of women and men of honour remained close to the Lusitanian princess, which undoubtedly helped create a climate of trust, unlike the experience of Joanna of Castile, known as Joanna the Mad, who, on her arrival at the court of Philip the Fair in 1496, was deprived of her retinue and confined to a diplomatic and potentially dramatic isolation. The lack of financial resources guaranteed by her dowry prevented the Infanta of Spain from establishing her own network and taking control of her household.[16] On the other hand, when the young brides entered the Burgundian family and their husbands' mothers were still alive, the dowager duchesses Margaret of Male for Margaret of Bavaria and Isabella of Portugal for Margaret of York played a key role in the transition and initiation into the customs and habits of the court and the duties of ducal wives. Margaret of Male seems to have chosen the members of her daughter-in-law's

---

12 Cf. Sommé, Isabelle de Portugal, see note 9, 22–23.
13 On the intellectual patronage of Isabella of Portugal, see in particular Charity C. Willard, Isabel of Portugal, patroness of humanism?, in: Franco Simone (ed.), Miscellanea di studi e recherche sul quattrocento francese, Turin 1967, 517–544. On the education of the young Charles de Charolais by his mother, see Monique Sommé, La jeunesse de Charles le Téméraire d'après les comptes de la cour de Bourgogne, in: Revue du Nord, 64, 254–255 (July–Dec.1982), 731–750.
14 Cf. Weightman, Margaret of York, see note 9, 24–25.
15 Cf. Georges Chastellain, Œuvres ed. by J. Kervyn de Lettenhove Bruxelles 1836–1866, II, 15.
16 Cf. Clara Kalogerakis's work in progress, in particular eadem, Les fides ecartelées: Jeanne de Castille et la cour de Bourgogne (1496–1506), in: Publications du Centre Européen d'Etudes Bourguignonnes, 62 (2022), 151–166.

household herself. The young Margaret of Bavaria quickly became attached to her and, as early as 1396, took her place at the meetings in Ardres when the duchess was unable to attend due to an attack of gout.[17] Isabella of Portugal, who had orchestrated the Anglo-Burgundian alliance from start to finish, was entrusted with the task of drawing up the marriage contract between her son and Margaret of York, and she came out of her seclusion at the Château de la Motte-au-Bois to welcome the young woman to Bruges and accompany her on her first steps in Flanders.[18] The young duchess maintained good relations with her mother-in-law and visited her regularly, as she had her own hotel with around 140 members. Isabella of Portugal's Lancastrian ancestry, which made her a cousin of Margaret's mother, undoubtedly played a role in the closeness between the two women, both of whom were particularly sensitive to England's cause and, as we shall see, very involved in their own affairs.[19] The integration of the duchesses presented here into the Burgundian court was achieved by several means. Their entourage was carefully selected by the House of Burgundy and the ladies-in-waiting were often the wives of the prince's officers. Were these measures designed to control them or, on the contrary, to facilitate their initiation into the ways of the court? Probably a little of both. In any case, the way in which the princesses were surrounded was not so different from that of the young princes, and suggests a desire to ensure an effective and lasting framework of government. The example of Margaret of York is particularly striking in this respect. Her ladies-in-waiting were under the command of Marie Countess de Charny, the illegitimate daughter of Philip the Good, whose husband Pierre de Beauffremont, lord of Charny, Seneschal of Burgundy and Knight of the Golden Fleece, was the captain of her bodyguard. On her arrival, Margaret was accompanied in her inaugural entries by Antoine, count de la Roche and first chamberlain of the court, David and Jean de Bourgogne, bishops of Utrecht and Cambrai

---

17 I would like to thank Jean-Baptiste Santamaria for this reference from 1388, according to which it was Marguerite de Male who sent a messenger "au Boiz en Beausse [pour] querir la dame dudit lieu pour servir madame de Nevers". ADCO B1473, fol. 62v. With regard to Ardres, an English document lists the lords, ladies and maidens who accompanied the king of France, including Margaret of Bavaria, the countess of Nevers. Paul Meyer and Siméon Luce, Documents et notices historiques. L'entrevue d'Ardres. 1396, in: Annuaire-Bulletin de la Société de l'Histoire de France, 18, 2 (1881), 209–224, 223.
18 Cf. Sommé, Isabelle de Portugal, see note 9, 61–63. Charles the Bold, who had full confidence in his mother, gave her full powers to negotiate the marriage in a letter dated 24 October 1467 : "[…] savoir faisons que nous, ayans, comme raison est, tout parfaicte et entiere confidence en notre tres chiere dame et mere, comme en icelle en qui geist le greigneur soing, regard en entente de notre personne et de tous noz affaires, et poure ce que a personne nulle a nous si feable qu'elle ne pourrions donner charge de telles et si grandes matières […] avons donné et donnons par ceste plain povoir et auctorité a notre dite dame et mère […]", cit. following Thomas Rymer, Foedera, London 1745, 11, 612–613.
19 Isabella of Portugal was the daughter of John of Avis and Philippa of Lancaster, herself the sister of Joan who had married Ralph Neville, the father of Cecile who married Richard Duke of York, by whom Margaret of York was born.

respectively, bastard sons of Philip the Good, Ferry de Clugny bishop of Tournai, Louis de Gruuthuse, Philippe de Croÿ, Antoine Rolin (son of the chancellor Nicolas), etc., many of whom were members of the ducal council. Men of trust and experience, such as Jean de Pernes to Isabella, a former servant of Philip the Bold who had advised his son Antoine in Brabant, again ensured a certain continuity in the business, despite the dispersion of lands in the Great Principality and the succession of princes. Nor should we underestimate the influence of the ecclesiastics who moved from one hotel to another, such as Nicolas Finet, chaplain to Isabella of Portugal, who later became almoner to Margaret of York and author of her spiritual guide *Le dialogue de la duchesse de Bourgogne à Jesus-Christ*.[20] In short, the princesses were trained to govern and applied themselves to it, but – just like young male princes – they always did so in the company of men who were experts in the affairs of the House of Burgundy and who were authorised to draw up decrees in the name of the princess, whose physical presence was necessary to ensure the authority and legitimacy of the orders issued. The Burgundian princess governed within a network of influence between her husband's court and her own.

2. "Madame en son conseil" or the art of governing in the company of men

In the Great Principality of Burgundy, the delegation of power was not only common but also necessary. The configuration of the space of political power was divided into two 'zones': the northern territories (Duchy of Brabant, County of Flanders, County of Hainaut, Holland, Zeeland, etc.) and the southern territories (Duchy of Burgundy, County of Burgundy, etc.). Correspondingly, the contemporary political culture, which shaped the representations and enactments of power, required the presence of a member of the ducal family in the lands of their lordship.[21] Even in the notoriously rebellious county of Flanders, the exercise of power was based on a political contract, the terms of which allowed the members of the county's representatives to challenge the prince's authority when it was deemed to be lacking. By the same token, the dukes were strongly encouraged to reside in Bruges or Ghent, or to leave their wives or heirs there.[22]

---

20 On Nicolas Finet, see Maureen Boulton, Aimer Dieu et flatter le prince, in: Elina Suomela-Härmä and Juhani Härmä (eds.), Aimer, haïr, menacer, flatter … en moyen français, Paris 2017, 65–74. On this treaty references, see note 52.
21 The two poles were made up of the southern countries (the Duchy of Burgundy, the County of Burgundy, the County of Nevers and the County of Rethel) and the northern countries, which included most of the counties of Flanders, Artois, Hainaut-Holland-Zeeland, Namur, the Duchies of Brabant and Luxembourg, the Lordship of Mechelen and the Duchy of Guelders.
22 On the political contract in the North and the consequences for Burgundian politics, see Elodie Lecuppre-Desjardin, The Illusion of the Burgundian State, Manchester 2022.

When John the Fearless made his Joyous Entry into Ghent on 20 April 1405, the deputies of the Four Members of Flanders sent him their demands, the first of which was that the presence of the duke or duchess should be recognised as having full authority in the absence of her husband. The princess was then to reside in the city of her choice and have full power, enlightened by a council of men familiar with the affairs of the land.[23] John the Fearless agreed, and indeed Margaret of Bavaria ruled in Ghent in her husband's absence from April 1407 to February 1409, as attested by the bailiff's accounts, before leaving for the southern territories.[24] The reports of the Four Members of Flanders indicate that in September 1408, on the eve of the Battle of Othée, in which John the Fearless took part alongside the bishop of Liège, the duchess negotiated with Chancellor Jean de Saulx for military aid to raise 6,000 men.[25] Each of these women exercised a delegation of power, which we can see as a technique of governance that was particularly necessary in the context of a composite principality.[26] So let us look at the nature of the political activities undertaken by these women.

The princesses were largely concerned with hotel matters and the administration of their estates. In this sense, they were driven by the desire to strengthen, exploit and protect their dower. Isabella of Portugal, for example, who had mastered double-entry bookkeeping, excelled not only in the administration of her own income but also in the financial management of the Great Principality, as attested by a reference to Jean Marlette, Receiver of Finances for Hainaut.[27] However, this was not the only power at the service of the Great Principality's interest. In addition to the administration of their hotels and estates, the duchesses were also responsible for military logistics. Whether it was Margaret of Bavaria, who was at the forefront of the French attacks on the Duchy of Burgundy in the early 1410s, Isabella of Portugal, who was behind the recapture of the Burgundian fortresses taken by the French in 1433–1434, or Margaret of York, who took over from her husband in Neuss to welcome the English troops at Calais in 1475, to name but a few examples, they all took part in the war effort. Most often this was a question of *faire finance*, for example raising the money needed for the payment of men, but it could also involve the coordination of military forces. In April 1434, Isabelle not only sent artillery to Mâcon to defend the city but also offered to come to the city in

---

23 Cf. Gilliodts van Severen (ed.), Inventaire des archives de la ville de Bruges, Bruges 1875, III, 507–515, 509.
24 Cf. Richard Vaughan, John the Fearless, Woodbridge 2005⁴, 16–17 (Archives Générales du Royaume, CC21788).
25 Cf. Marchandisse, Le pouvoir de Marguerite de Bavière, see note 9.
26 To open the comparison, see Gabriela Signori and Claudia Zey (ed.), Regentinnen und andere Stellvertreterfiguren vom 10. bis zum 15. Jahrhundert, Oldenbourg 2023; Sebastian Roebert, The Nominations of Elionor of Sicily as Queen-Lieutenant in the Crown of Aragon: Edition and Commentary, in: Mediaeval Studies, 80 (2018), 171–230.
27 On Isabella of Portugal's accounting expertise, see Sommé, Isabelle de Portugal, see note 9, 408–418.

person if the job required it ("de venir, si métier est, en ladite ville en sa personne").[28] Margaret of Bavaria and Isabella of Portugal seem to have taken a real interest in military matters. While the former ordered the display of arms and checked that the Dijon City Guard was in good order, the latter even visited the foundries to see that bombards were being made.[29] The princesses acted, signed their names with a firm will backed by the expression *bon plaisir*, but were always surrounded by a group of men who were experts in military and financial matters.[30] They all issued numerous orders to defend threatened cities and mobilise troops and funds to bolster the duke's armies.[31]

The other major area of agency – diplomacy – often conducted 'behind the curtain', is not always easy to document, as court chroniclers preferred to focus on the princes, whose actions they had to glorify. However, family networks and origins were often used to speed up the resolution of more or less delicate cases, and the foreign origins of princesses could become an asset.[32] At the Congress of Arras in the summer of 1435, Isabella did not take centre stage, but private meetings allowed messages to be passed on, and the duchess received Cardinal Albergati, the pope's mediator, and Henry Beaufort, bishop of Winchester, on several occasions.[33] The Franco-Burgundian reconciliation desired by the duchess made conflict with England inevitable, but very soon, in 1438, Isabella, played a leading role, along with her uncle Henri Beaufort, in the Gravelines conferences, which led to the re-establishment of good relations with England.[34] The duchess's partly English origins undoubtedly facilitated the negotiations, but it is worth noting that her interpersonal skills were put to good use for the Burgundian cause. Margaret of York also used her English origins to promote a rap-

---

28 For information on Margaret of Bavaria's involvement and responsibilities in Burgundy, see Marchandisse, Le pouvoir de Marguerite de Bavière, see note 9, 498–504. Duchess Isabella even offered to sell her own jewels to defend the city, cf. Marcel Canat (ed.), Documents inédits pour servir à l'histoire de la Bourgogne, Chalon-sur-Saône 1863, 1, 250.
29 Cf. Archives Départementales du Nord [ADN], B1969, fol. 27 (1440): "A maistre Pierre, fondeur canonnier, pour don a luy fait par madame la duchesse, quant elle a esté veoir le mole de la bombarde de Dijon que ledit maistre Pierre faisoit en la ville de Bruges." For other examples, see Sommé, Isabelle de Portugal, see note 9, 383 ff.
30 The limited space of this article does not allow us to develop this point, but there are many references in the documentation and a study of the network of these princesses (particularly Marguerite of Bavaria) remains to be carried out. Richard Vaughan argues that Margaret of Bavaria was certainly endowed with real political skills, even if her secretary Jehan de Maroilles accompanied her in many of her decisions, cf. Vaughan, John the Fearless, see note 24, 175.
31 We can compare this significant investment in warfare, which challenges gender stereotypes: Carlos Jesús Rodríguez Casillas (ed.), Mujer y Guerra en la Edad Media. El liderzgo military femenino en la Peninsula Ibérica y el ámbito mediterráneo, Caceres 2024.
32 It should be noted that the situation was more delicate for Michelle de France, second wife of Philip the Good, sister of the Dauphin Charles, the future Charles VII, who in 1419 ordered the assassination of her husband's father, John the Fearless, and who died in Ghent in 1422, rumoured to be a political assassination.
33 Cf. Antoine de la Taverne, Journal de la Paix d'Arras (1435), ed. by André Bossuat, Arras 1936, 80.
34 Cf. Christopher T. Allmand, The Anglo-French Negotiations (1439), in: Bulletin of the Institute of Historical Research, 40 (1967), 1–33.

prochement between her brother and her husband, while over time a way was found for the Burgundian princess to attempt to influence the situation in her native country. In the aftermath of the Nancy disaster, Margaret, then dowager duchess, advised her daughter-in-law to consider marrying her brother, the duke of Clarence, which showed that the cause of Yorkist England was still a priority. However, once Mary's marriage to Maximilian had been concluded, she placed her expertise at the service of the new ruling couple in a Great Principality deprived of many of its officers who had defected to the French court, even playing the role of ambassador to try to win support during the summer of 1480.[35] It was in fact she who signed the indenture contracts to recruit the English soldiers Maximilian needed.[36] While Wim Blockmans claims that the duchess of York never displayed an outspoken personal vision, and used her English connections to the benefit of her husband and then her son-in-law, it must be admitted that the efforts she made at the time of the so-called Perkin Warbeck affair were the result of a personal and firmly committed appreciation. Margaret was convinced of the legitimacy of the man claiming to be one of her nephews who had mysteriously disappeared in the Tower of London (or of the importance of the situation in destabilising the Tudor crown). So she supported the impostor who pretended to be Richard of York, the legitimate son of Edward IV, who had come to claim the throne of England, then in the hands of Henry VII Tudor, almost ten years after his disappearance.[37] On this occasion, the dowager duchess engaged in extensive international correspondence with Castile, Ireland, Scotland and Pope Alexander VI. The rhetoric used to persuade the pope on 8 May 1495 was not drawn from an emotional lexicon, but rather focused on the right of the kings of England to rule in harmony with the people, and on the superiority of the law of blood over the brutal imposition of a new regime.[38] As Margaret was the aunt of the so-called York, there is certainly a family element to this attitude, but it must be emphasised that this woman of power used all the tools of her time to achieve her ends. International diplomacy was undoubtedly a family affair, and princesses knew how to use their connections and the network of their ladies-in-waiting, sisters, aunts and cousins to influence the decisions of the princes in power, using tools worthy of the chancelleries of their male counterparts.

---

35 On how this ruling couple governed, see the article by Christina Lutter and Christof Muigg in this issue.
36 Details of the York family reunion can be found in: Weigthman, Margaret of York, see note 9, 134 ff.
37 For some thoughts on the diplomatic game played by Margaret of York and Margaret of Austria, see Wim Blockmans, Women and Diplomacy, in: Women of Distinction, see note 9, 97–101. The early years of the Tudor Dynasty were troubled, with Margaret repeatedly supporting the claims of 'impostors' such as Lambert Simnel and Perkin Warbeck, who posed as her missing nephews and pretenders to the crown. Cf. Gilles Lecuppre, L'imposture politique au Moyen Âge. La seconde vie des rois, Paris 2005.
38 Cf. the letter from Margaret of York to the pope, in: James Gairdner, Memorials of King Henry the Seventh, r. S. 10, London 1858, 393–399. For an analysis of the case, see Gilles Lecuppre, L'imposture politique au Moyen Âge, see note 37, 235–237, 241.

As part of this active diplomacy, their expected role of intercession also characterised their political action. Based on the biblical model of Esther's intervention with Ahasuerus and repeated many times in the plays that enlivened the Joyous Entries of the princesses, female intercession was based on stereotypes that made women peaceful mediators, like the Virgin Mary. As the embodiment of gentleness and clemency, it was she who had to bend the will of her husband, who, through her gentle words, would know how to prefer "mercy to rigorous justice". However, beyond the literary topoi deconstructed in particular by Jean-Marie Moeglin in the context of the episode of the citizens of Calais in 1347, the princess's diplomatic role in favour of peace was one of her prerogatives, as Christine de Pizan states in her *Épître à la reine:* "il appartient a haute princesse et dame estre moyenneresse de traictié de paix" (it belongs to a high princess and lady to be a mediator of peace).³⁹ And there is no doubt that the use of particular emotions was one of the tools used by these women in a context where diplomacy was mixed with family feelings, as we have just mentioned and as attested by the letter sent to Louis XI by Margaret of York and her daughter-in-law Mary of Burgundy, who, in the aftermath of the Battle of Nancy, appealed to the king of France, casting doubt on the death of the duke of Burgundy and not hesitating to present themselves as "desolate women" seeking the protection of a lord and peace for their land.⁴⁰ There are many examples of this, particularly in the case of the honourable and profitable fines negotiated at the end of urban revolts. Isabella of Portugal was particularly close to the cities, perhaps due to her Lusitanian culture, which had familiarised her with the world of merchants from an early age. She was a remarkable spokeswoman and negotiator for the cities of Flanders, particularly in 1438 after the great revolt in Bruges. In charge of peace talks between Bruges and Philip the Good, she managed to restore order and stability, albeit at the cost of 14,000 ridders granted by the city as a "token of gratitude". Intercession came at a price!⁴¹

However, as we will see in the next section, even in the same urban setting, negotiations could be carried out in a much harsher manner. Clearly, the way in which these princesses exercised their power was in no way inferior to the rigorous methods employed by their husbands. This last remark invites us to go beyond the stereotypes of the

---

39 Angus J. Kennedy, Christine de Pizan's Epistre à la reine (1405), in: Revue des langues romanes, 92 (1988), 256–258. On the Calais episode and Philippa of Hainaut's intercession with Edward III, see Jean-Marie Moeglin, Les bourgeois de Calais. Essai sur un mythe historique, Paris 2002. On the ritual aspects of these intercessions, see Nicolas Offenstadt, Les femmes et la paix à la fin du Moyen Âge: genre, discours, rites, in: Société des historiens médiévistes de l'Enseignement supérieur public (ed.), Le règlement des conflits au Moyen Âge, Paris 2001, 317–333.
40 Joseph Kervyn de Lettenhove, Une lettre inédite de Marie de Bourgogne et de Marguerite d'York à Louis XI, in: Bulletins de l'Académie Royale des Sciences, des Lettres et des Beaux-Arts de Belgique, 21 (1854), 104–111. On the use of emotions, see Tracy Adams, Married Noblewomen as Diplomats: Affective Diplomacy, in: Susan Broomhall (ed.), Gender and Emotions in Medieval and Early Modern Europe. Destroying Order, Structuring Disorder, Ashgate 2015, 51–65.
41 Van Severen, Inventaire des archives de la ville de Bruges, see note 23, 5, 168.

irenic woman in order to grasp a style of government that was perhaps more specific to the Burgundian court than to the *agency* of a princess.

3. Authoritarian devotees?

In the limited space of this article, I would like to draw attention to two examples from Lille involving Isabella of Portugal and Margaret of York. In the first case, the management and interests of the members of the household, which we have presented as one of the prerogatives of the duchesses, led Isabella of Portugal to force well-endowed middle-class women into marriage. Concerned with the comfort of the members of her household, the duchess sought matrimonial alliances within the court, which occasionally led her to exert very strong pressure on bourgeois families whose daughters' inheritances could provide a comfortable retirement for former officers.[42] This remark may seem anecdotal, since this type of information is widely scattered in chronicles and correspondence, but it reveals an aspect of the duchess's power that might be specific, since in these cases the initiative seems to have been hers, while the prince, for his part, became the executor of her will, even if this meant entering sensitive diplomatic territory. We will now examine the case of a forced marriage in Lille, which I have discussed elsewhere and which is reported in Georges Chastelain's *Chroniques*. It is said that this forced marriage can be traced back to a ducal will, but was in reality the result of a decision by the duchess.[43] In the spring of 1456, the duke intervened on behalf of a certain Colinet de la Thieuloye, who had 'fallen in love' with the daughter of a brewer from Lille. The woman in question, Jeanne Robaut, had been kidnapped and sent to the castle of Antoing, in the imperial lands, forcing the family to appeal to the Parliament of Paris. The archer at the origin of this affair was a protégé of Isabella, who took great care to defend and support the members of her household, not hesitating to interfere with local justice.[44] Although the duchess took the initiative in these nego-

---

42 I will not go into the administration of finances by Isabella of Portugal, which has been perfectly studied, see Sommé, Isabelle de Portugal, see note 9, 408–419. The mention of Jean Marlette in the 1436 aid account is explicit: "… ordonné par madame la duchesse, ayant regart au fait et gouvernement des finances de mondit seigneur" (ordered by the duchess with authority to govern the finances of my lord).
43 On this case, see Elodie Lecuppre-Desjardin, Affaires de cœur, affaire de cour : Quand le prince use de son 'bon plaisir' pour forcer au mariage dans la Grande Principauté de Bourgogne à la fin du Moyen Âge, in: Benjamin Deruelle and Michel Hébert (eds.), Arbitraire et arbitrages. Les zones grises du pouvoir (XIIe–XVIIIe siècle), Villeneuve d'Ascq, Québec 2024, 127–142.
44 Other similar situations might suggest a system, and Isabella used her power to arrange a marriage between one of her protégés and Livine Van der Haegen, the daughter of a wealthy Ghent family. On this topic, see Walter Prevenier, La stratégie et le discours politique des ducs de Bourgogne concernant les rapts et les enlèvements de femmes parmi les élites des Pays-Bas au XVe siècle, in: Jan Hirschbiegel and Werner Paravicini (eds.), Das Frauenzimmer. Die Frau bei Hofe in Spätmittelalter und früher Neuzeit, Stuttgart 2000, 429–437, 434. Examples of interference in local justice systems

tiations, her method was similar to that of her male counterparts, relying on force and threats.[45] The same authoritarian rigour was to be seen a few years later, again in Lille, this time as part of the religious reforms supported by Margaret of York.

At the court of Burgundy, the cult of Saint Colette of Corbie and her works were handed down from princess to princess.[46] The reform of the Poor Clares, which arose in the wake of the Franciscan Observance movement, was supported from the very beginning of the Colettian movement by Margaret of Bavaria through the saint's Franciscan confessor, Henri de Beaume, whose family was in the service of the duke.[47] Isabella of Portugal continued this work by founding reformed convents, notably in Hesdin (1435) and Ghent (1437). Later, in 1451, she arranged for the establishment of a convent of Grey Nuns (*Soeurs grises*) in Lille, located in the *rue des malades*, a notorious area known for its brothels, through the intermediary Jean de Luxembourg, who was well acquainted with the affairs of the city.[48] The purchase of a plot of land with the princess's money, followed by the support of the city magistrate, helped expand the influence of the Grey Nuns, who played a major role in charitable work and support for the disadvantaged. Following in the footsteps of her mother-in-law and the Burgundian devotional tradition that favoured reform movements, it is hardly surprising that Margaret of York was so involved.[49] However, urban sources reveal a very different approach to that of Isabella. After obtaining a bull from Pope Sixtus IV on 4 October 1483, confirmed by Innocent VIII on 11 May 1490, Margaret repeatedly demanded the foundation of a new convent of Poor Clares, this time cloistered and corresponding to the new movement of the Poor Clares of the Ave Maria.[50] Since this came at a time when some of the Grey Nuns also wanted to leave, the city magistrate did not accept the

---

 can be found in: Monique Sommé (ed.), La correspondance d'Isabelle de Portugal, duchesse de Bourgogne (1430–1471), Stuttgart 2009, 124 for example.

45 In this case, the victim's parents were forced to move their property out of the duke's jurisdiction, and the father, fearing the duke's repression, fell ill. Cf. Elodie Lecuppre-Desjardin, Affaires de coeur, affaire de cour.

46 On Saint Colette of Corbie and the aristocratic network that supported the reform of the Pauvres Claires (Poor Clares), see Joan Mueller and Nancy Warren, A Companion to Colette de Corbie, Leiden 2016.

47 On the network of nobility around Colette de Corbie, particularly at the Court of Burgundy, see Anna Campbell, Networks of Influence: Women and Power in Fifteenth-Century France, in: Reading Medieval Studies, 45 (2019), 109–131. The duchess encouraged the creation of convents in Auxonne (1412), Poligny (1415) and Seurre (1422). A comparison with the case of Paola Malatesta, discussed in the article by Isabella Lazzarini in this issue, can be made with regard to this avant-garde religiosity, even if the foundations in Mantua are in no way linked to the reform of Colette of Corbie.

48 Cf. ADNord, 101 H2, p. 1 [10 Nov. 1451].

49 Cf. Andrea G. Pearson, Margaret of York, Colette of Corbie, and the possibilities of female agency, in: Cynthia J. Brown and Anne-Marie Legaré (eds.), Les femmes, la culture et les arts en Europe, entre Moyen Âge et Renaissance, Turnhout 2016, 357–365.

50 Cf. ADNord 101 H4 nr. 1 et 3. Cf. Caroline Saletzky's master II thesis, Des dévotes au tribunal des hommes : le procès des sœurs grises hospitalières à Lille à la fin du Moyen Âge, defended in Lille in 2017 under the supervision of Elodie Lecuppre-Desjardin.

request of its *redoutée dame douairière*, and instead invited her to accompany the nuns who had expressed their wish to leave the existing establishment. However, the princess was stubborn, and in March 1486, according to a register of the city resolutions, she called on her son-in-law Maximilian to put pressure on the city authorities.[51] The latter refused, citing the poverty of the city, which could not afford to set up a new institution that would have to rely on the charity of its already overburdened citizens. Margaret was undoubtedly fulfilling a mission of which she was reminded in the *Dialogue de la duchesse de Bourgogne avec Jésus-Christ:*

> "You will do what you have to do for the common good in all your affairs, principally in the state of the Church and spirituality, so that the cloisters be reformed and the regular observance be in force especially in the four orders of the mendicants who have to preach to the others."[52]

Moreover, her position as a widow encouraged her, according to the codes of the time, to show a mobilising devotion that gave her a kind of social and political status. Her intransigence was already evident in Mons, where, between 1481 and 1485, she persuaded the magistrate to evict the prostitutes living around the Hôtel de Bavière. When prohibition failed, the duchess gave in and settled for some form of regulation, before renewing her efforts in 1485 and eventually obtaining the establishment of a house for repentant prostitutes under the rule of the bishop of Cambrai, Henri de Berghes. As Eric Bousmar points out, the princess's actions were somewhere between "required piety and personal involvement, between charitable concerns and social and political ulterior motives".[53]

4. Conclusion

This last remark invites us to conclude and answer the questions raised at the beginning, but not without pointing out that the subject is immense and has only been touched upon. However, a number of observations can be made from these few examples.

---

51 Cf. Lille (AM), register 275, fol. 71: "[…] et depuis icelle dame eust obtenu lettres du roi des Romains notre sir adrechans a iceux eschevins, par lesquelles nonobstant lesdits excuses il requiere que ledit accord soit fait […]". The refusal of March 1486 repeated that of October 1484.
52 Le Dyalogue de la duchesse de Bourgongne a Jhesu Crist, London British Library Add. Ms 7970, fol. 99. ("Tu feras ce que tu poras qui en toy sera pour le bien commun en tous tes affayres, principalement en l'estat de l'eglise et espirituel affin que les cloistres soyent reformés et la reguliere observance soit en vigueur meismement es quatre ordres des mendians qui ont a preschier aux aultres.").
53 Eric Bousmar, Marguerite d'York et les putains de Mons, entre charité dévote et offensive moralisatrice (1481–1485). Autour d'une fondation de repenties, in: Publications du Centre Européen d'Études Bourguignonnes, 44 (2004), 81–102, 102. Cf. also Marguerite's mix of financial interests and devout intentions in: Mario Damen, Charity against the Odds. Margaret of York and the Isle of Voorne (1477–1503), in: Dominique Eichberger, W. Hüsken and Anne-Marie Legaré (eds.), Women at the Burgundian Court. Presence and Influence, Turnhout 2010, 57–71.

First, the duchesses of Burgundy displayed an undeniable authority, prepared by a careful education, validated by delegations of power imposed by the very structure of the Burgundian composite space, supported – even guided – by councils populated by secular and religious men. Expected to act in the areas of courtly family affairs, peaceful intercession and devotional investment, to name but a few, they proved to be invaluable lieutenants in times of war, personally involved in the defence of the territories entrusted to them.

Second, the question of whether the princess's foreign status played a role in the expression of this agency seems to be part and parcel of the family policy of networking typical of dynastic governments in Europe and beyond.[54] The alliances forged and strengthened never ceased to mix up what in modern times has come to be known as 'the public' and 'the private', and it is easy to understand how belonging to the House of Lancaster or York made Isabella of Portugal and Margaret of York more sensitive to the English cause and more capable of negotiating than their Franco-Burgundian husbands. On the other hand, the fact that Isabella of Portugal was always thought of as a foreigner, legitimised by her marriage alliance, undoubtedly favoured her position in the eyes of the Flemish cities, which were particularly wary of the Burgundian princes whom they deemed greedy for their wealth. The Lusitanian princess, on the other hand, who was sensitive to the needs of the urban commerce, became the privileged interlocutor between the urban communities and the prince, both for negotiating reconciliation and for fairly calculating the extraordinary taxes to be levied.

However, as the introduction to this special issue encourages us to do, when questioning the room for manoeuvre of these princesses, we must recognise that it was indeed within the power couple they formed with their husbands that these women were able to develop their range of action. Martha Howell's hypothesis that the agency of medieval women must be assessed within the then normative framework of the time seems to be confirmed. As the representative of the ducal authority when the prince was absent, as it was often the case in the Burgundian composite state, the princess owed her legitimacy to govern to the prince, but certainly took advantage of this distance to develop her own capacity to act.

Whether in the field of war, matrimonial intrigues or religious reform, women acted like men. Although these women did not carry swords and did not, for the most part, engage in physical combat, they knew how to use the same rigour and will that is usually attributed to men when it came to winning their cases. But, of course, the use of emotions and the attitudes expected of their sex enrich a grammar of action that was put into strategic practice. So, for the time and place in question, would the *agency* of the princesses developed within these power couples be the adoption of patriarchal rules for the benefit of female interests? This is certainly a position that invites us to reconsider these women in the context of an "analytique du pouvoir", as envisaged by Michel

---

54 Cf. Jeroen Duindam, Dynasties. A Global History of Power, 1300–1800, Cambridge 2015.

Foucault, at the crossroads of existing cooperation, shifting relationships and, I would add, active personalities.[55]

---

[55] Martin Saar, Pouvoir, in: Jean-François Bert and Jérôme Lamy (eds.), Michel Foucault. Un héritage critique, Paris 2014, 131–136.

Christina Lutter and Christof Muigg

Gendered Power Politics in a Nascent Empire.
The Case of Maximilian of Habsburg (1459–1519) and Mary of Burgundy (1457–1482)[1]

1. Introduction

Around 1500, Europe's political landscape saw major territorial changes effected by long-term conflicts and military expansion. In the heart of the continent, the reign of Maximilian I is a case in point. From 1493 onwards, Maximilian was acting king (and from 1508 emperor) of the Holy Roman Empire, and simultaneously ruler of the Habsburg lands. In the former position he claimed a role as defender of Christendom against the Ottomans which reflected the idea of the emperor's eminence in Latin Christianity. In the latter position, he used these roles to advance his family's dynastic position in a pronounced manner.[2]

This is testified both by his own two marriages, to Mary of Burgundy and Bianca Maria Sforza of Milan, and even more by his far-reaching dynastic projects involving the Castilian and Bohemian lines. These dimensions required forms of shared rule, and thus Maximilian after the early deaths of his first wife Mary and his son Philipp delegated government in the "Habsburg Netherlands" to his daughter Margaret, who was then followed by her niece Mary (of Hungary), Maximilian's granddaughter.[3] Dynastic politics was a family business. Kin of both genders – spouses, sons and

---

1 This contribution is based on work within the Special Research Program (SFB 92) *ManMax: Managing Maximilian (1493–1519) – Persona, Politics, and Personnel Through the Lens of Digital Prosopography,* Speaker: A. Zajic, funded by the Austrian Science Funds (FWF), Project *Gendering Maximilian – Gendered Dimensions of Court Organisation and Representation* (PI C. Lutter), details at: https://manmax.hypotheses.org/the-team.
2 On the political situation in Europe around 1500 see the introduction to this special issue with further bibliography, esp. on p. 11–13. The classic study on Maximilian I. is Hermann Wiesflecker, Maximilian I, das Reich, Österreich und Europa an der Wende zur Neuzeit. 5 vols., Vienna 1971–1986. For a recent overview see Manfred Hollegger and Markus Gneiß, Maximilian I. (1459–1519). Herrscher und Mensch einer Zeitenwende, Stuttgart 2023²; Markus Debertol et al. (eds.), Per tot discrimina rerum. Maximilian I. (1459–1519), Wien/Köln/Weimar 2022.
3 Cyrille Debris, 'Tu, Felix Austria, Nube'. La dynastie de Habsbourg et sa politique matrimoniale à la fin du moyen âge, Turnhout 2005; on the topos see Alexander Kagerer, Macht und Medien um 1500. Selbstinszenierungen und Legitimationsstrategien von Habsburgern und Fuggern, Berlin/Boston 2017, 46–49.

daughters, aunts, and nieces – were key partners in the shared agenda of the dynasty. What is more, medieval monarchical rule was composite, as male and female rulers alike were legitimated and accompanied by formal councils and supported by offices holders and a large number of advisors, courtiers, and staff of both genders.[4]

The sequence of female governors of the Netherlands is a key example of successful Habsburg women rulers who interacted at eye level with their male relatives as peers.[5] Others were less fortunate: both Mary of Burgundy and her son Philip the Fair died in their mid-twenties; Bianca Maria Sforza's political agency suffered as a result of her husband's inauspicious Milan enterprise. However, dynastic, and personal 'success' or 'failure' did not just depend on political circumstances and only partly on 'individual' qualities. Rather, they were formed by a variety of role models, cultural traditions, and educational norms that in turn were deeply gendered. Starting with legal norms that regulated access to rule, the range and limitations of education and training, and long-standing traditions of thinking about gender and rule, any ruler's political agency was enabled and limited by representations of gender.

In this contribution, we will focus on the effects of gendered representations of pre-modern rule, comparing Maximilian himself and his first wife Mary of Burgundy. Until about two decades ago, Maximilian's and Mary's imageries have developed in a fundamentally unbalanced manner. While research and bibliography on the emperor is enormous, the Burgundian heiress – not least due to her early death – gained much less attention until recently. What is more, recent scholarly assessments underline the extent to which their images and the representations of their marriage were shaped by Maximilian's propaganda that in turn significantly influenced modern historiography "in a way that has led to (Mary's) almost being written out of history". This imbalance was reinforced by diverging foci of regional and national historiographies written in different languages, which privileged different strands of reception. Hence, a comparative reconsideration of the gendered quality of the heterogeneous and ambivalent assessments of both political *personae* during their lifetime, and the many layers of

---

4 For a global overview see Jeroen Duindam, Dynasties. A Global History of Power, 1300–1800, Cambridge 2016; on what follows with ample references: Christina Lutter, Gendering Late Medieval Habsburg Dynastic Politics: Maximilian I and His Social Networks, in: Austrian History Yearbook, 55 (2024), 1–16, at: https://doi.org/10.1017/S0067237824000274, access: 14 Oct. 2024. On the various forms of couples' shared ruling practice see the contributions by Julia Burkhardt and Isabella Lazzarini in this special issue, as well as, for instance, Sebastian Roebert, Die Königin im Zentrum der Macht. Reginale Herrschaft in der Krone Aragón am Beispiel Eleonores von Sizilien (1349–1375), Berlin 2020, 17–23, and Cristina Andenna, Stellvertretung im Königreich Sizilien-Neapel und die Stellung der ersten angevinischen Königinnen als Vikarinnen des Königs, in: Gabriela Signori and Claudia Zey (eds.), Regentinnen und andere Stellvertreterfiguren. Vom 10. bis zum 15. Jahrhundert, Berlin 2023, 85–110, 98 f.
5 Cf. William Monter, An Experiment in Female Governance. The Habsburg Netherlands 1507–1567, in: History Research, 3, 6 (2013), 441–452.

memory and historiography that constructed their images over the centuries has only begun recently.[6]

Following the general outline of this special issue, we will therefore ask which legal norms and cultural expectations confronted the adolescent Maximilian and Mary when they assumed their political tasks and responsibilities. Which shared or divergent role models and traditions were available to them as they fashioned their own political *personae?* Which political challenges counterbalanced or overruled gendered dynastic thinking? We will argue that gender as an analytical category does not just help to systematically compare representations of female and male rulers within complex power relations. As a relational category, it also allows us to move beyond gendered binaries and open them up to the practical dimensions of the 'making of' pre-modern rule that was always shared by various individuals and representative bodies.[7] The beginning of the couple's short shared rule (1477–1482) provides a case in point, as the composite quality of the Burgundian territories epitomized contemporary issues of the balance of power between 'internal' and 'external' influences, of the political participation of elites organized into political bodies, and discussions about princely qualities and the 'common good' that was at stake in composite principalities or monarchies.[8]

---

6 Cf. Michael Depreter et al., Mary of Burgundy. Agency, Government, and Memory, in: id. et al. (eds.), Marie de Bourgogne. Figure, principat et postérité d'une duchesse tardo-médiévale, Turnhout 2021, 13–23; the quote at 23. Similary Christina Antenhofer, Maximilian und die Frauen: Bilder und Narrative, in: Debertol et al., Per tot discrimina rerum, see note 2, 83–100; Christina Lutter, Zur Repräsentation von Geschlechterverhältnissen im höfischen Umfeld Maximilians, in: Johannes Helmrath, Ursula Kocher and Andrea Sieber (eds.), Maximilians Welt. Kaiser Maximilian I. im Spannungsfeld zwischen Innovation und Tradition, Berlin 2018, 41–60, 51.

7 Seminal is Joan Wallach Scott, Gender: A Useful Category of Historical Analysis, in: American Historical Review, 91, 5 (1986), 1053–1075. Cf. programmatically Theresa Earenfight, Without the Persona of the Prince: Kings, Queens and the Idea of Monarchy in Late Medieval Europe, in: Gender & History, 19, 1 (2007), 1–21; Heather J. Tanner (ed.), Medieval Elite Women and the Exercise of Power, 1100–1400, Moving Beyond the Exceptionalist Debate, Cambridge 2019. This point is also made by Lazzarini in this special issue. Depreter et al., Mary of Burgundy, see note 6, highlight the interactions of gendered rule, state-building, and the politics of memory in the given context.

8 On this tradition throughout the 15th century see Elodie Lecuppre-Desjardin in this special issue. Cf. John H. Elliott, A Europe of Composite Monarchies, in: Past & Present, 137 (1992), 48–71; Charlotte Backerra, Personal Union, Composite Monarchy, and 'Multiple Rule', in: Elena Woodacre et al. (eds.), The Routledge History of Monarchy, London 2019, 89–111; on the duchy of Burgundy see Jelle Haemers, For the Common Good. State Power and Urban Revolts in the Reign of Mary of Burgundy, 1477–1482, Turnhout 2009; Elodie Lecuppre-Desjardin, Le royaume inachevé des ducs de Bourgogne (XVIe–XVe siècles), Paris 2016; Jonas Braekevelt, Constitutions, State and Estates: Interactions Between Princely Restrictions and Reforms, Privileges of the Governed and the Control of Absolute Power in the Burgundian Countries, in: François Foronda and Jean-Philippe Genet (eds.), Des chartes aux constitutions. Autour de l'idée constitutionnelle en Europe, XIIe–XVIIe siècle, Paris 2019, 233–251.

2. A hero in defence of the Burgundian dynasty?

When Maximilian arrived in the Low Countries in August 1477 to marry the probably most attractive bride of her generation, the duchy had already been in a profound crisis for some time caused by Duke Charles the Bold's aggressive attempts to extend and all at once centralize the Burgundian territories. His incessant wars and the constant fiscal pressure on cities and principalities had thus already previously met substantial resistance. His death on the battlefield of Nancy against the towering army assembled by Lorraine and the Swiss on 5 January 1477 left his only child and sole heiress Mary not just an illustrious domain, but defeated armies, an empty treasury, discontented representatives of his subjects among cities and nobility, and a powerful external enemy, Louis XI of France, who immediately took advantage of the situation and invaded Burgundian territories.[9]

Mary thus had to defend her heritage against the French king's aspirations built like her own on dynastic claims. Supported by Margaret of York, Charles's widow and Dowager Duchess of Burgundy, she first and foremost negotiated the support of her subjects, represented by the Estates General, to reinvigorate her military forces after the recent devastating losses. Within only a few weeks of her father's death, she revoked many of his fiscal and administrative measures and granted both the Estates General and regional representative bodies of the disparate Burgundian lands several privileges in exchange for their recognition of her claim as legitimate heiress and their active support against the enemy.[10]

She agreed to marry Maximilian, son of Emperor Frederick III, a match that her father and Frederick had begun to negotiate a decade before. If the twenty-year old Mary (*1457) was the most sought-after bride of her time, the slightly younger Maximilian (*1459) was the prime candidate among many suitors. Mary was not just the heiress of highly attractive territories, notwithstanding the crisis unleashed by her father, but also an affluent bride who welcomed her groom from a 'foreign' land and an economically modest background, despite his rank as the emperor's son. Prestigious clothes were among the many gifts she sent her future spouse in the months before their first personal encounter.[11] Mary's quality as a "diplomatic weapon of universal value"

---

9 Cf. Wim Blockmans and Walter Prevenier, The Promised Lands. The Low Countries Under Burgundian Rule, 1369–1530, Philadelphia, PA. 1999, 174–205, especially 193–195. On the financial situation see Jelle Haemers, A Troubled Marriage: Maximilian and the Low Countries, in: Debertol et al., Per tot discrimina rerum, see note 2, 421–431.
10 The classic study on Mary's eponymous *Great Privilege* of 11 February 1477 is Wim Blockmans, Le Privilège général et les privilèges regionaux de Marie de Bourgogne pour les Pays-Bas 1477. Het algemene en de gewestelijke privilegien van Maria van Bourgondie voor de Nederlanden, Kortrijk-Heule 1985. On Margaret's support for Mary and Maximilian see Lecuppre-Desjardin in this special issue, p. 60.
11 Cf. Patrik Pastrnak, Travelling Grooms: A Royal Progress or A Wedding Journey?, in: Anthony Musson and J. P. D. Cooper (eds.), Royal Journeys in Early Modern Europe. Progresses, Palaces and

due to her hereditary status parallels Maximilian's status as saviour of the duchess and her heritage against King Louis XI of France.[12] While many welcomed the young Archduke of Austria as their defender against the French danger, he was no more than a 'foreign' prince consort, confronted with substantial opposition among both towns and nobility. Yet, in the campaigns of 1478 and 1479, he stood his ground and won significant battles, laying the foundation of the larger-than-life image of the hero that was later epitomized in his *Works of Fame (Ruhmeswerk)*.[13]

One of the ideals that governed his new task and title was chivalry, a formative cultural tradition amongst medieval Europe's nobility. The extent to which this tradition shaped Maximilian's self-fashioning throughout his lifetime, and influenced the way he has been perceived until today is epitomized in his popular epithet, "the last knight".[14] The role model of chivalric knighthood was a corner stone in young Maximilian's education, and yet the Burgundian context provided new models for this powerful construction of princely masculinity. Shaped by the examples of the Valois dukes of Burgundy Philip the Bold, John the Fearless, Philip the Good, and eventually Charles the Bold, it gained new force when he was faced with the eminent necessity of defending the duchy against the military power of France.[15]

Like his father-in-law, Maximilian was an ambitious commander who personally led the Burgundian armies and fought alongside his soldiers. He achieved his first substantial victory in the Battle of Guinegate (17 August 1479), where he emerged not just as a talented leader but also as a skilled fighter on the battleground. He exploited the pike square, a tactical formation of the Swiss infantry, which had famously defeated one

---

Panache, New York 2023, 113–126, 120. Wealth was a key factor for agency, as Lazzarini shows in this special issue.

12 For the quote see Richard Vaughan, Charles the Bold. The Last Valois Duke of Burgundy, Woodbridge 2002, 126 (orig. 1973); for an in-depth analysis see Sonja Dünnebeil, Mary, a "Diplomatic Weapon of Universal Value" for Charles the Bold, in: Depreter et al., Marie de Bourgogne, see note 6, 225–236; and ead., Handelsobjekt Erbtochter. Zu den Verhandlungen über die Verheiratung Marias von Burgund, in: ead. and Christine Ottner-Diesenberger (eds.), Außenpolitisches Handeln im ausgehenden Mittelalter. Akteure und Ziele, Wien 2007, 159–184. In fact, children of both genders were for the most part objects in dynastic planning and strategic hopes for the future.

13 On Maximilian's *Ruhmeswerk* consisting of several fictional accounts of his life and genealogy, partly crafted with the Emperor's own participation, see Jan-Dirk Müller, Gedechtnus. Literatur und Hofgesellschaft um Maximilian I., Munich 1982; Larry Silver, Marketing Maximilian. The Visual Ideology of a Holy Roman Emperor, Princeton 2008; examples of recent assessments are Kagerer, Macht und Medien, see note 3, and the introduction by Howard Louthan and Jonathan Green, Theuerdank. The Illustrated Epic of a Renaissance Knight, London 2022.

14 For instance, the exhibition at the Metropolitan Museum of Art in New York on the 500th anniversary of Maximilian's death (2019) and the catalogue were titled The Last Knight: The Art, Armor, and Ambition of Maximilian I., ed. by Pierre Terjanian, New Haven/London 2019. Cf. the bibliography quoted in note 13, here esp. Silver, Marketing Maximilian, 147–168.

15 Cf. Karl-Heinz Spieß, Idealisiertes Rittertum. Herzog Karl der Kühne von Burgund und Kaiser Maximilian I., in: Martin Wrede (ed.), Inszenierung der heroischen Monarchie. Frühneuzeitliches Königtum zwischen ritterlichem Erbe und militärischer Herausforderung, München 2014, 57–75.

Fig.1: Wedding Maximilian I and Mary of Burgundy 1477, Albrecht Dürer, Woodcarving, 1515, Detail of the "Ehrenpforte". Source: Wikimedia Commons / public domain

of Maximilian's ancestors, the Habsburg duke Leopold III, in 1386, and the mobile fortress of wagons used by the Hussite armies in the 1420s to stop heavily armed cavalry.[16] However, while Maximilian was probably aware of these precedents, it was in fact Jacques de Savoie, Count of Romont, a commander in many previous campaigns and loyal servant of Mary after 1477, who advised Maximilian to strengthen the infantry after the Swiss model. This later led to the establishment of a new type of mercenary, the German "Landsknecht", and Maximilian's reputation as "father of the Landsknechte".[17]

---

16 Cf. Alexander Querengässer, Before the Military Revolution. European Warfare and the Rise of the Early Modern State, 1300–1490, Oxford 2021, 152.
17 Malte Prietzel, „Letzter Ritter" und „Vater der Landsknechte". Fürstliche Gewaltausübung als Praxis und Inszenierung, in: Helmrath/Kocher/Sieber, Maximilians Welt, see note 6, 209–224; Michael

Despite these tactical innovations, the pivotal moment at Guinegate was probably Maximilian's decision to dismount his horse, join his pikemen and fight side by side with them. This act, apparently at odds with traditional fighting conventions, all at once epitomized Maximilian's exceptional bravery as a warrior, and formed a cornerstone of his military reputation.[18] His commanders joined him in foot combat, boosting the infantry's courage through exemplary prowess.[19] Military leadership, fighting skills in hand-to-hand combat, and personal bravery became central elements of Maximilian's self-representation, together with a strategic mind that integrated various military tactics, thus demonstrating exemplary prudence and skilfulness. They all rested upon – and yet modified – time-honoured chivalric values shaped over centuries.[20] Later, Maximilian's indubitable military competence was rendered unequivocal by the chroniclers he employed for the *Works of Fame* and eventually in historiography.

3. Monitoring princely masculinity – The Order of the Golden Fleece and the *correction*

Military success and ambition were eponymous features of the warring duke Charles the Bold, whose model Maximilian adopted and later passed on to his grandson and successor as Emperor, Charles (V).[21] But while his father-in-law provided an exemplary role model that became crucial in Maximilian's own representation and practice, it also built on a powerful Burgundian tradition rooted in medieval models of chivalry. In 1430, Mary's grandfather Philip the Good had founded the Order of the Golden Fleece intended to produce social and political integration within the elites of his heterogeneous territories and to forge their loyalty to the Burgundian dynasty. The Order's goal was to foster knightly practice, conceived of as service to God, and it thus followed the

---

Depreter, Les armées "bourguignonnes" après Nancy. Ruptures et continuités structurelles d'un instrument politique, in: id. et al., Marie de Bourgogne, see note 6, 251–274.
18 Cf. Wiesflecker, Maximilian, vol. I, see note 2, 144–149; Matthias Pfaffenbichler, "wie der (…) kunig ain schlacht tet und die gewann (…)" – Maximilian als Kriegsmann, in: Sabine Haag, Alfred Wieczorek, idem, and Hans-Jürgen Buderer (eds.), Kaiser Maximilian. Der letzte Ritter und das höfische Turnier, Regensburg 2014, 53–61; for a comparative perspective see Thomas Menzel, Der Fürst als Feldherr. Militärisches Handeln und Selbstdarstellung zwischen 1470 und 1550. Dargestellt an ausgewählten Beispielen, Berlin 2003, 130. Details on the battle in Ernst Richert, Die Schlacht bei Guinegate. 7. August 1479, Berlin 1907, 87–90.
19 Cf. Wiesflecker, Maximilian, vol. I, see note 2, 148; Richert, Guinegate, see note 18, 57.
20 Cf. Prietzel, „Letzter Ritter", see note 17; Silver, Marketing Maximilian, see note 13, 147–168; for a comparative perspective see István P. Bejczy (ed.), Princely Virtues in the Middle Ages. 1200–1500, Turnhout 2009.
21 Cf. Spieß, Idealisiertes Rittertum, see note 15; Maria Golubeva, Between the Courts of Burgundy and Vienna: Models of Military Competence in Dynastic Historiography, c. 1470–1700, in: Wrede, Inszenierung, see note 15, 317–333.

ideals of piety, loyalty, and chivalry.²² By admitting exclusively male members of the nobility, the Order all at once served as an instrument to reinforce social hierarchies, legitimize the power of the ruling elites, and assemble them at the Burgundian court around the duke.²³

When Charles the Bold died, both the duchy and the Order lost their sovereign. Since the duke had no male heir, and women were not admitted to the sovereign's position, the Order's statutes demanded that the heiress's husband should inherit this role.²⁴ Hence, Mary's marriage to Maximilian was of utmost importance for the continuity of the Order, while allowing the prince consort to establish his authority and precedence despite his foreign origin. As a result of this mutual dependency, the young Maximilian was appointed as sovereign of the Order at Bruges on 30 April 1478 – less than a year after the couple was married in Ghent on 19 August 1477 – during the Order's first assembly after Charles' death. The inauguration of the new sovereign was celebrated with enormous splendour, showing off the integrity of the Order and the loyalty of the Burgundian nobility to the prince consort at a moment when some of its members had already taken sides with Louis XI. It was designed to instil hope that the duchy's crisis could be overcome. The public ceremonies demonstrated the new regent's power before the duchy's subjects and the King of France.²⁵

While the meticulously staged layout and sequence of the inauguration ceremonies permitted Mary only a position on the side lines, notwithstanding her crucial position as the duchy's legitimate heiress, which linked the Burgundian dynasty to the role of the prince consort as the Order's sovereign, these ceremonies also underlined the reciprocity between Maximilian's pre-eminence as sovereign of the Order and his role as

---

22 Cf. Gert Melville, Rituelle Ostentation und pragmatische Inquisition: Zur Institutionalität des Ordens vom Goldenen Vlies, in: Heinz Duchhardt and Gert Melville (eds.), Im Spannungsfeld von Recht und Ritual. Soziale Kommunikation in Mittelalter und Früher Neuzeit, Köln 1997, 215–271, 220.

23 Cf. Leonhard Horowski, xxxj chevaliers sans reproche: Der Orden vom Goldenen Vlies als Instrument burgundischer Elitenpolitik, in: Sacra Militia: Rivista di storia degli Ordini militari, 1 (2000), 187–233; D'Arcy J.D. Boulton, The Knights of the Crown. The Monarchical Orders of Knighthood in Later Medieval Europe (1325–1520), Woodbridge/New York 2000; for a comparative perspective see Andreas Ranft, Ritterorden und Rittergesellschaften im Spätmittelalter: Zu Formen der Regulierung und Internationalisierung ritterlich-höfischen Lebens in Europa, in: Kaspar Elm and Cosimo D. Fonseca (eds.), Militia Sancti Sepulchri: Idea e istituzioni, Vatican City 1998; on the gendered nature of chivalric practice and its effects on social inclusion and exclusion see Ruth Mazo Karras, From Boys to Men. Formations of Masculinity in Late Medieval Europe, Philadelphia, PA. 2003, 20–66.

24 Cf. Sonja Dünnebeil (ed.), Die Protokollbücher des Ordens vom Goldenen Vlies, vol. 1, Stuttgart 2002, 229.

25 Cf. Sonja Dünnebeil, The Order of the Golden Vlies in the Year 1478 – Continuity or Recommencement, in: Anne van Oosterwijk and Wim Blockmans (eds.), Staging the Court of Burgundy. Proceedings of the Conference "The Splendour of Burgundy", London 2013; 59–66, 62f., and ead., Maximilian I. und der Orden vom Goldenen Vlies, in: Debertol et al, Per tot discrimina rerum, see note 2, 101–116, 104f.

primus inter pares among the brethren.[26] Propagating the idea of an elite Christian knightly brotherhood, the Order symbolized the union of Christian virtue, gendered courtly practice, and martial fortitude, while its practical mission was to provide a moral framework for, and control of its members' political and personal conduct. Accordingly, the Order's regular meetings were supposed to have both an integrative and a corrective function for its members: all members including the sovereign regularly had to undergo the ritual of the *correction*. In Maximilian's case, this tool of social monitoring was used specifically to control the 'foreign' prince consort's actions.[27]

Maximilian underwent his first *correction* in 1481 during the Order's assembly at 's-Hertogenbosch, during the on-going war against France. On this occasion, the brethren underlined that Maximilian, despite his youth and foreign origin, had prudently managed to govern the troubled duchy, and praised him for avoiding gambling and debauchery, the classic sins of young men. However, the brethren criticised the duke's recurrent daring bravado on the battlefield and recommended that he should henceforward seek the Order's advice before waging war.[28] Their critique echoes fifteenth-century political thought on military prudence. For instance, in *Le livre de faiz d'armes* Christine de Pizan defines "common sense" as a key trait of leadership.[29] Likewise, moderation was considered a quality essential to the ability to assess contradictory values according to the circumstances. In such assessments, above all in matters of war and other costly endeavours, the Order wished to be involved.[30] Hence, the *corrections* provided a symbolic frame and a practical means for debating shared values, identifying transgressions of moral standards and political mistakes as well as their public perception. Every act of *correction* negotiated and reaffirmed the ideals of the leading elites, including those of the sovereign, against the political needs of the day.

It is not surprising that the matters raised in Maximilian's *correction* of 1481 resembled those put forward against Charles the Bold in 1468.[31] Fortitude and bravado

---

26 Details in Dünnebeil, Continuity or Recommencement, see note 25, 60–62.
27 Cf. Bernhard Sterchi, Über den Umgang mit Lob und Tadel. Normative Adelsliteratur und politische Kommunikation im burgundischen Hofadel, 1430–1506, Turnhout 2005; on the opposition to Maximilian within the Order see Sonja Dünnebeil, Maximilian I. und der Orden vom Goldenen Vlies, in: Debertol et al, Per tot discrimina rerum, see note 2, 101–116, esp. 105f.
28 Cf. Sterchi, Lob und Tadel, see note 27, 435f.; Dünnebeil, Maximilian I. und der Orden, see note 27, 105 both with ample quotes from the protocol books; Petra Schulte, Die Exemplifizierung der politischen Ethik im Herzogtum Burgund, in: Christine Reinle and Harald Winkel (eds.), Historische Exempla in Fürstenspiegeln und Fürstenlehren, Frankfurt am Main 2011, 69–98.
29 Cf. François Le Saux, War and Knighthood in Christine de Pizan's Livre de faits d'armes et de chevallerie, in: Corime Saunders, François Le Saux and Neil Thomas (eds.), Writing War. Military Literary Responses to Warfare, Suffolk 2004, 93–106, 100.
30 Cf. Dünnebeil, Protokollbücher 1, see note 24, 199; Sterchi, Lob und Tadel, see note 27, 433 on Charles's the Bold *correction*, and 436 on Maximilian's, each time including warfare without consulting with the Order.
31 Cf. Sterchi, Lob und Tadel, see note 27, 364; 432–436; Dünnebeil, Maximilian und der Orden, see note 27, 105.

were so close that it was sometimes difficult to distinguish between the two. Maximilian's *correction* thus demonstrates the ambiguity of princely masculinity in the context of warfare. While the offensive political and military expansionism of the period made warfare an inevitable challenge for male and female rulers alike, military practice was a sphere traditionally dominated by men. The Order's chivalric ideology sustained this practice through an old and yet refined cultural tradition.

Like other contemporary princes, Maximilian had been well trained and prepared for warfare since childhood. Martial values and military practice already formed an integral part of his *habitus* already before his Burgundian experience.[32] Yet, not every prince at the time drew on the available models in the same manner. Probably unlike his own father, Frederick III, but comparable to his father-in-law, Charles the Bold, Maximilian obviously conceived of himself both as a virtuous knight and as a strategically thinking warlord – and like his father-in-law, he enacted these role models throughout his lifetime. In his response to the *correction* of 1481, though, Maximilian promised to improve, and enjoined the Knights of the Order to assist him in his moral efforts to balance the several role models embodied by their shared vision of ideal knights and rulers.[33] Despite his excessive warfare he negotiated all of these models and made them a cornerstone of his large-scale endeavours of representation: after all, "Halt Maß" ("Be moderate") became his motto, epitomized in the towering image of the *Weisskunig*, and even the role of counsellors and representative bodies is underlined by his alter ego, Knight *Theuerdank*, who like Princess *Ehrenreich* and her father habitually seek advice before making crucial decisions.[34]

4. The princesse naturelle: 'damsel in distress' or powerful duchess?

When the French diplomat and chronicler Philippe de Commynes compared Mary's position to that of her prince consort, he underlined the importance of her quality as *dame du pays* in popular perception.[35] The underlying concept of the 'natural' prince or princess was a key motif in contemporary political discourse about dynastic continuity

---

32 For a comparison see Robert Nye, The Transmission of Masculinities: The Case of Early Modern France, in: Philip S. Gorski (ed.), Bourdieu and Historical Analysis, Durham 2013, 286–302.
33 Cf. Sterchi, Lob und Tadel, see note 27, 436; Spieß, Idealisiertes Rittertum, see note 15; Golubeva, Models of Military Competence, see note 21; Todd W. Reeser, Moderating Masculinity in Early Modern Culture, Chapel Hill, NC 2006, 11–39.
34 The named figures are the protagonists of the fictional epics *Weisskunig* and *Theuerdank* that form part of Maximilian's *Works of Fame*, cf. above in footnote 13. Dünnebeil, Maximilian und der Orden, see note 27, 108 on the motto „Halt Maß" in the context of the Order.
35 "Car ce peuple de Gand et aultres villes l'avoient en plus grant reverance que le mary, a cause qu'elle estoit dame du pays." Philippe de Commynes, Mémoires, Livre VI, chap. 6, ed. by Joël Blanchard, Paris 2001, 466.

as a requirement for the stability, peace and justice of any rule, and was thus crucial in the process of Mary's succession.[36] Women, who ruled either in their own right or as regents for male relatives, were a political reality in pre-modern Europe. Learned political discourse and the many examples of female rulers generated competing role models and gave rise to debates.[37]

Succession laws were equally heterogeneous and became contested in times of struggle over territorial hegemony and expansion. Some polities, like the Duchy of Burgundy, allowed dynastic inheritance of women and men alike (albeit the latter mostly by default), while others like France excluded women from hereditary succession. As the Burgundian dukes formed a cadet line of the French Valois dynasty, Mary's succession after her father's sudden death was a gateway for French claims to succession according to the Salic Law.[38] The ensuing conflict, relying on both arguments and arms, shows that dynastic succession could not be taken for granted. On the contrary, arguments in favour of succession were only constructed within these struggles and reflected in richly layered contemporary and later chronicles of courtly and urban background as well as in literature, visual and material culture.[39] Mary's position as *princesse naturelle* by virtue of dynastic inheritance was neither taken for granted at home, but rested on her subjects' loyalty expressed in the political and financial support of her territories' representatives – not least for the military initiatives of her new husband. Hence, dependencies were complex. Unless Mary were accepted as heiress, the 'foreign' prince consort would not have been accepted as military leader of the Burgundian armies, nor would the Estates General have supported his campaigns with their money and forces. The interplay between the strife for dynastic continuity, the challenges of the imminent war with France, urban revolts from 1477 onwards, and the

---

36 Cf. Éloise Adde and Jonathan Dumont (eds.), Naturalisation and Legitimation of Power (1300–1800), Paris 2024; Jonathan Dumont and Elodie Lecuppre-Desjardin, Construire la légitimité d'un pouvoir féminin, in: Depreter et al., Marie de Bourgogne, see note 6, 41–60, for a comparative perspective see Michel Pauly (ed.), Die Erbtochter, der fremde Fürst und das Land. Die Ehe Johanns des Blinden und Elisabeths von Böhmen in vergleichender europäischer Perspektive, Luxembourg 2013.
37 On the famous *Querelle des femmes* that developed since the days of Christine de Pizan and Jean Gerson see Gisela Bock and Margarethe Zimmermann (eds.), Die europäische Querelle des Femmes im 15. und 16. Jahrhundert. Querelles. Jahrbuch für Frauenforschung, Bd. 2, Stuttgart/Weimar 1997. From the abundant bibliography: Heide Wunder (ed.), Dynastie und Herrschaftssicherung in der Frühen Neuzeit. Geschlechter und Geschlecht, Berlin 2002; Zeitenblicke, 8, 2 (2009): Gynäkokratie. Frauen und Politik in der höfischen Gesellschaft der Frühen Neuzeit, ed. by Katrin Keller; Earenfight, Persona, see note 7, and most recently Signori/Zey, Regentinnen, see note 4.
38 On the process of its legal construction see Derek Whaley, From a Salic Law to the Salic Law: The Creation and Re-Creation of the Royal Succession System of France, in: Woodacre et al., History of Monarchy, see note 8, 443–464; Eliane Viennot, La France et le pouvoir. L'invention de la loi salique (Vè–XVIè siècle), Paris 2006.
39 Cf. part 1 in Depreter et al., Marie de Bourgogne, see note 6, 27–190.

interests of an ambitious nobility constituted an open field of negotiation and action with fundamental effects on Mary's and Maximilian's positions alike.

Fig. 2: Mary of Burgundy, daughter of Charles the Bold; portrait by the circle of the Master of the Legend of St. Madeleine c. 1530–1540. Source: Wikimedia Commons / public domain

Hence, in the aftermath of her father's death, Mary and her court deliberately used the image of the young, orphaned virgin threatened by her relative and godfather Louis XI to win the loyalty and support of her subjects. The gendered image of a 'damsel in distress' relying on male representatives of the Burgundian elite and later on her husband became a persistent popular trope that exploited chivalric Burgundian courtly culture, partly because it was deployed for various interests both during the wars against France, and later in the upheavals against Maximilian.[40] Contrasting her manifold other representations as a duchess during her short lifetime, it was perpetuated in texts and images after her early death in 1482. Maximilian's own *Ruhmeswerk* played a key role in

---

40 Most recently Olga Karaskova-Hesry, L'image de la duchesse: Marie de Bourgogne (1477–1482) dans des œuvres de Jean Molinet, in: Sandra Hindman and Elliot Adam (eds.), Au prisme du manuscrit. Regards sur la littérature francaise du Moyen Age (1300–1550), Turnhout 2019, 181–201; Lisa Demets, Gendering Political Ideology in Late Medieval Bruges: Mary of Burgundy as City Maiden in the Manuscripts of the Excellente Cronike van Vlaenderen, in: Depreter et al., Marie de Bourgogne, see note 6, 83–101, and Lecuppre-Desjardin in this special issue.

this long-term process by idealizing and 'objectifying' his wife as an exemplary consort and heroine of virtue and honour, worthy of his eternal love and protection.[41]

Recent scholarship has drawn a nuanced image of the political *persona* of Mary during her short reign as Duchess of Burgundy.[42] A key dimension of her self-fashioning was the long-standing tradition of women regents in the Burgundian lands, personified by a line of duchess consorts who provided important role models for Mary, and later also for her daughter Margaret and her grand-daughter Mary.[43] While they all acted as regents by virtue of their marriages to Burgundian dukes or through designation by their husbands to rule during their absence, the sudden death of Charles the Bold made it necessary for Mary to shape a new role as duchess in her own right.[44]

Mary's succession testifies to the political agency that the young duchess developed in the desperate circumstances after 5 January 1477. For example, Mary immediately used her father's ducal seal until she had created her own coins and seals.[45] Her image as a hunter and falconer on horseback was modelled on the equestrian iconography of her male predecessors portrayed as armoured knights, the classic representation of princely masculinity. It thus differed significantly from the seals of other Burgundian women regents. As Ann Roberts and Andrea Pearson argue, this choice suggests Mary's awareness that in her quality as Duchess of Burgundy she actively stepped into her father's rights as the country's sovereign, except on the battlefield. Choosing the image of the hunter instead of the warrior suggests an attempt to bridge the gap between claims to lordship held by men on the one hand and the claim to women's succession on the other.[46]

To become effective in practical politics, these images had to meet contemporary perceptions that were informed by underlying role models and negotiated in various strands of contemporary political discourse. Hence, the ambiguity between these and

---

41 Cf. Ann M. Roberts, The Posthumous Image of Mary of Burgundy, in: Andrea Pearson (ed.), Women and Portraits in Early Modern Europe. Gender, Agency, Identity, Aldershot 2008, 55–70; Antenhofer, Maximilian und die Frauen, see note 6, and Lutter, Repräsentation, see note 6.
42 Cf. Haemers, For the Common Good, see note 8; Depreter et al., Marie de Bourgogne, see note 6, with ample bibliography.
43 Cf. Dagmar Eichberger, Margaret of Austria: A Princess with Ambition and Political Insight, in: eadem (ed.), Women of Distinction. Margaret of York, Margaret of Austria (Exhibition catalogue), Leuven 2005, 49–55; eadem, Women at the Burgundian Court. Presence and Influence, Turnhout 2010; Monter, Experiment, see note 5.
44 Cf. Lecuppre-Desjardin in this special issue, and Dumont/Lecuppre-Desjardin, Construire la légitimité d'un pouvoir féminin, see note 36, 44.
45 Cf. Olga Karaskova, "Ung Dressoir de cinq degrez": Mary of Burgundy and the Construction of the Image of the Female Ruler, in: Juliana Dresvina and Nicholas Sparks (eds.), Authority and Gender in Medieval and Renaissance Chronicles, Newcastle 2012, 319–344, 329.
46 Cf. Andrea Pearson, Rulership, Ridership, and the Perils of Sealing, in: Depreter et al., Marie de Bourgogne, see note 6, 115–136; Ann M. Roberts, The Horse and the Hawk. Representations of Mary of Burgundy as Sovereign, in: David S. Areford and Nina A. Rowe (eds.), Excavating the Medieval Image, Aldershot 2004, 135–150.

other representations – for example in Mary's Joyous Entries and patronage politics – of a young duchess strategically fighting for acceptance in a challenging political situation, and her portrayal as a 'damsel in distress' dependent on male advisors and rescued by her marriage to a virtuous knight, underlines the fact that the conflicts around the Burgundian lands involved much more than claims of dynastic succession. Like elsewhere after a ruler's sudden death, the eminent necessity of novel dynastic arrangements and important military decisions involved disputes around the balance of power between representatives of the ruling dynasty and those of the subjects of their lands. In the Burgundian case, these were embodied by the Estates General, but also involved particular interests of regional elites. Alongside practical considerations, these negotiations were always accompanied by considerations of the nature of ideal rulers as they related to issues of a polity's territorial integrity and were represented in their political *personae*.

Mary's *Great Privilege* of 11 February 1477 is a case in point. Traditional historiography claimed that the privilege was imposed on a young, female, and therefore weak ruler by the duchy's powerful representatives.[47] However, considering the complex power balance at stake, recent scholarship has convincingly argued that the privilege in fact documents the result of a negotiated consent of the multiple parties involved. Mary's concessions revoked many of her father's decisions, strengthened the estates' constitutional rights including their consent to declarations of war, and helped her consolidate her rule in the face of imminent danger. Her subjects' loyalty to the dynasty and to Mary as ruling duchess secured dynastic continuity and increased Mary's agency.[48] As an expression of the consensus between the ruler and the representatives of her territories, the privilege thus can be read as an example of Mary's political prudence. Shared rule and the distribution of power and specific responsibilities balanced gendered role models.

5. Conclusion: governing composite polities – beyond binaries

When Mary and Maximilian married in August 1477, courtly propaganda emphasized the perfect match of their backgrounds, beauty and youth.[49] From a dynastic perspective, the couple's greatest achievement lay in its immediate success to ensure progeny. Philipp the Fair was born in 1478, less than a year after the marriage; Margaret followed in 1480, and a third child, born in 1481, died early. The political consensus

---

47 On the political context of the *Great Privilege* and further concomitant privileges see above, p. 70 with footnote 10; Wiesflecker, Maximilian, vol. 1, see note 2, 114: "Die Führung des schwankenden Staates fiel auf die schwachen Schultern eines zwanzigjährigen Mädchens, Maria von Burgund, die langehin das Ungeheuerliche der letzten Wochen nicht fassen konnte."
48 Cf. Blockmans/Prevenier, Promised Lands, see note 9, 196–198.
49 Cf. Antenhofer, Maximilian und die Frauen, see note 6; Lutter, Repräsentation, see note 6, 51.

that Mary had achieved with the estates laid the basis for Maximilian's successful military campaigns. And yet, his rights were limited from the start, and framed by gendered norms and values just as much as were those of his wife. The matrimonial contract denied him any right of succession. The couple's future children would be the sole legitimate heirs to the Burgundian duchy through their mother.[50] While the prince consort was celebrated as hope incarnate on the battlefield, and Mary's first testament (September 1477) granted her husband her properties in case of her premature death without children, he also personified the estates' fear of foreign domination via marriage.[51]

In fact, Maximilian soon started to live up to these fears. He undid the privileges granted by his wife and returned to her father's policy of excessive warfare, central control, and heavy taxation.[52] He denied negotiations with protesting parties, above all among the Flemish cities, which resulted in a series of upheavals that he answered with violence. The conflicts peaked when Mary unexpectedly died in a riding accident (1482) and eventually led to Maximilian's imprisonment in Bruges (1488), while his son and heir Philipp was in custody of a regency council. Warfare against France and the Flemish revolts lasted over a decade, devastated the country, led to the decline of some of its most flourishing cities and the near-bankruptcy of the court and the cities. Supported by his armies and local factions Maximilian eventually prevailed in 1492, two years prior to Philipp's majority, was again recognized as regent for his son and revoked the *Great Privilege* of 1477. And yet it was the Estates General who now like then contributed fundamentally to solving the conflicts of 1482, 1488, and 1492, and to establishing a form of shared rule with the regent, based on regional customs and privileges that de-centred any gendered princely precedence.[53]

After Philipp's early death in 1506, Maximilian's daughter Margaret took over the regency of the Burgundian lands from her father. Her prudent government built on this type of shared rule with the very same Estates General became a model for three generations of *gouvernantes* in the "Habsburg Netherlands", a period more peaceful and prosperous than the previous decades.[54]

---

50 Cf. Matrimonial contract of August 18, 1477, edited in: Inge Wiesflecker-Friedhuber (ed.), Quellen zur Geschichte Maximilians I. und seiner Zeit, Darmstadt 1996, 38. On the importance of fertility for the standing of a princess or queen, see Lazzarini (p. 20) and Burkhardt (p. 39) in this special issue.
51 Cf. Wiesflecker, Maximilian, vol. 1, see note 2, 134; Anne Foerster, Regierende Herrscherwitwen und das Risiko eines fremden Herrschers: Zum Verhältnis von Dynastie und Geschlecht, in: Signori/Zey, Regentinnen, see note 4, 11–30.
52 On what follows: Blockmans/Prevenier, Promised Lands, see note 9, 198–205; Haemers, Troubled Marriage, see note 9, 421 f.
53 Cf. Haemers, Troubled Marriage, see note 9, 422–427 on the reasons for Maximilian's success; Blockmans/Prevenier, Promised Lands, see note 9, 203–205 on the role of the representative institution.
54 Monter, Experiment, see note 5.

Fig. 3: Christine de Pizan (1364–1430) presents her book to Margaret of Burgundy (1393–1442). Illustration from *The Treasure of the City of Ladies*, Paris BN fr. 1177, folio 114 ca. 1475. Source: Wikimedia Commons / public domain

Earlier, against the background of the destruction brought about by the Hundred Years' War, Christine de Pizan had famously advised "good and wise" queens and princesses "to be the means of peace and concord, to work for the avoidance of war".[55] Margaret knew Christine's writings as did those exemplary women rulers she had encountered during her childhood and youth,[56] including Margaret of York, who was responsible for young Margaret's education in Mechelen and who remained a trusted advisor until her death in 1503. It was her who together with her stepdaughter Mary in 1477 had negotiated the *Great Privilege* with the Estates General to restore the loyalty of the Burgundian territories and secure their integrity and 'common good'. The Estates' resistance then was in the first place directed against Charles the Bold's aggressive politics of warfare, a politics built on models of masculinity, which Maximilian shared

---

55 Christine de Pizan, The Treasure of the City of Ladies. Or the Book of the Three Virtues. Translated with an Introduction and Notes by Sarah Lawson, revised edition, London 2003, 23 f. Cf. Lecuppre-Desjardin in this special issue, p. 61 with further bibliographical references.
56 Cf. the contributions in Eichberger, Women of Distinction, see note 43.

and followed and which led to the same fundamental crises in Burgundy that Claudia Opitz describes for sixteenth-century France.[57]

Charles the Bold and Maximilian accentuated these images of masculinity in their military and financial politics, while their female successors seem to have primarily drawn on an alternative imagery as developed by Christine. And yet, these – at first glance again binary – gendered patterns remained ambivalent in political rhetoric as well as in pragmatic practice. While Christine regularly wrote about the ideal of good and wise rulers of both genders, she knew that women actively participated in warfare.[58] Likewise, the necessity of negotiating the 'common good' among various parties was highlighted both by the male representatives of the Low Countries (and elsewhere) and by several generations of princesses alike. And so, Maximilian's own image oscillated between the larger-than-life knightly hero and the moderate peacemaker who consulted with his counsellors prior to crucial decisions of peace and war.

Hence, female and male rulers alike constructed and fashioned their images according to political necessities. In doing so they drew on available – not just but always also gendered – role models, adapted them to the needs of the day and modified them throughout their lives. Many different people participated in these processes of image construction, and yet their 'products' were again read, judged and used ambivalently by contemporary audiences and historiography alike. A close look into the interactions of the many – including nascent institutional – actors that shaped European politics around 1500 does not only show the complex relations between gendered representations and practices of power. It also testifies to the fact that male rulers did never represent a 'neutral' norm, while their female equivalents featured the – albeit many – 'exceptions' from it. Gendered expectations and image politics formed an integral part of political representation and impacted power politics that in turn affected men and women alike.

---

57 Cf. Claudia Opitz-Belakhal, "Krise der Männlichkeit" – ein nützliches Konzept der Geschlechtergeschichte?, in: L'Homme. Zeitschrift für Feministische Geschichtswissenschaft (L'Homme. Z. F. G.), 19, 2 (2008), 31–50, 43–49.
58 Among them were several 15th century Burgundian duchesses, as underlined by Lecuppre-Desjardin in this special issue. Cf. Michèle Guéret-Laferté, Jeanne la Preuse, Jeanne la Sainte. La "Pucelle" dans le Ditié de Jehanne d'Arc de Christine de Pizan, in: François Neveux (ed.), De l'hérétique à la sainte. Les procès de Jeanne d'Arc revisités, Caen 2016, 213–226; On Joan of Arc as military leader see Kelly DeVries, A Woman as Leader of Men: Joan of Arc's Military Career, in: Bonnie Wheeler and Charles T. Wood (eds.), Fresh Verdicts on Joan of Arc, New York/London 1996, 3–19; On early modern representations of warrior women see Chassica Kirchhoff, The Martial Maid: Armoured Women in the European Imaginery, in: Stefan Krause (ed.), Iron Men. Fashion in Steel (Exhibition Catalogue), Köln 2022, 49–63.

Picture credits

Figure 1 Wedding Maximilian I and Mary of Burgundy 1477, Albrecht Dürer, Woodcarving, 1515, Detail of the "Ehrenpforte". Source: Wikimedia Commons / public domain, online accessible at: https://commons.wikimedia.org/wiki/File:Het_Bourgondische_huwelijk_Maximiliaan_trouwt_met_Maria_van_Bourgondi%C3%AB_Triomfboog_van_keizer_Maximiliaan_I_(serietitel),_RP-P-OB-1481.jpg

Figure 2 Mary of Burgundy, daughter of Charles the Bold; portrait by the circle of Master of the Legend of Saint Madeleine c. 1530–1540. Source: Wikimedia Commons / public domain, online accessible at: https://commons.wikimedia.org/wiki/File:Maria_Karoli_Filia.jpg

Figure 3 Christine de Pizan (1364–1430) presents her book to Margaret of Burgundy (1393–1442). Illustration from *The Treasure of the City of Ladies* Paris BN fr. 1177, folio 114 ca. 1475. Source: Wikimedia Commons / public domain, online accessible at: https://commons.wikimedia.org/wiki/File:Christine_de_Pizan_presents_her_Book_to_Margaret_of_Burgundy.jpg?uselang=de

Oliver Auge und Laura Potzuweit

Geschlechtsspezifische Ehelosigkeit und Herrschaft: Drei Beispiele aus dem spätmittelalterlichen Ostseeraum

1. Hinführung

In der idealtypischen Vorstellung einer mittelalterlichen Herrscherpersönlichkeit,[1] sowohl auf königlicher als auch auf fürstlicher Ebene, nimmt der Eheschluss, in der Regel aus generativen, ökonomischen oder politischen Gründen, eine zentrale Position ein.[2] Ein solches legitimiertes Zweier-Bündnis galt in der allgemeinen Wahrnehmung,

---

1 Vgl. die überpersonelle Ebene des Begriffs „Herrschaft": „Doch wird im SpätMA der H.schaftsbegriff in wachsendem Umfang auch in einem polit. Sinne generalisiert und schließlich im 15. Jh. mit der Begriffsprägung ‚Landesherrschaft' mit der territorialen Dimension von H.schaft fest verbunden." Dietmar Willoweit, Art. „Herr, Herrschaft", in: Lexikon des Mittelalters, 4 (1989), 2176–2179, 2176.

2 Vgl. die zahlreichen Publikationen zu dynastischen Heiraten, Eheschlüssen, -verhandlungen und -verträgen in Auswahl, z. B. Oliver Auge, Dynastiegeschichte als Perspektive vergleichender Regionalgeschichte. Das Beispiel der Herzöge und Grafen von Schleswig und Holstein (Anfang 13. bis Ende 17. Jh.), in: Zeitschrift der Gesellschaft für Schleswig-Holsteinische Geschichte, 135 (2010), 23–46; ders., Der dynastische Heiratsmarkt einer umkämpften Region. Ehen und Ehepolitik der Herzöge von Schleswig von Abel bis Adolf VIII., in: Zeitschrift der Gesellschaft für Schleswig-Holsteinische Geschichte, 138 (2013), 7–31; ders., Die Familien- und Heiratspolitik der Schauenburger Dynastie (bis ca.1500), in: ders. u. Detlev Kraack (Hg.), 900 Jahre Schauenburger im Norden. Eine Bestandsaufnahme, Kiel/Hamburg 2015, 211–232; ders., Das Haus Hessen und der „echte Norden". Frühneuzeitliche Eheverbindungen der Landgrafen nach Schleswig-Holstein, in: Lutz Vogel u. a. (Hg.), Mehr als Stadt, Land, Fluss. Festschrift für Ursula Braasch-Schwersmann, Neustadt an der Aisch 2020, 106–110; ders., Beobachtungen zu den Eheverbindungen zwischen den sächsischen und schleswig-holsteinischen Fürstenhäusern von der Mitte des 13. bis zum Beginn des 20. Jahrhunderts, in: Alexander Sembdner u. Christoph Volkmar (Hg.), Nahaufnahmen. Landesgeschichtliche Miniaturen für Enno Bünz zum 60. Geburtstag, Leipzig 2021, 305–335; ders., Das Haus Württemberg in der dynastischen Welt des 18. und 19. Jahrhunderts. Heiratsstrategien und Ehepolitik einer Aufsteigerdynastie, in: Zeitschrift für Württembergische Landesgeschichte, 80 (2021), 311–344; Melanie Greinert, Heiratspolitik als bestimmender Faktor dynastischer Größe. Das Konnubium der Gottorfer Dynastie, in: Oliver Auge u. Michael Hecht (Hg.), „Kleine Fürsten" im Alten Reich. Strukturelle Zwänge und soziale Praktiken im Wandel (1300–1800) (Zeitschrift für historische Forschung, Beiheft 59), Berlin 2022, 361–402; Karl-Heinz Spieß, European Royal Marriages in the Late Middle Ages. Marriage Treaties, Questions of Income, Cultural Transfer, in: Majestas, 13 (2005), 7–21; ders., Europa heiratet. Kommunikation und Kulturtransfer im Kontext europäischer Königsheiraten des Spätmittelalters, in: Rainer C. Schwinges, Christian Hesse u. Peter

insbesondere wenn eine ausreichende Anzahl an (männlichen) Nachkommen daraus hervorgegangen war, unbedingt als ein Stabilitätsfaktor. Darüber hinaus füllten die Mann- sowie Frauenseite eine oftmals geschlechtlich determinierte Rolle innerhalb der Ehe aus, sodass sie sich beispielsweise in den Bereichen „Herrschaft" und „Repräsentation" komplementär ergänzen konnten.[3] In Anbetracht der großen Anzahl an Verheiratungen im Mittelalter zeigt sich ein vermeintlich bewusster beziehungsweise unbewusster Verzicht von Frauen und Männern auf eine derartige Verbindung abseits einer geistlichen Sphäre als erklärungsbedürftig, zumal er in einigen Fällen als eine signifikante Normabweichung[4] gewertet werden kann. Das galt vor allem, wenn die Nachfolgesituation ungeklärt und somit die Kontinuität der Landesherrschaft in sich bedroht schien.

In Summe ist die „weltliche Ehelosigkeit", die aufgrund ihrer Geschlechtsneutralität als Terminus gewählt wurde, als (raum-)übergreifendes und geschlechterspezifisches Thema bisher ein Forschungsdesiderat, wohingegen einige Ausprägungen, wie die geistliche Ehelosigkeit[5] sowie die Witwen- und Witwerschaft[6], bis dato in Untersu-

---

Moraw (Hg.), Europa im späten Mittelalter. Politik – Gesellschaft – Kultur (Historische Zeitschrift, Beiheft 40), München 2006, 435–464; Margarete Sturm-Heumann, Ein ungehobener Schatz: Eheverträge als genealogische und sozialgeschichtliche Quelle, in: Familie? Blutsverwandtschaft, Hausgemeinschaft und Genealogie. Beiträge zum 8. Detmolder Sommergespräch, Essen 2014, 131–155.

3 Vgl. dazu auch den Beitrag zu den „Power Couples in Central Europe around 1500" von Julia Burkhardt in diesem Band. In vielerlei Hinsicht erinnert dies konzeptionell auch an die von Heide Wunder geprägte Formulierung „Arbeitspaar" für die Frühe Neuzeit. Vgl. dazu Heide Wunder, „Er ist die Sonn', sie ist der Mond". Frauen in der Frühen Neuzeit, München 1992.

4 Zum Beispiel Ottheinrich von Pfalz-Neuburg (1502–1559), der nach dem Tod seiner Ehefrau Susanna von Bayern (1502–1543) und dem Ableben seines einzigen Bruders Philipp (1503–1548) ohne jedwede Nachkommen eine Nachfolgeregelung einem weiteren Konnubium vorzog. Vgl. Laura Potzuweit, Zwischen dynastischer Räson und persönlichen Beweggründen: Fürstliche Witwer und ihre Handlungsspielräume im spätmittelalterlichen Reich (1250–1550), Diss. Kiel 2023, [im Druck]. Vgl. das sogenannte European Marriage Pattern, einen um 1965 zuerst in den Sozialwissenschaften, dann u. a. auch in der Anthropologie und Geschichtswissenschaft verwendeten Begriff, der das Heiratsmuster in europäischen Gesellschaften beschreibt. Ein zentraler Punkt ist dabei, dass Westeuropa über alle Epochen hinweg ein eindeutig von anderen Regionen unterscheidbares Heiratsverhalten aufweist. Vgl. dazu grundlegend John Hajnal, European Marriage Patterns in Perspective, in: David Victor Glass u. D. E. C. Eversley, (Hg.), Population in History. Essays in Historical Demography, London 1965, 101–143.

5 Vgl. dazu z. B. Andreas Willbold, Zölibat. Schlüsseltexte aus den Anfängen bis zum 5. Jahrhundert, Regensburg 2023; Claudia Zey, Ohne Frauen und Kinder. Askese, Familienlosigkeit und Zölibat in den Streitschriften des 11. und 12. Jahrhunderts, in: Saeculum, 68 (2018), 303–320; Bernhard Fraling u. Karl Hoheisel, Art. „Ehelosigkeit", in: Lexikon für Theologie und Kirche, 3 (1995), 495–497; Charles Munier, Ehe und Ehelosigkeit in der alten Kirche (1.–3. Jahrhundert), Bern 1987.

6 Vgl. in Auswahl Oliver Auge u. Laura Potzuweit (Hg.), Witwerschaft. Der einsame Mann in Geschichte, Literatur und Film, Bielefeld 2024; Laura Potzuweit, Eine Frage von Haben und Brauchen. Finanzen als handlungsbedingende Faktoren fürstlicher Witwerschaft im Spätmittelalter, in: Oliver Auge (Hg.), Fürsten und Finanzen, Ostfildern 2024, 297–312; dies., Zwischen dynastischer Räson und persönlicher Motivation. Handlungsspielräume fürstlicher Witwer im Spätmittelalter (1250–

chungen mehr oder minder hinreichend Berücksichtigung fanden. Im Allgemeinen ist diesbezüglich sicherlich allein bereits aussagekräftig, dass die Verlinkung innerhalb der digitalen Version des Lexikons des Mittelalters keinen eigenen Eintrag „Ehelosigkeit" anbietet, sondern lediglich auf die Texte zu „Gelübde" und „Jungfräulichkeit" verweist.[7] Damit wird begrifflich bereits die allgemeine und unmittelbare Assoziation des ehelosen Lebens mit der geistlichen sowie der sexuellen (weiblichen) Enthaltsamkeit hergestellt.[8]

Nachfolgend soll dieser Aspekt der Ehelosigkeit[9] anhand von drei Beispielen des Ostseeraumes in den Betrachtungsfokus gerückt und vergleichend untersucht werden, wobei nicht nur deren Beweggründe und die zugrunde liegende Qualität Berücksichtigung finden sollen, sondern auch der Frage nachgegangen wird, ob geschlechterspezifische Charakteristika diese Phase im Leben des Herrschers beziehungsweise der Herrscherin prägten.[10] Genossen etwa ehelose Herrscher einen größeren Handlungsspielraum als ihre ehelosen, weiblichen Pendants? Welche Unterschiede in der

---

1550), in: Mitteilungen der Residenzen-Kommission der Akademie der Wissenschaften zu Göttingen. Neue Folge, 8 (2019), 121–127; Oliver Auge u. Friederieke Maria Schnack, Fürstliche Witwer im spätmittelalterlichen Reich zwischen dynastischer Räson und persönlicher Motivation: Ein Problemaufriss, in: Archiv für Kulturgeschichte, 101, 2 (2019), 289–315; Oliver Auge, Nina Gallion u. Thomas Steensen (Hg.), Fürstliche Witwen und Witwensitze in Schleswig-Holstein, Husum 2019; Martina Schattkowsky (Hg.), Witwenschaft in der Frühen Neuzeit. Fürstliche und adlige Witwen zwischen Fremd- und Selbstbestimmung, Leipzig 2003.

7 Brepols. Lexikon des Mittelalters – online, unter: apps.brepolis.net/lexiema/test/Default2.aspx, Zugriff: 12.2.2024. Vgl. dagegen Alfred Perrenoud, Art. „Ehelosigkeit", in: Historisches Lexikon der Schweiz, unter: https://hls-dhs-dss.ch/de/articles/016110/2005-07-05/, Zugriff: 15.3.2024.

8 Innerhalb dieses Beitrags wird unter dem Begriff „Ehelosigkeit" schlicht der Sachverhalt verstanden, wonach sich die Herrscherin bzw. der Herrscher in keiner ehelichen Verbindung befand. Eingeschlossen sind demnach sowohl das Junggesellentum als auch die Verwitwung, da sich gravierende Unterschiede in beiden Fällen bis dato im Hinblick auf die Wahrnehmung und Folgen der Ehelosigkeit nicht erkennen lassen. Dies inkludiert nicht die Möglichkeit, gleichzeitig eine außereheliche Beziehung zu führen.

9 Der Begriff „Ehelosigkeit" impliziert nicht, gerade im Fall der Verwitwung, dass der verstorbene Partner bzw. die verstorbene Partnerin unmittelbar mit dem Tod auch aus dem Herrschaftsanspruch bzw. -selbstverständnis ausschied, wie z.B. anhand des Beispiels von Maximilian I. (1459–1519) und seiner ersten Frau Maria von Burgund verdeutlicht werden kann (siehe dazu u.a. den Beitrag von Christina Lutter und Christof Muigg in diesem Band).

10 Linda Dohmen verwies in ihrem Beitrag u.a. darauf, dass im Frühmittelalter der männliche *dux*-Titel für Herrscherinnen Verwendung fand, obwohl die weibliche Form *ducissa* bekannt war. Zurecht erklärte sie gleichermaßen, dass ein „grammatikalisch männlich wirkende[r] Titel" nicht als „soziale Männ[lichkeit]" missverstanden werden dürfe und Herrschaft als ausschließlich männlich konnotiert gelten solle. Vgl. dazu Linda Dohmen, Dux dominaque Iudita – Frauen als Regentinnen und Herzöge im 10. Jahrhundert?, in: Gabriela Signori u. Claudia Zey (Hg.), Regentinnen und andere Stellvertreterfiguren vom 10. bis zum 15. Jahrhundert, Berlin 2023, 31–52, 47. Vgl. Claudia Opitz-Belakhal, Macht und Geschlecht in der Vormoderne. Forschungsergebnisse und -desiderate einer Geschlechtergeschichte des Politischen, in: Matthias Becher, Achim Fischelmanns u. Katharina Gahbler (Hg.), Vormoderne Macht und Herrschaft. Geschlechterdimensionen und Spannungsfelder, Göttingen 2021, 13–32.

Erwartungshaltung Dritter ergaben sich für den ledigen König/Fürsten im Vergleich zur ledigen Königin/Fürstin?[11]

2. Fallbeispiel I: Waldemar IV. Atterdag von Dänemark

Im Fall Waldemars IV. Atterdag (ca. 1320–1375)[12], König von Dänemark, beschäftigte seine Ehelosigkeit im Anschluss an das Ableben seiner Gemahlin Helvig von Schleswig[13] († 1374) sogar Kaiser Karl IV. (1316–1378), der sich am 13. Mai ihres Sterbejahres an die *venerabiles* in Dänemark wandte, mit der Aufforderung, den königlichen Witwer von einer neuen ehelichen Verbindung zu überzeugen.[14] Da Waldemars einziger Sohn Christoffer bereits 1363 verstorben war, sollte eine weitere Hochzeit vor allem einem generativen Zweck dienen, weil der Luxemburger das Machtvakuum nach dem Tod des Königs von Dänemark und die gleichzeitigen Herrschaftsambitionen der Mecklenburger Herzöge im skandinavischen Teil des Ostseeraumes einhegen wollte. In der Tat hatte Waldemars Enkel, Albrecht IV. († 1388), der Sohn seiner Tochter Ingeborg (1347– ca. 1370) aus deren Heirat mit Heinrich III. von Mecklenburg (um 1337–1383), in diesem Zusammenhang die aussichtsreichsten Chancen auf die Übernahme der dänischen Königswürde, zumal Waldemar Albrecht II. von Mecklenburg (1318–1379) die Thronübernahme des ge-

---

11 Siehe als Vergleichsfolie für einen Raum abseits der vermeintlich ‚klassischen' Herrschaftszuschreibung v. a. Philippe Goridis, Gefährten, Regenten, Witwer. Männliche Herrschaft im Heiligen Land der Erbköniginnen, in: Claudia Zey (Hg.), Mächtige Frauen? Königinnen und Fürstinnen im europäischen Mittelalter (11.–14. Jahrhundert), Ostfildern 2015, 163–197.
12 Grundlegend u. a. Niels Bracke, Die Regierung Waldemars IV. Eine Untersuchung zum Wandel von Herrschaftsstrukturen im spätmittelalterlichen Dänemark, Frankfurt am Main 1999.
13 Der Eheschluss begründet sich durch die unsichere Stellung Waldemars in Dänemark sowie durch den Aspekt der Einflussnahme auf Schleswig mit dem langfristigen Ziel der Rückgewinnung des Herzogtums. Vgl. Oliver Auge, „Das tat sie mit großer Klugheit" – Margrete I., die Herrscherin dreier Reiche / „det magede hun med stor klogskab" – Margrete I., herskerinde over tre riger (1353–1412), in: ders., Lars Henningsen, Frank Lubowitz u. Broder Schwensen (Hg.), Zwischen Macht und Schicksal. Acht Herrscherinnen des Nordens aus acht Jahrhunderten (1200–2000) / Mellem magt og skæbne. Otte herskerinder i norden fra otte århundreder (1200–2000), Handewitt 2013, 32–55, 33. Vgl. Auge, Der dynastische Heiratsmarkt, wie Anm. 2, 7–31.
14 „Karolus Quartus diuina fauente &c. Rex Bohemie. Venerabiles deuoti dilecti &c. Mentis studio, quo circa profectum et vtilitatem regni Dacie mouetur nostra serenitas, vos vniuersos et singulos requirimus et hortamur attente, quatenus persuasionibus consultius, quibus expedit, velitis et debeatis inducere serenissimum Principem dominum vestrum Regem Dacie, fratrem nostrum carissimum, vt pro grato prolis fructu suscitando sibi faciat consortem matrimonio copulari, cuius presentia suo tempore preditum vt eius regnicole consolentur, et se in Regem Dacie procuret nihilominus coronari. Ne, quod absit, eo sine prole decedente, gwerrarum in regno suscitentur dissidia, Regnicole quoqve predicti tribulationibus maioribus aggrauentur." Zit. nach: Carl Andreas Christensen (Hg.), Diplomatarium Danicum 3, 9: 1371–1375, København 1982, Nr. 367; Peter Frederik Suhm, Historie af Danmark 13: Fra Aar 1340 til 1375, København 1826, 872f.

meinsamen Enkelsohnes in Dänemark noch zu Lebzeiten zugesichert hatte.[15] Schließlich rief der Kaiser auch die Stände des Königreiches nach dem Tod des dänischen Herrschers zur Unterstützung des Mecklenburgers Albrecht IV. mit der Begründung auf, einen inneren Thronkonflikt vermeiden zu wollen sowie dem Verweis darauf, dass Albrecht IV. als Sohn der älteren Tochter Waldemars IV. Atterdag einen berechtigteren Anspruch besitze.[16] Dieser Richtungswechsel ergab sich wahrscheinlich, weil dessen zweiter Enkel Olav (1370–1387), Sohn der jüngeren Waldemartochter Margarethe, über seinen Vater zudem die Nachfolge in Norwegen antreten konnte, sodass, wenn er sich auch in Dänemark hätte durchsetzen sollen, zwei skandinavische Reiche in seiner Hand vereint gewesen wären.

Die Ehelosigkeit des Königs in Verbindung mit dem Fehlen eines entsprechenden männlichen Nachkommens wurde demnach insgesamt, über die Grenzen Skandinaviens hinaus, als eine Problemstellung aufgefasst, weniger jedoch aufgrund innerer Instabilität, sondern vielmehr wegen der Auswirkungen auf das herrschaftliche Gleichgewicht im Ostseeraum. Das Fehlen beziehungsweise der Verzicht auf ein weiteres Konnubium war folglich, wie auch der Eheschluss als solcher, Bestandteil einer öffentlichen Sphäre und unterlag gegebenenfalls der Intervention Dritter.

Trotz der kaiserlichen Einflussnahme schloss Waldemar IV. Atterdag allerdings keine zweite Ehe, wobei zu berücksichtigen ist, dass er bereits knapp eineinhalb Jahre später, am 24. Oktober 1375, selbst verstarb. In Anbetracht des Schreibens Karls IV. kann somit durchaus von einer Erwartungshaltung an den verwitweten Herrscher gesprochen werden, wenn auch diese vordergründig durch das Fehlen eines männlichen Nachkommens bedingt war, und nicht so sehr durch seine Ehelosigkeit. In diesem Kontext muss sich daher zwingend die Frage anschließen, ob eine Kinder- und Nachfolgerlosigkeit nicht ebenfalls bei einer Herrscherin zum Hinweis auf oder zur Bitte um einen neuerlichen Eheschluss geführt hätte.

---

15 Vgl. Verein für Meklenburgische Geschichte und Alterthumskunde (Hg.), Meklenburgisches Urkundenbuch XVIII: 1371–1375, Schwerin 1897, Nr. 10229, 78f.; Christensen, Diplomatarium, wie Anm. 14, Nr. 131. Vgl. Ralf-Gunnar Werlich, Margarete – Regentin der drei nordischen Reiche, in: Gerald Beyreuther, Barbara Pätzold u. Erika Uitz (Hg.), Fürstinnen und Städterinnen. Frauen im Mittelalter, Freiburg/Basel/Wien 1993, 110–141, 115, der grundsätzlich in Frage stellt, ob Waldemar IV. Atterdag diese Vereinbarung umsetzen wollte. Vgl. auch Oliver Auge, Um den Sieg betrogene Verbündete? Der Stralsunder Frieden von 1370 und die norddeutschen Fürsten, in: Hansische Geschichtsblätter, 139 (2021), 1–37, 15–17.
16 Vgl. Christensen, Diplomatarium, wie Anm. 14, Nr. 531. In Auszügen auch Wilhelm Mantels, Kaiser Karls IV. Hoflager in Lübeck vom 20.–30. Oktober 1375, in: Hansische Geschichtsblätter, 1 (1874), 107–141, insbesondere 120f.

3. Fallbeispiel II: Margarethe I. von Dänemark[17]

Anders als von Karl IV. zunächst skeptisch erwartet und schließlich dann scheinbar doch gewollt, konnten sich jedoch nicht die Herzöge von Mecklenburg mit ihrem Protagonisten Albrecht IV. in Dänemark durchsetzen, sondern Waldemars jüngste Tochter Margarethe (1353–1412)[18], die seit 1363 mit dem König von Norwegen, Håkon VI. (1340–1380), verheiratet war.[19] Der Ehe entstammte ein gemeinsamer, bereits erwähnter Sohn namens Olav. Durch die Heirat erlangte Margarethe den Titel einer „Königin von Norwegen und Schweden", da ihr Schwiegervater Magnus Eriksson (1316–1374) sowie ihr Mann trotz der Wahl Albrechts III. von Mecklenburg (ca. 1340–1412) zum schwedischen König 1364 weiterhin Anspruch auf die Krone Schwedens erhoben. Ungeachtet der Zusagen Waldemars IV. Atterdag wurde schließlich auch Olav zum König von Dänemark gewählt, nicht der Mecklenburger Albrecht IV.[20] Nach dem Tod ihres Vaters nahm Margarethe zudem den Titel „Tochter und Erbin Königin Waldemars" an,[21] wobei sich in dieser Formulierung durchaus ein gewisser Herrschaftsanspruch verbarg und dies sogar noch zu Lebzeiten ihres Sohnes Olav.[22] Spätestens mit dem Ableben Håkons VI. gingen dann sämtliche Ansprüche in Norwegen und Schweden auf den einzigen gemeinsamen Sohn über, wobei Margarethe als Regentin für den gerade Zehnjährigen agierte, wodurch sich ihre Spielräume nochmals erweiterten.[23] Offenbar zog sie sich auch nach dessen Mündigkeit nicht aus der Herrschaft zurück, ähnlich wie später im Fall ihres Ziehsohnes Erik.[24]

In dieser Zeit scheint sie keine weitere Ehe angestrebt zu haben, obwohl sie im Todesjahr ihres Sohnes lediglich 34 Jahre alt war und durch dessen Geburt ihre Gebärfähigkeit bereits unter Beweis gestellt hatte. Angesichts der Kronen, die sie mit in

---

17 In strenger, begrifflicher Hinsicht kann sicherlich die Frage gestellt werden, ob Margarethe, da sie nicht als Königin gekrönt und auch nicht als solche bezeichnet wurde, nicht spätestens mit der Mündigkeit Eriks letztlich keine offizielle Herrschaft mehr innehatte.
18 Grundlegend u. a. Vivian Etting, Margrete den første. En regent og hendes samtid [Margrete die Erste. Eine Regentin und ihre Zeitgenossen], København 2021⁴; Kirsten Christiansen u. a. (Hg.), Margarete I., Regent of the North. The Kalmar Union 600 Years. Essays and Catalogue, Copenhagen 1997; Werlich, Margarete, wie Anm. 15; Auge, Margrete I., wie Anm. 13, 32–55.
19 Ausführlich zum Machtkampf vgl. Anders Bøgh, Sejren i kvindens hånd. Kampen om Magten i Norden ca. 1365–89 [Der Sieg in den Händen der Frauen. Der Kampf um die Macht im Norden ca. 1365–89], Aarhus 2003.
20 Vgl. Aksel Erhardt Christensen, Kalmarunionen og nordisk politik 1319–1439 [Die Kalmarer Union und die nordische Politik 1318–1439], København 1980, 87–89, 96–103; Auge, Margrete I., wie Anm. 13, 36; auch ders., Betrogene Verbündete, wie Anm. 15, 23–27; Werlich, Margarete, wie Anm. 15, 117.
21 Christensen, Diplomatarium, wie Anm. 14, Nr. 541.
22 Vgl. Auge, Margrete I., wie Anm. 13, 36, wonach sie sich kurzzeitig auch als „Dänemarks, Schwedens und Norwegens Königin" bezeichnete, vgl. Christensen, Diplomatarium, wie Anm. 14, Nr. 532, 541.
23 Vgl. Auge, Margrete I., wie Anm. 13, 37.
24 Vgl. Auge, Margrete I., wie Anm. 13, 38.

eine solche Verbindung eingebracht hätte – wenigstens hatte sie als ‚Erbtochter' die vermeintlich günstigste Ausgangslage –, ist dieser Umstand ungewöhnlich, zumal sie mittels eines Konnubiums angeheiratete Verbündete generiert hätte, um mit deren Unterstützung ihrem Haus auf Dauer zumindest die Herrschaft in Dänemark und Norwegen zu sichern. Sicherlich stellt sich im Umkehrschluss die Frage, ob überhaupt ein geeigneter, rangähnlicher Heiratskandidat zu diesem Zeitpunkt zur Verfügung stand, sodass schlicht das Fehlen eines solchen ihre Ehelosigkeit in diesem Moment bedingt haben könnte.

Ungeachtet dessen konnte sie sich allerdings in herrschaftlicher Hinsicht nach dem überraschenden Ableben Olavs in allen drei skandinavischen Reichen durchsetzen, vermutlich insbesondere, da sie als Gemahlin und Tochter zweier Herrscher im skandinavischen Herrschaftsraum etabliert sowie anerkannt und gleichermaßen die Nachfolge durch ihren Großneffen Erik geklärt worden war:[25] Während die Huldigung als Reichsverweserin in Dänemark („Danmarks fuldmægtige frue, husbonde og formynder")[26] unmittelbar erfolgte, wurde ihr diese erst im Februar 1388 auch in Norwegen zuteil, da in der Erbmonarchie keine Ansprüche der Herzöge von Mecklenburg griffen. In Schweden sollte es hingegen noch einen weiteren Monat dauern, bis Margarethe dort ebenfalls die Rolle einer Reichsverweserin übernahm.[27] Die direkte Konkurrenz zu Albrecht III. gelangte erst durch dessen Niederlage in der Schlacht von Åsle bei Falköping am 24. Februar 1389 sowie seine anschließende Gefangenschaft zu einem Abschluss. Die langjährige, vom schwedischen Adel mehr und mehr ungeliebte ‚Fremdherrschaft' des Mecklenburgers war mitentscheidend, dass Margarethe sowie Erik als Alternative akzeptiert wurden.

Anstatt jedoch dauerhaft die Position einer alleinigen Herrscherin – im Grunde genommen auch bereits als Herrscherin einer Personalunion aus Dänemark, Norwegen und Schweden – zu bekleiden, konnte Margarethe ihren Großneffen Bogislaw von Pommern [Erik VII. (Erich von Pommern)] (1382–1459), Enkel ihrer älteren Schwester Ingeborg, als König in den drei skandinavischen Reichen durchsetzen.[28] Dieser war nur unwesentlich jünger als ihr verstorbener Sohn Olav. Dennoch hätte sie auch zu diesem Zeitpunkt noch eine zweite Ehe anstreben können, schließlich war sie gerade erst 36 Jahre alt. Allerdings zeugen die Herrschaftsregelung und die Verbringung Eriks in den Norden davon, dass sie dies nicht beabsichtigte. Ihr Handeln – die

---

25 Ihr rasches und zielstrebiges Handeln unmittelbar nach Olavs Tod wurde offenbar dann auch als Kontrastfolie zum gängigen Frauenbild wahrgenommen, das man in Momenten der Trauer mit (lähmender) Emotionalität in Verbindung brachte. Vgl. Auge, Margrete I., wie Anm. 13, 40.
26 Vgl. die Formulierung bei Thomas Riis (Hg.), Diplomatarium Danicum 4, 3: 1386–1388, København 1993, Nr. 222.
27 Vgl. Thomas Riis, Art. „Margarete, Königin von Norwegen, Reichsverweserin von Dänemark (1353–1412)", in: Lexikon des Mittelalters, 6 (1993), 234f.; Auge, Margrete I., wie Anm. 13, 40.
28 Vgl. Thomas Riis, Art. „Kalmarer Union", in: Lexikon des Mittelalters, 5 (1991), 875–877; Oliver Auge, Ein Integrationsmodell des Nordens? Das Beispiel der Kalmarer Union, in: Werner Maleczek (Hg.), Fragen der politischen Integration im mittelalterlichen Europa, Ostfildern 2005, 509–542.

(Aus-)Wahl eines geeigneten Nachfolgers – evoziert Assoziationen mit einem männlich konnotierten Herrschaftsverhalten, weniger mit der vermeintlich passiven Rolle von Königinnen und Witwen, deren Möglichkeiten seitens der Forschung lange Zeit auf Wiederverheiratung oder lebenslangen Rückzug auf das Wittum reduziert worden sind. In diesem Kontext wurde Erik wiederum annähernd übergangslos die Rolle des verstorbenen Olavs übertragen. Spätestens zu diesem Zeitpunkt stellte sich eine weitere Ehe Margarethes somit aber als dynastisch unnötig dar.

Obwohl Margarethe mit Begründung der Kalmarer Union „die formelle Generalquittung ihrer Amtsführung"[29] erhalten hatte, zog sie sich anschließend nicht aus dem Herrschaftshandeln zurück, sondern blieb neben ihrem Ziehsohn Erik in politischen Belangen bis zu ihrem Tod weiterhin aktiv wie zum Beispiel im Konflikt mit dem Deutschen Orden um die Ostseeinsel Gotland[30] oder im Rahmen der Streitigkeiten um das Herzogtum Schleswig[31]. Im Unionsbrief von 1397, der vermutlich nie ratifiziert wurde, war ihr durchaus eine solche Freiheit quittiert worden: „Framdeles scal wor fru drotning Margretæ. styra oc besidiæ radhe. oc beholde i henne lifdaghe whi<i>ndrit meth al koningxlich ræt engte wnden taket. efter henne vilghe alt thet som henne fadher. oc henne søn henne wnte oc gafue i thorræ lifuende liff."[32] Ebenso verweisen die nachfolgenden Ausführungen auf ihre fortwährend zentrale Rolle, da ihr von Seiten Eriks und des lokalen Adels die Sicherheit ihrer Besitzungen sowie ein gewisser Schutz zugesichert wurden:

> „[O]c at koningen oc rikesens men i thisse thry koningxrike. hielpe henne thetta forscrefne at besidiæ oc beholde oc beskyrme oc werghe. oc at heynæ i goth tro i henne lifdaghe wtan arct

---

29 Riis, Margarete, wie Anm. 27, 234 f. Er bezeichnet sie auch als „die eigtl. Leiterin der Regierung" (ebd.).
30 Vgl. dazu u. a. Laura Potzuweit, Zwischen erobertem und ererbtem Besitzanspruch. Die Insel Gotland im 14. und 15. Jahrhundert, in: Jahrbuch für Regionalgeschichte, 40 (2022), 30–42; dies., Im Zentrum von Ostsee und Anspruch. Der Deutsche Orden, die Krone Dänemark und der Besitzkonflikt um die Insel Gotland im 14. und 15. Jahrhundert, in: Norbert Kersken u. Paul Srodecki (Hg.), Viele Welten des Ostseeraumes. Politischer, wirtschaftlicher und kultureller Austausch vom Hochmittelalter bis zum Beginn der Neuzeit, Marburg 2024, 157–164; Detlef Kattinger, Die Verhandlungen zwischen König Albrecht von Mecklenburg, dem Deutschen Orden, dem Unionskönigtum und den Hansestädten um die Gotland-Frage. Eine Studie zum Kräfteverhältnis im Ostseeraum am Beginn des Unionszeitalters, in: Zenon Hubert Nowak (Hg.), Der Deutsche Orden in der Zeit der Kalmarer Union 1397–1521, Torún 1999, 47–68.
31 Vgl. dazu u. a. Frederic Zangel, Landesherr und Ritterschaft während des Konfliktes um das Herzogtum Schleswig (1410–1435), in: Zeitschrift der Gesellschaft für Schleswig-Holsteinische Geschichte, 136 (2011), 39–66; Ernst Daenell, Die staatsrechtliche Stellung Schleswigs zu Dänemark im Zeitalter Waldemar Atterdags, Margarethes und Erichs des Pommern, in: Zeitschrift der Gesellschaft für Schleswig-Holsteinische Geschichte, 33 (1903), 329–338; Auge, Margrete I., wie Anm. 13, 38 f., 43–46.
32 Zit. nach: Aage Andersen (Hg.), Diplomatarium Danicum 4, 6: 1396–1398, København 1998, Nr. 345, 282: „Ferner soll unsere Frau Königin Margrete nach ihrem Willen mit allem königlichen Recht ungehindert nutzen und besitzen, herrschen und behalten, was ihr Vater und ihr Sohn ihr gaben zu ihren Lebzeiten" (eigene Übersetzung).

om thet nødh gørs. Wille oc nokræ henne i thisse forscrefne stykke wforrætæ. eller henne her i amot at gøre arghæ eller hindræ i nokræ modæ tha wille <w>i i goth tro. meth al macht wære henne ther i behelpelike at scipæ henne ræt ouer thom. som thet gøre oc wnne wi h[e]nne at hwn ma takæ gudh til hielp. oc thom henne hielpe wilghæ. at sta ther amot. oc werghæ sich wforwit."[33]

Letztlich lässt sich in Bezug auf Margarethe resümieren, dass die Herrschaft über die drei skandinavischen Königreiche erst mit ihrem Tod im Jahr 1412 vollständig auf ihren Großneffen überging.[34] Im Vergleich erinnert diese Co-Herrschaft, die keines Ehemannes für Margarethe bedufte, nicht nur an die Zusammenarbeit zwischen ihrem Sohn Olav und ihr, sondern ebenso an die gemeinsame Regierung ihres Ehemannes Håkon VI. mit Magnus Eriksson in Norwegen ab 1355/58, wo nach der Mündigkeit des Sohnes die Geschäfte nicht an diesen übergeben wurden, sondern der Vater sowohl die Titulatur behielt als auch seine Herrschaftsaufgaben mit Håkon teilte.[35] Ob dieses Miteinander ein Vorbild für Margarethes und Eriks herrschaftliches Zusammenspiel darstellte, kann allerdings nicht abschließend beurteilt werden. In der Rezeption der Regierungszeit von Margarethe fallen im Kontrast zu ihren männlichen Verwandten dann jedoch wiederum die abwertenden Bemerkungen auf, die offenbar explizit auf ihre Weiblichkeit requirieren, wenn sie unter anderem als „verschlagen" und „listig" angesehen wurde.[36]

Auch angesichts dessen kann Margarethe sicherlich nicht als ein ‚klassisches' Beispiel einer (ungekrönten) Herrscherin gelten. Dennoch ebnete sie zweifellos den Weg

---

33 Zit. nach: Aage Andersen, Diplomatarium Danicum 4, 6, wie Anm. 32, 282: „Und der König und die Männer des Reiches in diesen drei Königreichen sollen ihr helfen, das Vorgenannte zu besitzen und zu bewahren und zu beschützen und zu bewachen und sie werden sie in gutem Glauben zu Lebzeiten beschützen, wenn es nötig ist, ohne Arg. Sollte ihr jemand wegen dieser Vorschriften Unrecht tun oder sich ihr in irgendeiner Weise widersetzen, sie verletzen oder sie daran hindern, so werden wir ihr nach Treu und Glauben und mit all unserer Macht beistehen, um für sie Gerechtigkeit gegen diejenigen zu erwirken, die dies tun; und wir ermahnen sie, dass sie sich an Gott und diejenigen wenden möge, die ihr helfen werden, ihr zu widerstehen und sie unbedingt zu schützen" (eigene Übersetzung).
34 Vgl. für diesen Zeitraum insbesondere Jens E. Olesen, Erich von Pommerns Alleinherrschaft 1412–1439/40, in: Detlef Kattinger, Dörte Putensen u. Horst Wernicke (Hg.), „huru thet war talet j kalmarn". Union und Zusammenarbeit in der Nordischen Geschichte. 600 Jahre Kalmarer Union (1397–1997), Hamburg 1997, 199–239.
35 Vgl. Harald Gustafsson, The Forgotten Union. Scandinavian dynastic and territorial politics in the 14th century and the Norwegian-Swedish connection, in: Scandinavian Journal of History, 42 (2017), 560–582, 564.
36 Johann Martin Lappenberg, Chronicon Holtzatiae, auctore Presbytero Bremensi, Kiel 1862, Cap. XXVIII, 95 („astutissima mulier"); Cap. XXXIII, 111(„astuta"); Anonymi veteris Rerum Danicarum & Svecicarum Chronologia ab An. 826 ad An. 1415, in: Jacobus Langebek (Hg.), Scriptores Rerum Danicarum Medii Ævi I, Kopenhagen 1772, 387–398, 398 („incredibili astutia", „nec poterat aliqvis illius astutiæ resistere"). Auch Auge, Margrete I., wie Anm. 13, 33, wonach „[b]esonders die mittelalterlichen Geistlichen, welche Chroniken schrieben, […] sich offenkundig schwer damit [taten], dass es eine Frau zu solcher Machtfülle gebracht hatte".

für die Frau ihres Neffen, Philippa von England (1394–1430)[37], die erste gekrönte Unionskönigin, die mit weitreichenden Besitzungen in Schweden bedacht und ebenfalls als Regentin in der Abwesenheit Eriks eingesetzt worden war, beispielsweise von August 1423 bis Mai 1425. Innerhalb seines Nachfolgekonzepts wurde ihr für den Fall seines Todes entsprechend auch eine zentrale Rolle zugewiesen.[38] Wenn auch umstritten bleiben muss, wie groß der Einfluss Margarethes auf das Rollenverständnis und die Rollenauslegung Philippas war,[39] ist auffällig, dass die Situation der Waldemartochter, explizit nach dem Tod ihres Mannes und Sohnes, und ihr Umgang mit dieser den Bestimmungen in der späteren Nachfolgeregelung zumindest ähneln.[40] Da Philippa kinderlos vor ihrem Mann verstarb, kamen diese Festlegungen jedoch nie zum Tragen.

In dieser Übersicht soll nicht unerwähnt bleiben, dass die Ehefrau von Eriks Nachfolger Christoph von Pfalz-Neumarkt (Christoph von Bayern) (1416–1448), Dorothea von Brandenburg (1430–1495), unmittelbar nach dem Tod ihres Mannes dessen Nachfolger Christian I. (Christian von Oldenburg) (1426–1491) ehelichte, somit die Ehelosigkeit in ihrem Fall keine Rolle spielte, sondern sich die Stabilität ihrer Position langfristig gerade aus ihrem Konnubium sowie ihren Söhnen als Nachkommen speiste.[41] Allerdings stellte die Heirat mit der verwitweten Dorothea auch eine Grundbedingung der Stände für die Übernahme der Krone durch Christian dar, um so die Kosten für ihre Witwenversorgung einzusparen, sodass hier weniger von ihrer *agency* ausgegangen werden sollte.

---

37 Grundlegend zu Philippa siehe Marie-Louise Flemberg, Filippa. Engelsk prinsessa och nordisk unionsdrottning [Philippa. Englische Prinzessin und nordische Unionskönigin], Stockholm 2014.
38 Vgl. Laura Potzuweit, A Queen in Margaret's Shadow? Philippa of England (1394–1430) as daughter, wife, and regent, in: Norbert Kersken (Hg.), Regentinnen im östlichen Europa, [in Vorbereitung].
39 Sicherlich sind zumindest Philippas Zuwendungen an das schwedische Kloster Vadstena in unmittelbarer Orientierung an Margarethe erfolgt, vgl. Flemberg, Filippa, wie Anm. 37, 155 f.
40 Vgl. Jens E. Olesen, The Governmental System in the Union of Kalmar, 1389–1439, in: Thomas Riis (Hg.), Studien zur Geschichte des Ostseeraumes 1, Odense 1995, 49–66, 53 f.; Ralf-Gunnar Werlich, Bogislaw IX. von Pommern-Stolp – ein Pommer in den dynastischen Plänen der nordischen Reiche in der ersten Hälfte des 15. Jahrhunderts, in: Pommern. Geschichte – Kultur – Wissenschaft. 2. Kolloquium zur Pommerschen Geschichte 13. und 14. September 1991, 37–58; Flemberg, Filippa, wie Anm. 37, 199–204.
41 Vgl. grundlegend Carsten Jahnke, Dorothea von Brandenburg (um 1431–1495): Verdrängt, vergessen und doch überaus machtvoll / Dorothea af Brandenborg (omkring 1431–1495): Fortrasngt, bortglemt men alligevel magtfuld, in: Oliver Auge, Lars Henningsen, Frank Lubowitz u. Broder Schwensen (Hg.), Zwischen Macht und Schicksal. Acht Herrscherinnen des Nordens aus acht Jahrhunderten (1200–2000) / Mellem magt og skæbne. Otte herskerinder i norden fra otte århundreder (1200–2000), Handewitt 2013, 56–75; ders., Dorothea von Brandenburg: Die zentrale Fürstin der dänischen und schleswig-holsteinischen Geschichte, in: Oliver Auge, Uta Kuhl u. Jan Ocker (Hg.), Fürstinnen in Schleswig-Holstein. Handlungsspielräume im Spannungsfeld zwischen Dynastie, Familie und Individuum, Kiel 2024, 39–55.

4. Fallbeispiel III: Heinrich V. von Mecklenburg

In einer gewissen Parallelität zu Margarethe erscheint die langjährige Ehelosigkeit Herzog Heinrichs V. von Mecklenburg (1479–1552) ebenfalls als dynastisches Kalkül, da aus seinen zwei ersten Heiraten bereits zwei Söhne, Magnus (1509–1550) und Philipp (1514–1557), hervorgegangen waren. Um die Nachfolge nicht durch die Ansprüche weiterer legitimer männlicher Nachkommen zu destabilisieren, verzichtete der Herzog nach dem Tod seiner zweiten Ehefrau Helene von der Pfalz (1493–1524) für ca. 27 Jahre auf eine dritte eheliche Verbindung, zumal die beiden Söhne bereits 15 beziehungsweise neun Jahre alt waren.[42] Damit entsprach Heinrich V. dem von Karl-Heinz Spieß in Bezug auf fürstliche Witwer beobachteten Verhalten, wonach bei einer ausreichenden Anzahl an potentiellen männlichen Nachfolgern auf eine weitere Hochzeit verzichtet wurde, um deren Ansprüche nicht durch Nachkommen aus zweiten, dritten oder gar vierten Verbindungen zu gefährden und den Familienhaushalt finanziell zu überfordern.[43] Überspitzt formuliert sollte die Ehelosigkeit des Herrschers den innerdynastischen Frieden bewahren und damit stabilisierend wirken.

Die ‚Söhnelosigkeit' durch die geistige Beeinträchtigung Philipps in Folge eines Turnierunfalls im Herbst 1537 und zudem das Ableben des älteren Sohnes Magnus führten dann aber doch zu einem Ende der dynastisch kalkulierten Ehelosigkeit Heinrichs V. Im Mai 1551 ging er im fortgeschrittenen Alter von 72 Jahren eine dritte Ehe mit Ursula von Sachsen-Lauenburg († 1578) ein. Allerdings verstarb der Mecklenburger bereits neun Monate später, ohne noch einen weiteren Nachkommen in dieser Verbindung gezeugt zu haben.

Inwiefern eine unmittelbare Erwartungshaltung von außen, wie im Fall Waldemars IV. Atterdag, schriftlich oder mündlich an den Herzog herangetragen worden war, ist nicht überliefert, jedoch zeugt die überaus rasche Neuverheiratung nach dem Tod seines Sohnes Magnus davon, dass er die Dringlichkeit zum Erhalt der eigenen Linie erkannt hatte, die Söhnelosigkeit überwinden zu müssen, zumal er selbst schon hochbetagt war.

Die Ehelosigkeit als dauerhafter Status war zuvor nicht als herrschaftsgefährdender Zustand wahrgenommen worden, da die Landesherrschaft in der nächsten Generation

---

42 Für den Betrachtungszeitraum liegt keine allgemein gültige Aussage zu einer ‚ausreichenden' Anzahl an Nachkommen vor, ab der ein Herrscher bewusst auf weitere Kinder verzichtete. In einigen Fällen war dieses vermeintliche Soll bereits mit zwei Söhnen erreicht. Vgl. Laura Potzuweit, Dynastische Räson, [im Druck]; Karl-Heinz Spieß, Familie und Verwandtschaft im deutschen Hochadel des Spätmittelalters. 13. bis Anfang des 16. Jahrhunderts, Stuttgart 2015².

43 Vgl. Karl-Heinz Spieß, Fürsten und Höfe im Mittelalter, Darmstadt 2008, 50; ders., Familie, wie Anm. 42, 421; ders., Konstellationen und Motive bei der Wiederverehelichung von fürstlichen Witwern im spätmittelalterlichen Reich, in: Auge/Potzuweit, Witwerschaft, wie Anm. 6, 45–70, 69f.

als gesichert angesehen werden konnte.[44] Auch als absehbar wurde, dass sein jüngerer Sohn Philipp eine nicht mehr heilbare Einschränkung erlitten hatte und daher für die Nachfolge ungeeignet war, beendete Heinrich V. seine Ehelosigkeit nicht, da ihm ja weiterhin sein Sohn Magnus als personelle Alternative zur Verfügung stand. Dieser war am 26. August 1543 mit der 18-jährigen Elisabeth, Tochter Friedrichs I. von Dänemark-Norwegen (1471–1533), verheiratet worden. Demnach wurde Heinrichs langjährige Ehelosigkeit nicht durch die Erkrankung seines jüngeren Sohnes in Frage gestellt, sondern durch die Ehe seines älteren Sohnes sowie die damit verbundene generative Erwartung weiterhin ermöglicht.

5. Zusammenfassung

In herrschaftlicher Perspektive ist weltliche Ehelosigkeit somit sowohl als zustandsbewahrend als auch als zu überwindender Zustand zu erklären, insbesondere in Kombination mit einer Erben- beziehungsweise präziser einer Söhnelosigkeit, wie am Beispiel Waldemars IV. Atterdag gezeigt. Gerade in diesem Fall wird deutlich, dass nicht allein eine Ehe, sondern auch eine Ehelosigkeit keine primär persönliche Angelegenheit des Herrschers war, sondern den ganzen eigenen Herrschafts- und Machtbereich betraf, hier sogar über dessen Grenzen hinaus. Ehelosigkeit wurde als vermeintliches ‚Problem' für die Stabilität in der Region „Ostseeraum" wahrgenommen.

Als Frau eröffneten sich Margarethe, nachdem ihr Ehemann sowie der gemeinsame Sohn und Thronanwärter verstorben waren, in ihrer Ehelosigkeit gänzlich neue Handlungsmöglichkeiten:[45] Sie konnte selbst zwar nicht zur Königin der Kalmarer Union gekrönt werden, weswegen sie diese offizielle Rolle ihrem Großneffen Erik überantwortete, jedoch hat sie zweifellos als Architektin dieser nordischen Personalunion zu gelten. Faktisch hatte sie zudem bis zu Eriks Mündigkeit im Jahr 1400 und sogar darüber hinaus die Herrschaft über die drei skandinavischen Reiche inne. Dennoch zeigt sich anhand ihres Beispiels auch einschränkend, dass sie zwar ehelos und gleichzeitig machtvoll war, dies allerdings vor allem, weil sie Erik nach außen als Ersatz für ihren aus dem Leben geschiedenen eigenen Sohn Olav vorweisen konnte. Darüber hinaus konnte sie als Tochter Waldemars IV. Atterdag bereits ein gewisses ‚Standing'

---

44 Zum problematischen Verhältnis Heinrichs V. zu seinem Bruder Albrecht VII. (1486–1547) vgl. jüngst Oliver Auge, Mecklenburg und das Reich um 1500, in: Martin Buchsteiner u. Michael Busch (Hg.), „Prelaten Manne unde Stede". Aspekte ständischer Herrschaft im nördlichen Deutschland, Lübeck 2024, 15–34.
45 Im Kontrast dazu vgl. Judith M. Bennett u. Ruth Mazo Karras (Hg.), Women, Gender, and Medieval Historians, in: dies., The Oxford Handbook of Women and Gender in Medieval Europe, Oxford 2013, 1–20, 4, wonach Kontinuitäten in weiblichen Lebensläufen durchweg auffälliger seien als Veränderungen.

vorweisen, weswegen an dieser Stelle zu fragen bleibt, welche Handlungsspielräume sich im Vergleich für ehelose Frauen aus instabilen beziehungsweise schwächeren Dynastien ergaben.

In Summe zeigt sich Ehelosigkeit auf herrschaftlicher Ebene demnach aber nicht zwingend als ein defizitärer Zustand. Sie bot vielmehr, wie bei Heinrich V. von Mecklenburg, einen alternativen Lebensentwurf, wenn die dynastischen ‚Hausaufgaben' der generativen Vermehrung und sozialständischen Sicherung erledigt waren, was sowohl für die königliche als auch fürstliche Ebene zu gelten hat. Gerade im Fall Margarethes ging es sogar um eine Erweiterung ihres Spielraumes, vornehmlich durch ihr neues Rollenverständnis nicht mehr als Ehefrau oder Witwe, sondern primär als Reichsverweserin. Um von den hier in aller Kürze angeführten Einzelfällen ausgehend jedoch allgemeinere Merkmale, Gemeinsamkeiten und Unterschiede zwischen der weiblichen und männlichen Ehelosigkeit herausstellen zu können, bedarf es zukünftiger Forschungsarbeiten auf Basis eines größeren Personenkorpus.[46] Dennoch zeigen sich ehelose Herrscherpersönlichkeiten grundsätzlich als funktionsfähige Figuren des öffentlichen Raumes, auch ohne ein eheliches Pendant.[47] ‚Gewollte' oder ‚ungewollte' Ehelosigkeit stellen sich gesamtheitlich dann schließlich auch als gar nicht so seltenes Phänomen über die genannten Beispiele sowie die norddeutschen und skandinavischen Grenzen hinweg dar.[48] Mit Malcolm IV. „the Maiden" von Schottland (1141–1165) trägt einer sein Unverheiratet-Sein sogar im – vermeintlich negativ konnotierten – Beinamen.

---

46 Vgl. zum männlichen Junggesellentum im sog. Reichsfürstenstand demnächst Oliver Auge, Christian Hoffarth u. Laura Potzuweit, Der Fürst ohne Frau: Fürstliche Junggesellen im spätmittelalterlichen Reich zwischen dynastischer und persönlicher Handlungsmotivation (1350–1550). Eine Projektskizze, in: Archiv für Kulturgeschichte, [im Druck].
47 Siehe hierzu beispielsweise Kurfürst Friedrich (den Weisen) von Sachsen (1463–1525), der als Landesherr zeitlebens unverheiratet blieb. Vgl. z. B. Armin Kohnle u. Uwe Schirmer (Hg.), Kurfürst Friedrich der Weise von Sachsen. Politik, Kultur und Reformation, Stuttgart 2015.
48 Vgl. dagegen Perrenoud, der von lediglich 6 % bis 10 % an ledigen Frauen, jedoch gesamtgesellschaftlich, vor dem 18. Jahrhundert ausgeht: „Avant le XVIIIe s., des ordres de grandeur de 6 à 10 % chez les femmes, un peu moins chez les hommes, paraissent vraisemblables". Perrenoud, Ehelosigkeit, wie Anm. 7.

Sabine Veits-Falk

Amtsärztinnen in Bosnien und Herzegowina (1892–1918). Politik, Medizin, Kultur und Geschlecht

Die österreichisch-ungarische Monarchie ging Ende des 19. Jahrhunderts verblüffend ‚fortschrittlich' mit der Kategorie Geschlecht um, sofern es politisch-imperialistischen und kulturellen Zwecken dienlich war. Dies kann am Beispiel der Amtsärztinnen in Bosnien und Herzegowina aufgezeigt werden.[1] Fünf promovierte Medizinerinnen nutzten die Chance, noch bevor Frauen im Habsburgerreich Medizin studieren konnten, als staatlich angestellte Ärztinnen in Bosnien und Herzegowina, einem als ‚rückständig' und ‚uneuropäisch' dargestellten Herrschaftsgebiet der Monarchie, ihren Beruf auszuüben. Ihr Wirken rangierte zwischen Krankenversorgung, Gesundheitsfürsorge und ‚kultureller Mission' – Bereiche von habsburgischer Herrschaft und Wissenstransfer, die seit längerer Zeit mit Konzepten von „Kolonialismus" und „Orientalismus" in unterschiedlicher Ausprägung diskutiert und auch mit Geschlechtergeschichte verknüpft werden.[2]

1. Historischer Kontext

Mit der Okkupation von Bosnien und Herzegowina 1878 wurde Österreich-Ungarn eine innereuropäische Kolonialmacht. Nachdem der Russisch-Osmanische Krieg mit einem Sieg Russlands geendet hatte und die europäischen Mächte das Gleichgewicht Europas durch einen Machtzuwachs Russlands gefährdet sahen, wurden die Ergebnisse des kurz zuvor geschlossenen Friedens von San Stefano auf dem Berliner Kongress 1878

---

1 Vgl. dazu das Kapitel über die bosnisch-herzegowinischen Amtsärztinnen in: Sabine Veits-Falk, Die „Schweizer Ärztinnen" der Habsburgermonarchie. Weibliche Karrieren, Handlungsspielräume und Grenzüberschreitungen (ca. 1860–1945), unveröffentlichte Habilitationsschrift, Salzburg 2022, 265–304. Die Studie erscheint 2025 in der Reihe Mitteilungen des Instituts für Österreichische Geschichtsforschung, Ergänzungsband 70.
2 Vgl. dazu (mit weiterführenden Literaturhinweisen) Ninja Bumann, Die „muslimische Frauenfrage" im habsburgischen Bosnien-Herzegowina. Diskurse, Akteur*innen und Verflechtungen mit und in der islamischen Welt, in: Christoph Augustynowicz, Dietlind Hüchtker u. Börries Kuzmany (Hg.), Perlen geschichtswissenschaftlicher Reflexion. Östliches Europa, sozialgeschichtliche Interventionen, imperiale Vergleiche, Göttingen 2022, 199–204.

neu verhandelt. Ein Resultat war, dass das Osmanische Reich die Verwaltung von Bosnien und Herzegowina an Österreich-Ungarn abtreten musste und die Doppelmonarchie das Zugeständnis zur militärischen Okkupation, die schließlich 1908 in eine Annexion Bosniens und Herzegowinas mündete, erhielt.[3] Der k. u. k. Finanzminister Benjámin von Kállay übte als ‚de-facto-Gouverneur' dreißig Jahre die Oberaufsicht über die Verwaltung in den okkupierten Gebieten aus.[4] In Bosnien und Herzegowina lebte damals eine in verschiedenen Varianten serbokroatisch sprechende, konfessionell heterogene Bevölkerung. Die orthodoxen Serb:innen bildeten mit 40 Prozent die größte Bevölkerungsgruppe, die politische und wirtschaftliche Macht lag jedoch in den Händen der muslimischen Bevölkerungsgruppe (30 Prozent). Die katholischen Kroat:innen machten einen Bevölkerungsanteil von rund 25 Prozent aus und begrüßten die Okkupation, während die muslimische Bevölkerungsgruppe die Fortdauer der türkischen Herrschaft und die orthodoxe einen Anschluss an Serbien vorgezogen hätte.[5]

Wie seitens der *postcolonial studies* aufgezeigt wurde, hatte das Okkupationsgebiet allein schon aus territorialen, strategischen und wirtschaftlichen Gründen den Status einer innereuropäischen Kolonie, ohne dass hier näher auf unterschiedliche Definitionen und Ansätze eingegangen werden kann.[6] Ein wesentliches Ziel der habsburgischen Herrschaft bestand darin, Bosnien und Herzegowina zu modernisieren und zu ‚zivilisieren'. Gleichzeitig versuchte die k. u. k. Regierung die einheimische Gesellschaft zu stabilisieren, indem man traditionelle Strukturen soweit bestehen ließ, dass keine Unruhe und kein Widerstand aufkamen.[7] Ausdruck dieser Bestrebungen waren die Einführung eines Schulsystems, die Errichtung von Infrastruktur und öffentlicher medizinischer Versorgung sowie die Förderung von Gesundheit und Hygiene nach dem Vorbild der Kronländer der Monarchie.[8]

---

3 Vgl. Clemens Ruthner, Bosnien-Herzegowina als k. u. k. Kolonie. Eine Einführung, in: ders. u. Tamara Scheer (Hg.), Bosnien-Herzegowina und Österreich-Ungarn, 1878–1918. Annäherungen an eine Kolonie, Tübingen 2018, 15–44, 19 f.
4 Vgl. Pieter Judson, Habsburg. Geschichte eines Imperiums. 1740–1918. Aus dem Englischen von Michael Müller, München 2017^2, 420 f. (Orig. Harvard 2016); Ernst Bruckmüller, Österreichische Geschichte. Von der Urgeschichte bis zur Gegenwart, Wien/Köln/Weimar 2019, 398 f.
5 Vgl. Erich Zöllner, Geschichte Österreichs. Von den Anfängen bis zur Gegenwart, Wien 1984^7, 421.
6 Vgl. Johannes Feichtinger et al. (Hg.), Habsburg postcolonial, Wien 2023; Robin Okey, Taming Balkan Nationalism, Oxford 2009; Raymond Detrez, Reluctance and Determination. The Prelude to the Austro-Hungarian Occupation of Bosnia Hercegovina in 1878, in: Clemens Ruthner et al. (Hg.), WechselWirkungen. Austria-Hungary, Bosnia-Herzegovina, and the Western Balkans, 1878–1918, New York 2015, 21–40; jüngst auch: Hannes Gradits, The End of Ottoman Rule in Bosnia. Conflicting Agencies and Imperial Appropriations, London 2023; Leyla Amzi-Erdogdular, The Afterlife of Ottoman Europe. Muslims in Habsburg Bosnia Herzegovina, Stanford 2023.
7 Vgl. auch Marie-Janine Calic, Südosteuropa. Weltgeschichte einer Region, München 2016, 401.
8 Vgl. Brigitte Fuchs, „Ärztinnen für Frauen". Eine feministische Kampagne zwischen Wien, Prag und Sarajewo, in: Vesela Tutavac u. Ilse Korotin (Hg.), „Wir wollen der Gerechtigkeit und Menschenliebe dienen …". Frauenbildung und Emanzipation in der Habsburger Monarchie – der südslawische Raum und seine Wechselwirkung mit Wien, Prag und Budapest, Wien 2016, 94–127, 98.

Zahlreiche, wohl auch zur Rechtfertigung von vorzunehmenden Maßnahmen verfasste, Sanitätsberichte der Landesregierung, aber auch Stereotype bedienende Artikel in der Presse beschrieben den Gesundheitszustand der Bevölkerung und die hygienischen Praktiken in Bosnien und Herzegowina als völlig unzureichend und „desolat". Berichtet wurde etwa von Muslim:innen, die in schmutzigen Häusern und Hütten wohnten, selten ihre Kleidung und Wäsche wechselten, kaum Körperhygiene betrieben, sich von ungesunder, einseitiger Kost ernährten, Ess- und Trinkgeschirr gemeinsam benutzten und unmäßige Mengen an Kaffee und Tabak konsumierten.[9]

Die bosnisch-herzegowinische Militärverwaltung begann 1878 sogleich mit dem Aufbau eines Systems moderner Medizin und Hygiene. Zu dieser Zeit gab es mit dem Vakufspital in Sarajewo bloß ein einziges Krankenhaus in Bosnien und Herzegowina und nur sieben Ärzte in der gesamten, rund 1,1 Millionen Einwohner:innen zählenden Provinz.[10]

Wie die Sanitätserhebungen der 1880er Jahre ergaben, häuften sich in Sarajewo und im Kreis Banja Luka, wo der Anteil der muslimischen Bevölkerung besonders hoch war, Syphilis-Fälle.[11] Zu ihrer Bekämpfung wurde eine Kampagne für Hygiene und eine Verbesserung der medizinischen Versorgung vorgeschlagen. Um diese Maßnahmen umsetzen zu können, mussten allerdings religiös-kulturelle Vorbehalte überwunden werden: Aufgrund religiöser Vorschriften, die eine strikte Trennung zwischen den Geschlechtern forderten, wurde eine Untersuchung von muslimischen Frauen durch männliche Ärzte sowohl von muslimischen Frauen als auch Männern kategorisch abgelehnt. Für diese Aufgabe sollten nun Ärztinnen aus der Monarchie als Amtsärztinnen bestellt werden.

Dieses ungewöhnliche Modell, Ärztinnen zur medizinischen Betreuung von Frauen anderer religiös-kultureller Zugehörigkeit einzusetzen, war, wie ein internationaler Vergleich veranschaulichte, nicht völlig neu. In den 1870er Jahren betreuten britische Ärztinnen in Indien Frauen hinduistischen Glaubens, die sich ebenfalls nicht von einem männlichen Arzt behandeln lassen wollten und konnten. Auch in Russland wurden von den *zemstva*, den landständischen Selbstverwaltungsorganen, eigene Ärztinnen für Musliminnen im Ural und in den Gebieten Zentralasiens angestellt.[12]

---

9 Vgl. Landesregierung für Bosnien und die Herzegovina (Hg.), Das Sanitätswesen in Bosnien und Hercegovina 1878–1901, Sarajevo 1903, 3, 33–43.
10 Vgl. Landesregierung für Bosnien und die Herzegovina, Das Sanitätswesen, wie Anm. 9, 4.
11 Dabei handelte es sich nicht um eine sexuell übertragbare Variante, sondern um die endemische Syphilis, die v. a. durch mangelnde Hygiene verbreitet wurde. Vgl. Brigitte Fuchs, Orientalizing Disease. Austro-Hungarian Policies of „Race", Gender and Hygiene in Bosnia and Herzegovina, 1874–1914, in: Christian Promitzer, Sevasti Trubeta u. Marius Turda (Hg.), Health, Hygiene and Eugenics in Southeastern Europe to 1945, Budapest/New York 2011, 57–85, 69–76.
12 Vgl. Martina Gamper, „Die Aerztin gehört für die Frau." Niedergelassene Ärztinnen und Ärztinnen im Sozialwesen in Wien 1900–1938, unveröffentlichte Diplomarbeit, Wien 2001, 24f.; Fuchs, Orientalizing Disease, wie Anm. 11, 76.

Minister Kállay holte bei der aus Russland stammenden und in Salzburg praktizierenden Ärztin Rosa Kerschbaumer ihre fachliche Meinung dazu ein.[13]

1891 kam erstmalig in der Habsburgermonarchie die Stelle einer vom Staat beamteten Ärztin mit fixem Gehalt zur Ausschreibung. Da dies zu einem Zeitpunkt geschah, als in Österreich-Ungarn Frauen der Zugang zum Medizinstudium noch verwehrt war, wandte sich Minister Kállay direkt an österreichisch-ungarische Absolventinnen der Universität Zürich, wo die ersten aus der Monarchie stammenden Frauen bereits seit den 1870er Jahren Medizin studierten.

Zunächst wurde für die im Nordosten von Bosnien und Herzegowina gelegene, rund 11.000 Einwohner:innen zählende Kreisstadt Dolnja Tuzla der „Posten eines weiblichen Amtsarztes creirt".[14]

2. Die Ärztinnen

Wer waren nun die Ärztinnen, die sich auf dieses Wagnis einließen? Von den insgesamt neun Amtsärztinnen bis 1918 wird in diesem Beitrag vor allem auf die ersten Medizinerinnen eingegangen, die in der Schweiz Medizin studiert hatten und denen in verschiedener Hinsicht eine Pionierinnenrolle zukam. In den Quellen werden sie auch als „Schweizer Ärztinnen" bezeichnet, da der dort erworbene Doktortitel in der Monarchie nicht anerkannt war.

Sie kamen aus Böhmen, Mähren oder dem russischen Teilungsgebiet des ehemaligen Polens und stammten durchwegs aus großbürgerlichen Familien, in denen Töchter nach hegemonialen Weiblichkeitsentwürfen sozialisiert und erzogen worden waren. Mit dem Schritt, an einer Schweizer Universität Medizin zu studieren, hatten sie bereits das erste Mal die für sie vorgesehenen ‚weiblichen' Bahnen verlassen und einen als ‚männlich' – und mit ihrem Geschlecht als nicht kompatibel definierten – Bildungsweg eingeschlagen, wofür sie sowohl Widerstände aus ihrem sozialen Umfeld als auch Frauen diskriminierende institutionelle Strukturen überwunden hatten. Das selbstständige Verlassen ihres Herkunftsorts war als zusätzlich deviant erachtet worden, da (Bildungs-)Migration männlich konnotiert war. Generell zeigten sie alle eine hohe Bereitschaft zur Mobilität und hatten, als sie nach Bosnien und Herzegowina gingen, bereits Erfahrung darin, in einem fremden Umfeld als ‚unweiblich' erachtete Lebensziele zu verwirklichen.[15]

---

13 Vgl. Rosa Kerschbaumer, Über die ärztliche Berufsbildung und Praxis der Frauen, in: Jahresbericht des Vereines für erweiterte Frauenbildung in Wien, 1 (1888/89), Beilage 7; Sabine Veits-Falk, Rosa Kerschbaumer-Putjata (1851–1923). Erste Ärztin Österreichs und Pionierin der Augenheilkunde. Ein außergewöhnliches Frauenleben in Salzburg, Salzburg 2012².

14 Landesregierung für Bosnien und die Herzegovina, Das Sanitätswesen in Bosnien und der Hercegovina, wie Anm. 9, 17.

15 Vgl. Veits-Falk, Schweizer Ärztinnen, wie Anm. 1, 98–147.

Die erste, die die neu geschaffene Amtsärztinnen-Stelle in Dolnja Tuzla erhielt, war Dr. Anna Bayer (Bayerova) (1853–1924). Sie stammte aus Böhmen, war die Tochter eines Brauerei-Pächters, hatte 1875 ihr Medizinstudium in Zürich begonnen und 1881 in Bern abgeschlossen.[16] 1887 eröffnete sie als erste Frau in Bern eine Praxis als „Aerztin für Frauen- und Mädchenkrankheiten" und entschloss sich vier Jahre später für die Bewerbung als Amtsärztin.[17]

Ihr Dienstantritt als „erste Staatsärztin" in der Habsburgermonarchie im Jänner 1892 fand breite Beachtung in der Presse: In Anwesenheit sämtlicher Beamter wurde Anna Bayer von Statthaltereirat Vuković beeidet. In seiner Rede hob er „die Wichtigkeit hervor, welche die Frau als Arzt für das allgemeine Wohl habe". Minister Kállay habe erkannt, „daß ärztliche Frauenhilfe zuerst den Frauen jener Länder zu gewähren sei, denen Sitte und Religion verbieten, einen männlichen Arzt zu consultiren".[18] Vertreterinnen der österreichischen Frauenbewegung und Befürworterinnen des Frauenstudiums wie Marianne Hainisch interpretierten die Anstellung Anna Bayers als Signal, welches Anlass zur Hoffnung gab, dass in Österreich bald ein Medizinstudium für Frauen möglich sein werde.[19]

Für Anna Bayer selbst gestaltete sich hingegen die Realität weniger erfreulich: Erst nach einigen Anfangsschwierigkeiten konnte sie ihre Praxis aufnehmen. Sie begann mit der Betreuung muslimischer Frauen und Kinder in Dolnja Tuzla und Umgebung und konnte deren Vertrauen erwerben.[20] Die Probleme mit den Behörden setzten sich jedoch weiter fort. Bayer erhielt etwa behördliche Instruktionen nur mit großer zeitlicher Verzögerung und war in ihrem Berufsalltag mit Problemen in puncto Mobilität konfrontiert. So wurde beispielsweise von ihr erwartet, dass sie zur Behandlung der Patientinnen mit dem Pferd in die Dörfer ihres Bezirkes ritt, obwohl sie nicht reiten konnte. Sie hatte den – nicht unbegründeten – Eindruck, die Landesregierung boykottiere ihre Arbeit, und bat daher Minister Kállay, der ihre Ideen und Vorstellungen unterstützte, um Intervention. Nach überwundenen Erkrankungen an Diphterie und Grippe suchte Anna Bayer im Juli 1892 um Versetzung nach Sarajewo an, da sie das Klima in Dolnja Tuzla nicht vertrug. In Sarajewo sah sie der ihr vorgesetzte Kreisarzt

---

16 Geb. in Vojtěchov (heute zur Gemeinde Mšeno gehörig) bei Mělník. Vgl. Anna Honzáková, Dr. med. Anna Bayerová 1853–1924. První česká lékařka ve Švýcarech [Die erste tschechische Ärztin in der Schweiz], Praha 1937; Ctibor Nečas, Mezi muslimkami: Působení úředních lékařek v Bosně a Hercegovině v letech 1892–1918 [Unter Musliminnen. Die Tätigkeit der Amtsärztinnen in Bosnien und Herzegowina in den Jahren 1892–1918], Brno 1992, 20–49 [ich danke der Slawistin Monika Bankowski, Zürich, sehr herzlich für die Übersetzung]; Brigitte Fuchs u. Husref Tahirović, Dr. Anna Bayerová: The First Official Female Doctor in Bosnia and Herzegovina, in: Acta Medica Academica, 48, 1 (2019), 121–126.
17 Franziska Rogger, Der Doktorhut im Besenschrank. Das abenteuerliche Leben der ersten Studentinnen – am Beispiel der Universität Bern, Bern 2002², 48.
18 Die Presse, 8.3.1892, 4.
19 Vgl. Marianne Hainisch, Ein Mutterwort über die Frauenfrage, in: Jahresbericht des Vereines für erweiterte Frauenbildung in Wien, 4 (1891/92), 21–32, 32.
20 Vgl. Nečas, Mezi muslimkami, wie Anm. 16, 31.

allerdings nur für administrative Tätigkeiten und die Ausfertigung von Rezepten vor. Bayer verstand aber unter ihrer Aufgabe als Ärztin die medizinische Behandlung und Betreuung von Patientinnen aller Glaubensgemeinschaften sowie Aufklärungsarbeit und Wissensvermittlung in Hygiene, Ernährung, Kinder- und Krankenpflege. Als sie beim Kreisvorsteher diesbezüglich Stellung bezog, wurde sie wegen „unbotmäßiger Einwände" gerügt.[21] Danach reichte sie ihr Entlassungsgesuch ein. Der ‚Fall Bayer' zeitigte jedoch Konsequenzen: Auf Kállays Weisung hatten alle Beamten hinkünftig die Boykottierung der medizinischen Tätigkeit durch Überhäufung mit administrativer Arbeit zu unterlassen.[22] Im Februar 1893 endete nach 14 Monaten Anna Bayers Karriere als Amtsärztin und sie verließ Sarajewo.[23]

Bemerkenswert ist, dass Bayer sich selbstbewusst dagegen auflehnte, untergeordnete administrative Tätigkeiten, die ihr wohl auch aufgrund ihres Geschlechts aufgetragen wurden, und solche, die nicht ihren Vorstellungen vom Aufgabengebiet einer Amtsärztin entsprachen, zu verrichten und letztlich keine Kompromisse einging. Mit ihrem Widerstand gegen die oberhalb genannten Praktiken verhinderte sie, dass das Berufsbild der Ärztin von Beginn an ‚verwässert' wurde und trug gemeinsam mit einer Anordnung des Finanzministers wesentlich dazu bei, dass der Tätigkeitsbereich der Amtsärztin konkrete Konturen erhielt. Mit Recht hieß es im „Jahresbericht des Vereines für erweiterte Frauenbildung in Wien": „[…] und wenn sie auch nach Verlauf eines Jahres, durch Vorurtheile in der Ausübung ihrer Praxis gehemmt, dieses Land verliess, so war doch ihr Wirken von Bedeutung für ihre Nachfolgerinnen."[24]

Nach der zweiten Ausschreibung 1892[25] erhielt Theodora Krajewska die Stelle in Dolnja Tuzla in der Nachfolge von Anna Bayer und Bohuslava Keck bekam einen neu geschaffenen Posten in Mostar, der Hauptstadt der Herzegowina.

Dr. Bohuslava Keck (1854–1911) stammte wie Anna Bayer aus Böhmen und war die Tochter eines Gutsbesitzers. Nach ihrem Medizinstudium in Zürich (1874–1880) und vergeblichem Bemühen um Anerkennung ihres Schweizer Doktordiploms in Österreich-Ungarn hatte sie eine Hebammenausbildung in Wien absolviert. Sie gab ihre florierende Hebammen-Praxis in Prag auf und ließ sich auf die neue Herausforderung in Mostar ein.[26] Der Einstieg in ihre Tätigkeit als Amtsärztin gestaltete sich positiv. Mufti Džabić Ali Fehmi, später Führer der muslimischen autonomistischen Bewegung der Herzegowina und bedeutender Hochschullehrer in Konstantinopel,

---

21 Nečas, Mezi muslimkami, wie Anm. 16, 46.
22 Vgl. Nečas, Mezi muslimkami, wie Anm. 16, 42, 46.
23 Vgl. Fuchs/Tahirović, Anna Bayerová, wie Anm. 16, 124.
24 Vorkämpferinnen des österreichischen Frauenstudiums, in: Jahresbericht des Vereines für erweiterte Frauenbildung in Wien, 8 (1895/96), 35–48, 39.
25 Vgl. Internationale Klinische Rundschau, 1892, 1248.
26 Geb. 1854 in Bukol (heute Gemeinde Vojkovice). Vgl. Nečas, Mezi muslimkami, wie Anm. 16, 51–70; Husref Tahirović u. Brigitte Fuchs, Bogusławą Keckova: An Official Female Doctor in Bosnia and Herzegovina, 1893–1911, in: Acta Medica Academica, 48, 2 (2019), 232–249.

vertraute ihr gleich zu Beginn die Behandlung seiner Ehefrau an. Nach der Genesung der *muftinica* und weiteren Heilerfolgen wurde sie auch von anderen wohlhabenden Musliminnen zur Behandlung in deren Häuser gerufen. In der Folge suchten auch immer mehr Frauen aus den mittleren und unteren sozialen Schichten Kecks Ambulanz auf.[27] Dabei kamen der Ärztin ihre Erfahrungen als Hebamme ‚für Frauen aller Klassen' in Prag zugute. Auch Minister Kállay würdigte mehrfach ihre Tätigkeit. In ihren Jahresberichten schilderte Keck ihre Erfahrungen, Erfolge und Schwierigkeiten und betonte, in Mostar habe sich ihr Traum und Ideal, als „Ärztin der Frauen und Kinder" tätig sein zu können, erfüllt.[28]

Dr. Theodora Krajewska, geb. Kosmowska (1854–1935), die 1892 in Dolnja Tuzla zu arbeiten begann, war in Warschau geboren worden und hatte hier nach abgelegter Lehramtsprüfung 1874 als Lehrerin gearbeitet. Nach dem frühen Tod ihres Mannes hatte sie ein Medizinstudium begonnen und 1892 in Genf promoviert.[29] Dort beendete sie ihre Anstellung als wissenschaftliche Assistentin nach einiger Zeit aufgrund von Anfeindungen durch männliche Kollegen und eines Konflikts mit ihrem Doktorvater. Der „breite und humanitäre Geist dieser völlig neuen Institution" sei dabei eine Motivation für sie gewesen sich als Amtsärztin zu bewerben, erklärte Krajewska später.[30] Unmittelbar nach ihrer Ernennung reiste sie nach Wien, um dort die österreichische Staatsbürgerschaft zu erwerben, die ebenso wie die Kenntnis einer slawischen Sprache Voraussetzung für eine Anstellung als Amtsärztin war (alternativ hätte sie auch die ungarische Staatsbürgerschaft erwerben können). Zudem wollte sie hier Serbokroatisch lernen.[31] Schon in ihrem ersten Dienstjahr erwarb sie sich besondere Verdienste bei der Bekämpfung der Cholera im Kreisspital in Dolnja Tuzla.[32] Trotz großer Erfolge und Anerkennung ihrer Arbeit seitens der Landesverwaltung beschrieb Krajewska in ihrem Erinnerungsbuch die Zeit in Dolnja Tuzla als von nicht enden wollender Arbeit ge-

---

27 Vgl. Nečas, Mezi muslimkami, wie Anm. 16, 60; Tahirović/Fuchs, Bogusławą Keckova, wie Anm. 26, 235.
28 Fuchs, Ärztinnen für Frauen, wie Anm. 8, 107.
29 Vgl. Brigitte Fuchs u. Husref Tahirović, Teodora Krajewska, Official Female Doctor of Tuzla and Sarajevo: Medical Practitioner, Woman of Science, Polish Patriot and Feminist, in: Acta Medica Academica, 48, 3 (2019), 317–327; Nečas, Mezi muslimkami, wie Anm. 16, 71–94; Zofia Krzysztoforska-Weisswasser, Bildungs- und Emanzipationsbestrebungen der polnischen Frau in Galizien – Arbeit und Solidarität mit bosnischen Frauen, in: Tutavac/Korotin: „Wir wollen der Gerechtigkeit und Menschenliebe dienen …", wie Anm. 8, 128–159, 151–154; Fuchs, Ärztinnen für Frauen, wie Anm. 8, 108–110.
30 Theodora Krajewska, Expériences d'une femme-médecin à Donja Tuzla (Bosnie), in: Rosalie Schoenflies u. a. (Hg.), Der Internationale Kongreß für Frauenwerke und Frauenbestrebungen in Berlin 19. bis 26. September 1896, Berlin 1897, 185–190, 186.
31 Vgl. Krajewska, Expériences, wie Anm. 30, 186.
32 Vgl. Weibliche Aerzte in Bosnien, in: Wiener Medizinische Wochenschrift, 30 (1896), 1349–1351, 1350.

prägt, oft auch begleitet von Selbstzweifeln und Gefühlen der Einsamkeit.[33] Als sie das Angebot erhielt, eine Stelle als Amtsärztin in Sarajewo zu bekleiden, nahm sie diese mit 1. Oktober 1899 an.

Nicht zuletzt aufgrund der Erfolge und positiven Resonanz auf die Tätigkeit von Bohuslava Keck und Theodora Krajewska wurden 1899 zwei weitere Amtsärztinnen eingesetzt: Dr. Hedwig (Jadwiga) Olszewska (1855–1932) war die Nachfolgerin von Theodora Krajewska in Dolnja Tuzla. Sie stammte aus dem russischen Teilungsgebiet Polens[34] und hatte an der Sorbonne in Paris Medizin studiert. Nach kurzer Unterbrechung ihres Studiums aufgrund der Geburt ihres Sohnes promovierte sie 1894. Da die russischen Behörden ihr Doktordiplom nicht anerkannten, arbeitete sie zuerst in Požarevac (Königreich Serbien) als Assistenzärztin. Auf Empfehlung von Krajewska zur Amtsärztin berufen, erhielt auch sie die für ihre Anstellung notwendige österreichische Staatsbürgerschaft. Olszewska war unter anderem bei den Malaria- und Cholera-Epidemien 1893 bis 1899 sowie bei der Bekämpfung der Syphilis im Einsatz.[35]

Die neu geschaffene Stelle in Banja Luka erhielt Dr. Gisela Kuhn-Januszewska[36] (1867–1943), geborene Rosenfeld, die aus Mähren stammte. Die Tochter eines Landgutpächters hatte 1898 in Zürich ihr Medizinstudium abgeschlossen.[37] Als sie nach Bosnien kam, hatte sie bereits im Deutschen Reich einige Monate als Kassenärztin für Frauen und Kinder in Remscheid und Barmen (heute ein Stadtteil von Wuppertal) gearbeitet. Sie musste die Stelle jedoch aufgeben, da ihr die Aufsichtsbehörde die Kassenpraxis aufgrund einer fehlenden deutschen Approbation untersagte.[38] Während ihrer einjährigen Tätigkeit in Banja Luka von Juli 1899 bis Juli 1900 behandelte Gisela Kuhn-Januszewska 1431 Personen (936 Frauen, 479 Kinder und 16 Männer).[39] Um 1899 ließ sie sich von ihrem damaligen Ehemann, Heinrich Kuhn,

---

33 Vgl. Bogusława Czajecka (Hg.), Teodora z Kosmowskich Krajewska, Pamiętnik, Kraków 1989, 89–92. Das von Theodora Krajewska auf Polnisch verfasste Erinnerungsbuch mit einer kurzen Familiengeschichte und Schilderungen ausgewählter Ereignisse wurde 1989 erstmals publiziert.

34 Geb. in Kurzawka bei Sławatycze (bei Lublin); Nečas, Mezi muslimkami, wie Anm. 16, 95–101.

35 Vgl. Krysztoforska-Weisswasser, Bildungs-und Emanzipationsbestrebungen, wie Anm. 29, 154; Fuchs, Ärztinnen für Frauen, wie Anm. 8, 110.

36 In erster Ehe verheiratete Kuhn, in zweiter Ehe verheiratete Januszweska. Der hier verwendete Doppelname ist ein Terminus technicus, um die Namen, unter denen sie als Ärztin bekannt ist, miteinander zu verbinden.

37 Geb. in Drnowitz (Drnovice, Tschechien). Vgl. Brigitte Fuchs u. Husref Tahirović, Gisela Januszewska (née Rosenfeld), an Austro-Hungarian ‚Woman Doctor for Women' in Banjaluka, 1899–1912, in: Acta Medica Academica, 49, 1 (2020), 75–83; Nečas, Mezi muslimkami, wie Anm. 16, 102–105; Januszewska, Gisela, in: biografiA, unter: www.biografia.at, Zugriff: 13.1.2024; Gisela Januszewska, in: Frauen in Bewegung 1848–1938, unter: https://fraueninbewegung.onb.ac.at/node/3204), Zugriff: 13.1.2024.

38 Vgl. Johanna Bleker, Frauenpraxis. Die Berufsrealität deutscher Ärztinnen bis zum Beginn der Weimarer Republik, in: Trude Maurer (Hg.), Der Weg an die Universität. Höhere Frauenstudien vom Mittelalter bis zum 20. Jahrhundert, Göttingen 2010, 236–251, 244; Ärztinnen im Kaiserreich, unter: https://geschichte.charite.de/aeik/index.html, Zugriff: 13.1.2024.

39 Vgl. Landesregierung für Bosnien und die Herzegovina, Das Sanitätswesen, wie Anm. 9, 400f.

scheiden. Aus einer jüdischen Familie stammend, konvertierte sie zum Katholizismus und heiratete den aus Polen stammenden bosnisch-herzegowinischen Sanitätsrat und Distriktarzt Ladislaus Januszewski. Aufgrund der Eheschließung mit ihrem direkten Vorgesetzten musste sie zwar ihren Posten als Amtsärztin aufgeben, konnte aber als Privatärztin weiter praktizieren. Im März 1903 eröffnete sie im muslimischen Viertel von Banja Luka ein Ambulatorium, das von der Landesregierung finanziell unterstützt wurde. Die Kreisverwaltung sah keinen Grund, den freigewordenen Amtsärztinnen-Posten neu zu besetzen, denn mit Kuhn-Januszewskas Praxis waren die Kranken des Kreises versorgt. Im August 1912, nach der Pensionierung ihres Ehemanns, verließ sie nach 13 Jahren Bosnien und übersiedelte mit ihm nach Graz.[40] 1915 unterzog sich die 48-jährige Ärztin nach ihrer jahrelangen Tätigkeit als Amtsärztin an der Universität Graz der Wiederholung ihrer Medizinprüfungen, um das österreichische Doktorat zu erlangen. Als „rassische Jüdin" verfolgt, wurde sie 1942 in das Konzentrationslager Theresienstadt deportiert, wo sie ein Jahr später ermordet wurde.[41]

Als 1902 in der Kreisstadt Travnik eine weitere Amtsärztinnen-Stelle geschaffen wurde, erhielt diese Dr. Rosa Einhorn-Bloch (1872–1950), geborene Einhorn. Sie stammte aus dem Gouvernement Grodno im Russischen Reich, war die Tochter eines Rabbiners und hatte in Lausanne Medizin studiert.[42] Als Hospitantin an der dermatologischen Klinik des Syphilis-Spezialisten Isidor Neumann in Wien war sie vielleicht auf die Stelle aufmerksam gemacht worden. Auch sie musste zunächst die österreichische Staatsangehörigkeit erwerben. Einhorn-Blochs Wirken als Amtsärztin verlief anfänglich engagiert, danach mit Unterbrechungen und nicht friktionsfrei. Als sie im Sommer 1904 an einem medizinischen Kongress in St. Louis, Missouri (USA) teilnahm, kam sie nicht zum vereinbarten Zeitpunkt zurück. Im Dezember 1904 erfolgte ihre Amtsenthebung wegen Unzufriedenheit mit ihrem Verhalten und ihrer Leistung.[43] 1905 ging Rosa Einhorn-Bloch dann wieder nach Travnik, heiratete Gerichtsrat Sigismund Bloch und reichte ein Gesuch ein, eine Privatpraxis betreiben zu dürfen, was ihr auch genehmigt wurde. Vermutlich eröffnete sie ihre Praxis erst 1908, da im

---

40 Vgl. Nečas, Mezi muslimkami, wie Anm. 16, 104; Reinhold Aigner, Die Grazer Ärztinnen aus der Zeit der Monarchie, in: Zeitschrift des Historischen Vereines für Steiermark, 70 (1976), 45–70, 61f.
41 Verein für Gedenkkultur. Stolpersteine in Graz, Gisela Januszewska, unter: https://stolpersteine-graz.at/stolpersteine/januszewska, Zugriff: 18.10.2024); Dokumentationsarchiv des österreichischen Widerstandes, Gisela Januszewska, unter: https://www.doew.at/result, Zugriff: 18.10.2024.
42 Geb. in Suchowolo (im damaligen russischen Teilungsgebiet Polens). Vgl. Brigitte Fuchs und Husref Tahirović, Rosa Einhorn (1872–1950). A Woman Pioneer in Medicine between Bosnia (1902–1913), New York, and Palestine, in: Acta Medica Academica, 49, 3 (2020), 281–291; Barbara Martin, Als Ärztin in Bosnien-Herzegowina – zur Tätigkeit Rosa Bloch-Einhorns in Travnik von 1902 bis 1917 (?), 10, unter: https://de.scribd.com/document/386555172/Als-Arzt in-in-Bosnien-Herzegowina-Zur-Tätigkeit-Rosa-Bloch-Einhorns-in-Travnik-von-1902-bis-1917, Zugriff: 24.9.2024; Nečas, Mezi muslimkami, wie Anm. 16, 106–108.
43 Vgl. Martin, Rosa Bloch-Einhorn, wie Anm. 42, 24.

Oktober 1906 ihr Sohn zur Welt kam.[44] 1910 bemühte sie sich vergeblich um die erneute Einsetzung als Amtsärztin. Anders als Gisela Kuhn-Januszewska gelang es Rosa Einhorn-Bloch aber nicht, während ihres dreijährigen Aufenthalts in Travnik eine dem Aufgabengebiet einer Amtsärztin ähnliche Tätigkeit zu entfalten.[45]

Bis zum Ende der Monarchie waren noch vier weitere Amtsärztinnen in Bosnien und Herzegowina angestellt, deren Ausgangslage, Anforderungsprofil und Aufgaben sich nach der Jahrhundertwende änderten, da Frauen inzwischen in Österreich-Ungarn Medizin studieren und auch praktizieren konnten.[46] 1908 wurde die 29-jährige Dr. Kornelija Rakić (1879–1952), die serbischer Herkunft war und ein Medizinstudium in Budapest abgeschlossen hatte, zur Amtsärztin von Bihać ernannt. 1912 wurde sie nach Banja Luka und 1917 nach Mostar versetzt.[47] Mit September 1914 erhielt Dr. Rosalie Sattler-Feuerstein (1883–?) neben Theodora Krajewska die Stelle einer Amtsärztin in Sarajewo. Sie kam aus Czernowitz und hatte 1909 in Wien promoviert. Dass die 31-jährige Ärztin mit einem in verschiedenen Funktionen in Bosnien und Herzegowina tätigen Arzt verheiratet war, stellte nun kein Hindernis mehr dar. Dr. Rachel Weissberg (1884–1943) nahm im Mai 1918 die Stelle einer Amtsärztin in Travnik an. Sie wurde 1884 in Krakau geboren, wo sie auch Medizin studiert hatte.[48]

Der Ausbruch des Ersten Weltkriegs hatte massive Folgen für die Bevölkerung von Bosnien und Herzegowina, da das südliche Kroatien und Ostbosnien zum Kriegsschauplatz wurden. Aufgrund des erheblichen Mangels an männlichen Ärzten während der Kriegsjahre wurden die Amtsärztinnen auch zu Aufgaben herangezogen, die sonst den männlichen Kollegen vorbehalten waren, etwa zur Leitung eines Krankenhauses.[49] Mit dem Ende der Monarchie fand die Institution der Amtsärztinnen ihr Ende. Alle noch Ende 1918 in Bosnien und Herzegowina amtierenden Ärztinnen – Theodora Krajewska, Kornelija Rakić, Rosalie Sattler-Feuerstein, Hedwig Olszewska und Rachel Weissberg – wurden vom neuen Staat, dem Königreich der Serben, Kroaten und Slowenen, übernommen.

---

44 Vgl. Österreichisches Staatsarchiv, Allgemeines Verwaltungsarchiv, MdI, Sanitätsakten, 1911–1912, Karton 2930, Fasz. Rosa Einhorn Bloch, Curriculum Vitae, 2.
45 Vgl. Martin, Rosa Bloch-Einhorn, wie Anm. 42, 38.
46 Vgl. etwa Waltraud Heindl u. Marina Tichy, „Durch Erkenntnis zu Freiheit und Glück ..." Frauen an der Universität Wien (ab 1897), Wien 1990.
47 Vgl. Barbara Martin, Zur Tätigkeit von Kornelija Rakić als Amtsärztin in Bosnien-Herzegowina (1908–1918). Eine Spurensuche, 2, unter: https://de.scribd.com/document/360574359/Zur-Tatigkeit-von-Kornelija-Rakić-in-Bosnien-Herzegowina, Zugriff: 24.9.2024; Nečas, Mezi muslimkami, wie Anm. 16, 109f.
48 Vgl. Barbara Martin, Rosalie Sattler-Feuerstein und Rachel Weissberg – die beiden letzten von Österreich-Ungarn in Bosnien-Herzegowina eingesetzten Amtsärztinnen, unter: https://de.scribd.com/document/340141560/Rosalie-Sattler-Feuerstein-und-Rachel-Weissberg-die-beiden-letzten-von-Osterreich-Ungarn-in-Bosnien-Herzegowina-eingesetzten-Amtsarztinnen, Zugriff: 24.9.2024.
49 Vgl. Martin, Kornelija Rakić, wie Anm. 47, 17.

von	bis	Ort	Amtsärztin
1892	1893	Dolnja Tuzla	Anna Bayer
1893	1899	Dolnja Tuzla	Theodora Krajewskja
1893	1911	Mostar	Bohuslava Keck
1899	1922	Sarajewo	Theodora Krajewska
1899	1923	Dolnja Tuzla	Hedwig Olszewska
1899	1900	Banja Luka	Gisela Kuhn-Januszewska
1902	1904	Travnik	Rosa Einhorn-Bloch
1908	1912	Bihać	Kornelia Rakić
1912	1917	Banja Luka	Kornelia Rakić
1914	1918	Sarajewo	Rosalie Sattler-Feuerstein
1918	1920	Travnik	Rachel Weissberg
1918	1952	Mostar	Kornelia Rakić

Tab. 1: (Amts-)Ärztinnen in Bosnien und Herzegowina 1892–1952[50]

3. Medizinische Praxis und Forschung

Die „Instruktion für die Amtsärztinnen in Bosnien und Herzegowina" aus dem Jahr 1892[51] regelte die Pflichten der Medizinerinnen, die dem jeweiligen Kreisvorsteher unterstellt waren. Diese umfassten die medizinische Betreuung aller Frauen des betreffenden Amtskreises, ungeachtet deren ethnischer oder konfessioneller Zugehörigkeit. Besondere Fürsorge sollte jedoch Musliminnen zuteilwerden. Eine Amtsärztin musste bei ihrer Wohnung ein Ambulatorium betreiben, um dessen Einrichtung und Erhalt sie sich selbst zu kümmern hatte. Sie musste Hausbesuche bei Frauen in der jeweiligen Kreisstadt und deren näherer Umgebung machen und im Bedarfsfall auch in entfernt gelegenen Gegenden des Kreises medizinisch tätig werden. Mittellose Patientinnen hatten ein Recht auf unentgeltliche Behandlung und Medikamente auf Kosten der Gemeinde- beziehungsweise Kreiskasse. Jährlich waren ausführliche Rechenschaftsberichte zu verfassen, die der Kreisverwaltung und von dieser der Landesregierung in Sarajewo respektive dem k. u. k. Reichsfinanzministerium vorgelegt werden mussten. Eine Amtsärztin durfte auch männliche Patienten medizinisch betreuen, „wenn es sich um Kinder oder um solche Männer handelt, deren Frauen in ihrer Behandlung stehen, und welche bei diesem Anlasse auch ihre ärztliche Hilfe für sich

---

50 Vgl. Barbara Martin, Liste der 9 von Österreich-Ungarn eingesetzten Amtsärztinnen in Bosnien-Herzegowina 1892–1918), unter: https://de.scribd.com/document/336593960/Liste-der-9-von-Osterreich-Ungarn-eingesetzten-Amtsarztinnen-in-Bosnien-Herzegowina-1892-1918-unter-Berucksichtigung-des-spateren-Berufswegs-der-Ar, Zugriff: 24.9.2024.
51 Nečas, Mezi muslimkami, wie Anm. 16, 18, zit. nach: Arhiv Bosne i Hercegovine (ABH), ZMF, 544/B.H./1892.

anrufen".⁵² Der abzulegende Amtseid verpflichtete sie zu gewissenhafter Diensterfüllung, Gehorsam gegenüber den Vorgesetzten, Wahrung des Berufsgeheimnisses, strikter Einhaltung der Landesgesetze und Enthaltung von jeglicher politischen Tätigkeit.⁵³ Die Amtsärztinnen wurden somit Teil des Organisationsnetzes des ärztlichen Personals, das bisher in allen Bereichen und Funktionen ausschließlich aus Männern bestanden hatte.

Ein Bericht über das Sanitätswesen in den Jahren 1893 bis 1901, der insgesamt einen deutlichen Ausbau der medizinischen Infrastruktur belegt, dokumentiert die Arbeit der vier Amtsärztinnen, die in diesen acht Jahren wirkten. Bohuslava Keck, Theodora Krajewska, Hedwig Olszewska und Gisela Kuhn-Januszewska behandelten gemeinsam 19.148 Patient:innen, davon 67 Prozent Erwachsene und 33 Prozent Kinder. Unter den Erwachsenen machte der Anteil an Männern 2 Prozent aus. 54 Prozent ihrer Patient:innen wurden in der Statistik als muslimisch, 23 Prozent als orientalisch-orthodox, 21 Prozent als römisch-katholisch, 3 Prozent als israelitisch und 0,5 Prozent als evangelisch geführt.⁵⁴

Unter den behandelten Krankheiten rangierten Erkrankungen der Geschlechtsorgane (13 Prozent), des Stoffwechsels und Blutes (13 Prozent) sowie der Verdauungsorgane (13 Prozent) an erster Stelle, gefolgt von Entbindungen und Krankheiten im Wochenbett (11 Prozent). Infektionskrankheiten machten 8 Prozent und die Behandlung von Syphilis 6 Prozent aus.⁵⁵

Den Amtsärztinnen gelang es weitgehend, ihre Zielgruppen von der Notwendigkeit medizinischer Untersuchungen zu überzeugen. Mit präventiven Maßnahmen wie Impfungen und Instruktionen über Hygiene im Alltag konnten sie auch tatsächlich eine Verminderung von Krankheiten und eine Verbesserung der Gesundheit ihrer Patient:innen erreichen.

Wie das Beispiel von Bohuslava Keck zeigt, war der Arbeitsalltag der Amtsärztinnen oftmals körperlich überaus anstrengend und fordernd. Sie war nicht nur in Mostar stationiert, sondern praktizierte eine Zeit lang in kleineren Städten und musste auch entferntere Distrikte besuchen, in denen die Patientinnen an einem Sammelort zusammenkamen. Diese Orte erreichte sie mit einem einfachen Bauernwagen oder der Eisenbahn. Für Krankenvisiten in der näheren Umgebung benutzte sie ein Fahrrad, das sie sich mit einer eigens dafür erbetenen Gehaltserhöhung angeschafft hatte. Nach 1895 unternahm Keck jährlich eine sechswöchige Dienstreise, auf der sie ihrer Verpflichtung zur Bekämpfung von regional verbreiteten Krankheiten, besonders der Syphilis, nachkam. Dabei wurde sie von zwei Gendarmen und einem lokalen musli-

---

52 Weibliche Aerzte in Bosnien, in: Wiener Medizinische Wochenschrift, 30 (1896), 1349–1351, 1350.
53 Vgl. Nečas, Mezi muslimkami, wie Anm. 16, 16, zit. nach: ABH, ZVS, 102018/I/99, Eides-Urkunde.
54 Vgl. Landesregierung für Bosnien und die Herzegovina, Das Sanitätswesen, wie Anm. 9, 398.
55 Vgl. Landesregierung für Bosnien und die Herzegovina, Das Sanitätswesen, wie Anm. 9, 399.

mischen „Führer" begleitet, der die Ankunft der „doktorica" in den Dörfern ankündigte.[56]

Alle Amtsärztinnen nahmen regelmäßig Impfungen gegen verschiedene Infektionskrankheiten vor: 1902 führte Theodora Krajewska eine große Impfaktion in Sarajewo und Umgebung durch, bei der sie in der ersten Jahreshälfte auf dem Land 1.473 muslimische Frauen und Mädchen und 1.439 weibliche Personen in Sarajewo gegen Pocken immunisierte.[57] Der Impftätigkeit seiner Schwester Gisela Kuhn-Januszewska widmete der österreichische Schriftsteller Alexander Roda Roda sogar einen Absatz in seinem Familienroman: „Meine tapfre kleine Schwester ritt im ersten Winter ihres bosnischen Wirkens zwei Kreise ab, die Hälfte Bosniens, von Dorf zu Dorf, oft im Schnee bis an die Bügel, ließ sich von Gendarmen die Kinder in den Sattel reichen und impfte zwanzigtausend Kinder. Doch ja nicht Kinder der Moslime [sic] und der Christen mit demselben Besteck […]."[58]

Mit einer regional besonders augenscheinlich auftretenden Erkrankung, der Osteomalazie, einer schmerzhaften Störung des Knochenstoffwechsels, die zu einer Demineralisation und damit Erweichung der Knochen führt, setzten sich Theodora Krajewska und Gisela Kuhn-Januszewska in Forschung und Praxis auseinander. Als eine der ersten beschrieb Krajewska die Knochenerweichung, die vor allem bei Musliminnen auftrat und vor ihrer Amtstätigkeit von männlichen Ärzten, die Frauen nicht untersucht hatten, daher weder festgestellt noch beschrieben worden war.[59] Sie veröffentlichte einen ausführlichen Beitrag über „Osteomalacie in Bosnien (Kreis Dolnja Tuzla)" in der „Wiener medizinischen Wochenschrift".[60] Auch Gisela Kuhn-Januszewska publizierte einen wissenschaftlichen Artikel in der „Wiener klinisch-therapeutischen Wochenschrift"[61], in dem sie aber einen etwas anderen Standpunkt als Krajewska vertrat. Krajewska erklärte die große Anzahl an Osteomalazie-Fällen unter muslimischen Frauen vor allem als eine Folge ihrer Lebensweise. Sie heirateten früh und ihr Organismus werde durch sexuelle Ausbeutung in der Ehe, häufige Geburten und lange Stillzeit geschwächt, so Krajewska. Zusätzlich würden die Frauen die meiste Zeit in der Hocke oder Kauerstellung auf dem Boden in feuchten Räumen verbringen und hätten einen eklatanten Sonnen- und Bewegungsmangel. Januszewska war hin-

---

56 Nečas, Mezi muslimkami, wie Anm. 16, 59–61; Tahirović/Fuchs, Bogusławą Keckova, wie Anm. 26, 236.
57 Vgl. Jahresbericht der Amtsärztin Dr. Teodora Krajewska in Sarajevo für das Jahr 1902, in: Wiener Medizinische Wochenschrift, 53, 4 (1903), 1927.
58 Alexander Roda Roda, Roda Rodas Roman, München 1925, 519.
59 Vgl. Brigitte Fuchs, „Weiche Knochen". Medizinhistorische Diskurse über Ethnizität, Religion und Weiblichkeit in Bosnien und Herzegowina (1878–1914), in: Virus, 7 (2008), 69–83, 70–72, 78f.; Nečas, Mezi muslimkami, wie Anm. 16, 90.
60 T[heodora] Krajewska, Osteomalacie in Bosnien, Kreis Dolnja Tuzla, in: Wiener medizinische Wochenschrift 50, Nrn. 38–45 (1900).
61 Gisela Januszewska, Über Osteomalazie mit Anhang über Tetanie, in: Wiener klinisch-therapeutische Wochenschrift 1910, 503–510.

gegen überzeugt, dass die Knochenerweichung hauptsächlich durch Mangelernährung und zu wenig Sonnenlicht verursacht und durch Schwangerschaften und langes Stillen nur verschärft werde.[62]

Theodora Krajewska publizierte mehrfach in Fachzeitschriften und nahm an einigen medizinischen Kongressen teil, wo sie über ihre Erfahrungen als Amtsärztin berichtete und somit auch die Institution selbst und die Bestrebungen der österreichischen Regierung bekannt machte. Bohuslava Keck verfasste vier umfangreiche Artikelserien zur präventiven Gesundheitsfürsorge, die 1904 und 1905 in der in Mostar publizierten Zeitschrift „Osvit" (Aufklärung) erschienen,[63] und später noch weitere Beiträge, auch für deutsche und tschechische Zeitungen, über ihre Tätigkeit in Mostar.

Als Gisela Kuhn-Januszewska Banja Luka verließ, resümierte sie, es sei gelungen, die „zwei Geißeln der muselmanischen Frauen" zurückzudrängen: Die Osteomalazie trete nicht mehr so häufig und in der hochgradigen Form auf, da sich die ärztliche Versorgung verbessert habe, und Frauen würden schon in einem früheren Stadium einer Erkrankung ärztliche Hilfe suchen.[64] Damit war das Wirken der Amtsärztinnen auch Teil eines staatlich intendierten Medikalisierungsprozesses, „in dem die Heilkunde zu einer umfassenden öffentlichen Kontroll- und Regulierungsinstanz aufstieg, in dessen Verlauf die modernen Gesellschaften mit ihren Einzelindividuen zunehmend unter die Aufsicht der Ärzte als Diener des Staates gestellt" wurden.[65] Wie die Ethnologin Brigitte Fuchs kritisch kommentiert, rekurrierten die Errichtung des Systems der öffentlichen Gesundheitsfürsorge und besonders die von den Amtsärztinnen durchgeführten Kampagnen zur Bekämpfung der Osteomalazie und zur Eindämmung der Syphilis auch stark auf einen „Orientalismus" und „einen spezifisch feministischen, kolonialistischen Diskurs", der international geführt wurde.[66] Dabei wurde mit ‚typisch orientalischer', das heißt aus westeuropäischer Sicht ‚ungesunder', ‚rückständiger' Lebensweise als Krankheitsursache argumentiert.

4. Kulturelle Mission

An die medizinische Behandlung und Aufklärungsarbeit anknüpfend, sah der Habsburgerstaat, der in nahezu alle Belange des gesellschaftlichen Lebens eingriff, mit einer ‚kulturellen Mission' ein weiteres Handlungsfeld für die Amtsärztinnen vor. Um diese zu legitimieren, wurden die in Bosnien und Herzegowina lebenden Menschen als „das

---

[62] Vgl. Fuchs/Tahirović, Gisela Januszewska, wie Anm. 37, 81.
[63] Vgl. Nečas, Mezi muslimkami, wie Anm. 16, 67f.
[64] Martin, Kornelija Rakić, wie Anm. 47, 15.
[65] Wolfgang Uwe Eckart u. Robert Jütte, Medizingeschichte. Eine Einführung, Köln/Weimar/Wien 2007, 16.
[66] Fuchs, Weiche Knochen, wie Anm. 59, 78.

Fremde" imaginiert, das der Zivilisierung bedürfe.[67] Wie bereits Edward Said 1978 in seiner Studie zum Orientalismus, in der er den Begriff als eine Vorstellung von Orient und Okzident als höchst konträre, wenngleich imaginäre Anti-Welten definierte, hervorhob, war die soziale Situation von muslimischen Frauen ein viel diskutiertes und kritisiertes Thema des westlichen Europas.[68] Daher wurde auf „erzieherisches Wirken" der Amtsärztinnen,[69] besonders auf ihre soziale Kompetenz und geschlechtsspezifische Kommunikation, „von Frau zu Frau", gesetzt.[70] Nicht außer Acht gelassen werden darf dabei der Umstand, dass die Ärztinnen auch Zutritt zu den privaten Haushalten muslimischer Familien (Harem) hatten, der fremden, westlichen Männern verweigert war. So sollten sie die Rolle als Vermittlerin ‚westlicher' Werte direkt vor Ort erfüllen und auch über ihre Eindrücke von diesen klischeebehafteten Räumen berichten.

In diesem Sinn beschrieb Bohuslava Keck „ihre Mission auch als eine culturelle".[71] 1893 erhielt sie von zwei muslimischen Begs die Erlaubnis, deren Frauen und Töchter in einigen elementaren Schulfächern zu unterrichten. Da in Bosnien und Herzegowina der Besuch der Volksschule nicht obligatorisch war, betrug die Analphabetenrate 1910 bei Männern 82,9 Prozent, bei Frauen 93,35 Prozent und bei muslimischen Frauen sogar 99,6 Prozent.[72] Die Schulbindung war von Anfang an ein zentraler Ansatz der habsburgischen ‚Zivilisierungsmission', besonders auch bei Mädchen, denn durch westliche Bildung sollten Zivilisation und Fortschritt auch im privaten Rahmen Einzug halten. Der Widerstand gegen eine staatliche Bildung muslimischer Mädchen war in der Bevölkerung groß, da befürchtet wurde, der Einfluss westlicher Bildung würde Mädchen ‚verderben' und sie würden die Verbindung zu ihren Traditionen und ihrem Glauben verlieren.[73] Mit der Möglichkeit, einigen wenigen Frauen Privatunterricht zu geben, gelang es Keck, der vom Koran vermeintlich vorgegebenen Verurteilung der Frauen zu Unwissenheit zumindest in einem bescheidenen Ausmaß entgegenzuwirken und ein Signal zu setzen.[74] Im Schuljahr 1900/1901 erhielt sie überdies von der Landesregierung den Auftrag, an der höheren Mädchenschule in Mostar Hygiene, Anthropologie und häusliche Krankenpflege zu unterrichten und wurde dort zugleich zur Schulärztin ernannt. Da sie selbst gerne handarbeitete, gab Keck auch darin Kurse und konnte so – über als ‚typisch weiblich' bewertete, rollenkonforme Tätigkeiten –

---

67 Ruthner, Bosnien-Herzegowina, wie Anm. 3, 40.
68 Vgl. Bumann, „Muslimische Frauenfrage", wie Anm. 2, 199f.; Edward Said, Orientalismus, Frankfurt am Main 2012³.
69 Landesregierung für Bosnien und die Herzegovina (Hg.), Das Sanitätswesen, wie Anm. 9, 399.
70 Heinrich Renner, Durch Bosnien und die Herzegowina kreuz und quer, Berlin 1896, 469.
71 Vorkämpferinnen des Frauenstudiums, wie Anm. 24, 40.
72 Vgl. David Schlaeppi, Oesterreich-Ungarn in Bosnien und der Hercegovina von 1878–1914. Inaugural-Dissertation der Philosophischen Fakultät der Universität Bern, Bern 1921, 26f.
73 Vgl. Fabio Giomi, Forging Habsburg Muslim Girls. Gender, Education and Empire in Bosnia and Herzegovina (1878–1918), in: History of Education, 44, 3 (2015), 274–292.
74 Vgl. Fuchs, Ärztinnen für Frauen, wie Anm. 8, 107.

den Schulbesuch von Frauen popularisieren.[75] Auch Theodora Krajewska und Gisela Kuhn-Januszewska waren als Lehrerinnen für Hygiene an unterschiedlichen Mädchenschulen angestellt. ‚Moderne', gebildete, westliche christliche Frauen sollten also ‚orientalischen', ‚rückständigen' muslimischen Frauen Bildung und westliche Normen vermitteln.

In der in- und ausländischen Öffentlichkeit stießen die Amtsärztinnen auf großes Interesse.[76] In der österreichischen Presse wurde vielfach betont, dass es nun mit der Institution der Amtsärztinnen beeindruckende ‚lebende Beweise' gebe, dass Frauen für den Beruf der Ärztin, noch dazu unter schwierigsten Bedingungen, geeignet seien.

5. Fazit

Mit der Berufung von Amtsärztinnen hatte sich die Habsburgermonarchie in eine skurrile Lage manövriert. Die „Arbeiterinnen-Zeitung" schrieb von einem „Kuriosum, dass in Österreich weibliche Ärzte angestellt werden, in Bosnien und Herzegowina nämlich, wo sich mohamedanische Frauen nicht von einem Mann untersuchen lassen. Bei uns sind die Frauen weder zum Studium noch zur Praxis als Ärzte zugelassen".[77] Der Staat war demnach bereit, wenn es politische, ‚höhere' Ziele erforderten, bestehende Geschlechtergrenzen über den Weg von Sonderregelungen aufzuweichen. Dies geschah in einem vom Zentrum der Macht räumlich und kulturell weit entfernten Gebiet und beruhte auf einem Konzept, das eine gleichgeschlechtliche, weibliche medizinische Versorgung vorsah und vielleicht deswegen von männlichen Ärzten als weniger ‚gefährlich' oder ‚bedrohlich' eingeschätzt wurde. Zugleich wurden die Ärztinnen auch für politisch-imperialistische Zwecke eingesetzt, indem sie dazu beitragen sollten, ‚Fortschritt' und ‚Zivilisation' in Bosnien und Herzegowina zu verbreiten. Generell zählten sie zu den ersten, die auf dem Gebiet der Habsburgermonarchie als Ärztinnen praktizierten und das Berufsbild prägten.

---

75 Vgl. Nečas, Mezi muslimkami, wie Anm. 16, 60: Von einheimischen Frauen erhielt sie auch zahlreiche selbst angefertigte Werkstücke als Geschenk, die sie später dem Nationalmuseum in Prag übergab und die noch heute zum Museumsbestand zählen.
76 Vgl. etwa Prager Tagblatt, 6. 9. 1894, 6; Innsbrucker Nachrichten, 2. 10. 1895, 10; (Neuigkeits-) Welt Blatt, 26. 7. 1896, 13; Das Vaterland, 29. 7. 1896, 4; Bukowinaer Rundschau, 13. 12. 1896, 3; Der Hausbesitzer. Hausherren Zeitung, 1. 6. 1897, 20; Agramer Zeitung, 11. 11. 1897, 5; Neues Wiener Tagblatt, 25. 2. 1903, 6; Südsteirische Zeitung, 26. 5. 1895, 3; Agramer Zeitung, 22. 5. 1895, 5; The British Medical Journal, 3. 1. 1903, 58.
77 Arbeiterinnen-Zeitung, 1894, Nr. 15, 5.

Julia Heinemann

Verwandtsein als politische Ressource für Mütter, Söhne und Schwestern. Zur Relationalität von Herrschaft, Verwandtschaft und Geschlecht in der französischen Monarchie im 16. Jahrhundert

Die vormoderne französische Monarchie war patrilinear: Die sogenannte *Lex Salica*[1] wurde so interpretiert, dass Frauen nicht nur von der Sukzession als Königin ausgeschlossen waren, sondern weibliche Verwandte des Königs auch keine Thronansprüche an ihre Söhne weitergeben konnten. Zugleich finden sich in der französischen Monarchie aber seit dem 15. Jahrhundert auffällig häufig weibliche Regentinnen, während Männer für das Amt nicht mehr in Frage kamen.[2] Aus geschlechtergeschichtlicher Perspektive galt dieses Phänomen mächtiger Frauen in einer Monarchie, die Frauen theoretisch von der Herrschaft ausschloss, lange als paradox. Aus verwandtschaftlicher Perspektive jedoch lässt sich dieses Paradox auflösen. Denn weibliche Regentschaft kann als Effekt einer stärkeren Betonung vertikaler Linien in Verwandtschaftsformationen seit dem Spätmittelalter[3] verstanden werden, von denen insbesondere Mütter profitierten.

Ich möchte diese Verbindung einer geschlechtergeschichtlichen Perspektive mit einem verwandtschaftsgeschichtlichen Zugang zum Anlass nehmen, um über die Relationalität von Verwandtschaft, Geschlecht und Herrschaft in der Vormoderne nachzudenken. Der Fall der Königsfamilie in der französischen Monarchie des 16. Jahrhunderts, mit dem ich besonders vertraut bin,[4] wird zum Ausgangspunkt, um danach zu fragen, wie Verwandtsein gedacht und praktiziert wurde und inwiefern es

---

1 Die Validität und Auslegung der *Lex Salica* war nicht unumstritten, insbesondere die Frage, ob sie überhaupt für die Sukzession in der französischen Monarchie anwendbar war. Vgl. dazu z. B. Sarah Hanley, The Family, the State, and the Law in Seventeenth- and Eighteenth-Century France. The Political Ideology of Male Right versus an Early Theory of Natural Rights, in: The Journal of Modern History, 78, 2 (2006), 289–332; Craig Taylor, The Salic Law and the Valois Succession to the French Crown, in: French History, 15, 4 (2001), 358–377.
2 Zur Chronologie vgl. Fanny Cosandey, La reine de France. Symbole et pouvoir. XVe–XVIIe siècle, Paris 2000, 296–301.
3 Vgl. David Sabean u. Simon Teuscher, Kinship in Europe. Approaches to Long-Term Development (1300–1900), New York/Oxford 2007.
4 Die Ausführungen basieren, falls nicht anders angegeben, auf Julia Heinemann, Verwandtsein und Herrschen. Die Königinmutter Catherine de Médicis und ihre Kinder in Briefen, 1560–1589, Heidelberg 2020.

eine geschlechtsspezifische politische Ressource darstellen konnte. Ich nehme dafür drei historische Figuren schlaglichtartig vergleichend in den Fokus: königliche Mütter, Söhne (bzw. Brüder) und Schwestern (bzw. Töchter). Dieser Ausblick soll beispielhaft zeigen, wie Verwandtschaftsbeziehungen je nach Geschlecht und Position im Verwandtschaftsgeflecht unterschiedliche Handlungsspielräume und Herrschaftsansprüche eröffneten. Ich plädiere damit für eine relationale Perspektive, die Macht grundsätzlich vergeschlechtlicht denkt und zugleich Geschlecht nicht unhinterfragt ins Zentrum setzt, insbesondere wenn es sich um Herrschaft ausübende Frauen handelt. Und ich denke, dass Verwandtschaft dafür eine notwendige analytische Kategorie bildet. Denn eine Verknüpfung von geschlechtergeschichtlich orientierter Politikgeschichte mit neuer Verwandtschaftsforschung lässt uns neuartige Perspektiven entwickeln, die das komplexe Verhältnis von Geschlecht und Macht in der Vormoderne sichtbar machen.

Methodisch knüpfe ich an die *New Kinship Studies* an, die sich von biologistischen Vorannahmen zu Verwandtschaft distanzieren und stattdessen fragen, was Verwandtsein (*relatedness*) für historische Akteur*innen ist.[5] Mein Fokus richtet sich daher auf damit verbundene historische Praktiken und Konzepte. Ich verstehe Verwandtsein als Repertoire politischen Denkens und Handelns, ähnlich Bourdieus Votum, „daß Verwandtschaftsverhältnisse eine Sache sind, die man macht und aus der man etwas macht".[6] Konkret bedeutet dies, Konzepte wie das „Haus" oder die „Dynastie", die spezifische historische Begriffe waren und oft vorschnell zu analytischen Werkzeugen werden, zu hinterfragen, insbesondere in ihrer Bedeutung für einzelne Akteur*innen. Stattdessen frage ich nach verwandtschaftlichen Figuren in ihrer Relationalität: Was waren königliche Mütter, Söhne oder Schwestern in der französischen Monarchie? Mit dem Begriff der Figur ist eine standortgebundene, kontextualisierende Perspektive verbunden, in der die geschlechtliche Markierung eine unter vielen ist. Michaela Hohkamp konnte so etwa zeigen, dass Handlungsspielräume von und Erwartungen an frühneuzeitliche Schwestern sich je nach ihren Positionen im verwandtschaftlichen Gefüge stark unterschieden.[7]

---

5 Exemplarisch aus anthropologischer Perspektive: Janet Carsten, After Kinship, Cambridge 2004; Marilyn Strathern, After Nature. English Kinship in the Late Twentieth Century, Cambridge u. a. 1992.
6 Pierre Bourdieu, Sozialer Sinn. Kritik der theoretischen Vernunft, Frankfurt am Main 2014[8], 297.
7 Vgl. Michaela Hohkamp, Do Sisters Have Brothers? Or the Search for the „rechte Schwester". Brothers and Sisters in Aristocratic Society at the Turn of the Sixteenth Century, in: Christopher H. Johnson u. David Warren Sabean (Hg.), Sibling Relations and the Transformations of European Kinship, 1300–1900, New York/Oxford 2011, 65–84. Zum Begriff der Figur vgl. Almut Höfert, Michaela Hohkamp u. Claudia Ulbrich, Editorial, in: L'Homme. Europäische Zeitschrift für Feministische Geschichtswissenschaft (L'Homme. Z. F. G.), 28, 2 (2017), 9–13. Zur Relationalität von Geschlecht vgl. Andrea Griesebner u. Christina Lutter, Mehrfach relational. Geschlecht als soziale und analytische Kategorie, in: Wiener Zeitschrift zur Geschichte der Neuzeit, 2, 2 (2002), 3–5 sowie spezifischer zum Thema Christina Lutter, Herrschaft und Geschlecht. Relationale Kategorien zur

Die zweite Hälfte des 16. Jahrhunderts war in der französischen Monarchie von den Religionskriegen geprägt und für die Forschung einhellig eine Zeit der Krise.[8] Zugleich gilt sie als Inkubator einer Reihe von zukunftsweisenden Entwicklungen, wie dem Absolutismus, der Idee der Staatsräson und der Regentschaft der Königinmutter. Für diese schuf Catherine de Médicis 1560 einen Präzedenzfall, indem sie erstmals ohne vorherige Designation eines Königs Regentin für den minderjährigen Charles IX. wurde und als Königinmutter weit über ihre offizielle Regentschaft hinaus die Geschicke der königlichen Politik prägte. In politischen Theorien, im Parlament und unter den politischen Akteur*innen der Zeit wurde intensiv diskutiert, worauf königliche Autorität beruhe, was Souveränität sei, wer Anteil daran habe, und welche „loix fondamentales" für das Königreich wesentlich seien. Verwandtschaftliche Konzepte und Metaphern waren dabei zentral, um politische Ordnung zu entwerfen und umzusetzen.[9] Was bedeutete das nun für herrschaftstragende Akteur*innen der Zeit?

Fanny Cosandey hat eine Chronologie aufgezeigt, in der Königinmütter seit dem 16. Jahrhundert zentral für die französische Monarchie wurden:[10] Seit dem 14. Jahrhundert war Verwandtschaft mit dem König unabdingbar für die Regentschaft – häufig handelte es sich um Onkel – und seit dem 15. Jahrhundert wurden ausschließlich weibliche Verwandte für diese Funktion gewählt. Während ab 1483 mit Anne de France noch eine Schwester die Regentschaft für den minderjährigen Charles VIII. übernahm, wurden seit dem 16. Jahrhundert, beginnend 1515/1525 mit Louise de Savoie, der Mutter von François I., nur noch Mütter des Königs – im Fall von dessen Minderjährigkeit oder Abwesenheit – zu Regentinnen bestimmt. Auffällig ist, dass weniger die Weiblichkeit der Regentin – aus Sicht zahlreicher Rechtsgelehrter der Zeit ein Ausschlusskriterium für Herrschaft – in den Fokus gestellt wurde als ihre Position als Mutter. Louise de Savoie begründete ihre Herrschaftsposition gegenüber dem Parlament mit der Äußerung, die *Lex Salica* sei nur auf Frauen anzuwenden, nicht jedoch auf Mütter.[11] Catherine de Médicis berief sich in ihrer Korrespondenz kaum auf ihre Position als Königin beziehungsweise Königinwitwe, sondern legitimierte ihre Autorität als Mutter. So schrieb sie 1575, als sie während des fünften Religionskrieges für König Henri III. mit den Hugenotten verhandelte, sie habe auf die Forderung nach

---

Erforschung fürstlicher Handlungsspielräume, in: Matthias Becher, Achim Fischelmanns u. Katharina Gahbler (Hg.), Vormoderne Macht und Herrschaft. Geschlechterdimensionen und Spannungsfelder, Bonn 2021, 201–231.
8 Vgl. Arlette Jouanna, La France du xvie siècle. 1483–1598, Paris 2012.
9 Vgl. Sarah Hanley, Engendering the State. Family Formation and State Building in Early Modern France, in: French Historical Studies, 16 (1989), 4–27; Julia Heinemann, Conceptualizing Kinship in Sixteenth Century Political Theories. Bodin's and Hotman's Ideas of Monarchy, in: Erdmute Alber u. a. (Hg.), The Politics of Making Kinship. Historical and Anthropological Perspectives, New York 2022, 204–234.
10 Vgl. Cosandey, La reine, wie Anm. 2.
11 Vgl. Elizabeth McCartney, The King's Mother and Royal Prerogative in Early-Sixteenth-Century France, in: John Carmi Parsons (Hg.), Medieval Queenship, New York 1993, 117–141.

einer schriftlichen Vollmacht geantwortet: „pençant que aiant l'honneur d'estre vostre mere et plusieurs lettres escriptes de vostre main, qu'il n'en estoit poinct de besoing".[12] Catherine war zu diesem Zeitpunkt keine Regentin, aber sie sah sich aufgrund ihrer Position als Mutter und der Briefe ihres Sohnes zum Herrschaftshandeln berechtigt – und Henri arbeitete auch bis kurz vor ihrem Tod eng mit ihr zusammen. Regentschaftsdiskurse der Zeit betonten aus naturrechtlicher Perspektive die Uneigennützigkeit von Müttern, die diese besonders geeignet für die Regentschaft machen würden.[13] Aus Sicht der Verwandtschaftsforschung ist dies nicht überraschend, denn in einer patrilinearen Sukzessionsordnung konnten Mütter im Gegensatz zu männlichen Verwandten ihren Kindern die Herrschaft nicht streitig machen.[14] Eine so mächtige Position von Müttern war in diesem Sinne nur in einer patrilinearen Monarchie möglich, in der sie selbst nicht sukzessionsfähig waren. Der in der Verwandtschaftsforschung konstituierte Wandel seit dem Spätmittelalter hin zu einer vermehrten Betonung vertikaler Linien war insofern mit einer Stärkung der Position von Müttern verbunden.

Wesentlich für diese Autoritätsposition war zudem die leibliche Verbindung der Königinmutter mit den Königskindern. Während der doppelte Körper des Königs (natürlich und politisch) schon von Ernst Kantorowicz als wichtiges Element vormoderner politischer Theorie und Praxis beschrieben wurde, war es das Verdienst Regina Schultes, den „Körper der Königin" zum Thema zu machen: In England, einer kognatischen Monarchie, in der Frauen bei fehlenden männlichen Nachfolgern aus eigenem Recht Königinnen werden konnten, hatten diese ebenfalls einen doppelten Körper. Demgegenüber wurde in Frankreich, wo Frauen nur durch eine Ehe Königin wurden, ihr Körper vor allem leiblich-natürlich konzipiert, der zugleich aber immer den politischen Körper miteinschloss.[15] Wenn wir nun diese Frage auf die Königinmutter übertragen, wird es noch komplexer: Im Fall von Catherine de Médicis hatte diese durch die Ehe den natürlichen und politischen Körper ihres verstorbenen Gatten einverleibt, während sie als Königinmutter Königskinder im Bauch getragen und geschaffen hatte. Die Betonung der schöpferischen Eigenschaften einer Mutter und ihrer

---

12 „Da ich dachte, weil ich die Ehre habe, Eure Mutter zu sein, und mehrere handgeschriebene Briefe von Euch, sei das überhaupt nicht nötig." Catherine an Henri III., 21. 11. 1575, in: Lettres de Catherine de Médicis, hg. v. Hector de La Ferrière-Percy (Bd. 1–5), Gustave Baguenault de Puchesse (Bd. 6–10), Paris 1880–1909, Suppl. Bd. 10, 392.
13 Vgl. Fanny Cosandey, Puissance maternelle et pouvoir politique. La régence des reines mères, in: Clio. Histoire, femmes et sociétés, 21 (2005), 1–15, unter: https://clio.revues.org/1447, Zugriff: 16. 10. 2024.
14 Vgl. Christiane Klapisch-Zuber, La „mère cruelle". Maternité, veuvage et dot dans la Florence des xive–xve siècles, in: Annales. Economies, sociétés, civilisations, 38, 5 (1983), 1097–1105; Isabelle Chabot, Lineage Strategies and the Control of Widows in Renaissance Florence, in: Sandra Cavallo u. Lyndan Warner (Hg.), Widowhood in Medieval and Early Modern Europe, New York 1999, 127–144.
15 Vgl. Regina Schulte (Hg.), Der Körper der Königin. Geschlecht und Herrschaft in der höfischen Welt, Frankfurt am Main 2002.

leiblichen Verbundenheit mit den Kindern hatte den Vorteil, dass diese Aspekte dauerhaft waren und somit die andauernde Herrschaftsposition der Königinmutter als Notwendigkeit verstehen und umsetzen ließen, während Regentschaft nur eine temporäre Vertretung war. Die Frage, was eine Königinmutter als verwandtschaftliche Figur ist, geht so weit über die Frage nach ihrer ‚Weiblichkeit' hinaus.

Während für die Königinmutter das Gebären königlicher Kinder Herrschaftsansprüche begründete, war es für die königlichen Söhne und Töchter ihre Abstammung. Für Söhne eines französischen Königs waren Männlichkeit und Verwandtsein mit dem König grundsätzlich mit einem Herrschaftsanspruch verbunden. Ausschlaggebend für ihre tatsächlichen Herrschaftschancen und Handlungsspielräume war aber in erster Linie ihre Position im Verwandtschaftsgefüge, das heißt die Frage, ob sie erst- oder nachgeborene Söhne waren. Das mag banal klingen, vermag jedoch die Bedeutung von Geschlecht wiederum zu differenzieren. Im Fall der französischen Monarchie des 16. Jahrhunderts sind die Beispiele Henri III. und François d'Anjou aufschlussreich. Theoretisch waren erstgeborene Söhne in Verwandtschaftsordnungen mit männlicher Primogenitur in erster Linie Königssöhne, während nachgeborene Söhne in erster Linie Königsbrüder sein sollten, also loyal gegenüber dem Ältesten. Allerdings musste man immer mit dem Tod rechnen und dementsprechend konnten auch jüngere Söhne noch Könige werden. So folgte Henri III. 1574 seinem Bruder Charles IX. auf den Thron, der wiederum auf seinen Bruder François II. gefolgt war. Damit wurde Henri vom Königsbruder (und damals gerade gewählten König von Polen) zum französischen König. Das wiederum führte in den folgenden Jahren immer wieder zu teils bewaffneten Konflikten mit seinem jüngeren Bruder François. Dieser war als letztgeborener Sohn in einer ‚typisch' problematischen Situation in solchen patrilinearen Verwandtschaftsgefügen: einerseits als Königssohn zum Herrschen geboren und ein potentieller Thronfolger, andererseits jedoch aufgrund seiner Position in der Geburtenreihe nachrangig und eingeschränkt in seinen Ansprüchen. Von François wurde sozusagen erwartet, mehr Bruder als Sohn zu sein. Seine Versuche, dennoch zu eigener Herrschaft zu kommen – beispielsweise in den Niederlanden – zeugen von den Konflikten zwischen Herrschaftsanspruch qua Geschlecht und Abstammung bei gleichzeitiger Zurücksetzung qua Geburtenfolge. So vermag ein Fokus auf Verwandtschaftspraktiken wiederum die Bedeutung von Männlichkeit für Herrschaftsansprüche zu differenzieren. Dies verdeutlicht auch die Tatsache, dass der kinderlose Henri III. während seiner Regierungszeit immer wieder Vorwürfen angeblicher Homosexualität und ‚Verweiblichung' ausgesetzt war:[16] Einerseits zeigen diese Anschuldigungen, wie sehr weibliches Geschlecht mit Delegitimierung verbunden wurde, andererseits aber auch, dass die Männlichkeit eines Herrschers ebenfalls fragil sein konnte. Dennoch wird in der

---

16 Vgl. Catharine Randall, Masculinity, Monarchy, and Metaphysics. A Crisis of Authority in Early Modern France, in: Kathleen P. Long (Hg.), High Anxiety. Masculinity in Crisis in Early Modern France, Kirksville 2002, 211–231.

Forschung häufig ignoriert, dass auch männliche Herrscher ein Geschlecht hatten, während Regentinnen und Königinnen meist unter dem Schlagwort „weibliche Herrschaft" untersucht werden. Theresa Earenfight hat dies treffend auf vergeschlechtlichte Forschungspraktiken bezogen: „Queenship scholars, armed with feminist and gender theories, study queens, while kingship scholars, trained in law and political theory, study kings".[17]

So wie Königssöhne zugleich immer Brüder waren (und Neffen, Onkel, Cousins, etc.), waren Königstöchter immer zugleich Schwestern. Aufgrund ihres Ausschlusses von der Sukzession wurden sie mehr noch als ihre Brüder vor allem in ihrer Geschwisterfunktion gesehen; hinzu kam die zentrale Bedeutung von Schwestern als Ehefrauen. Allerdings bildete ihr Verwandtsein mit Königen auch für Töchter beziehungsweise Schwestern die zentrale politische Ressource und einen Herrschaftsanspruch. So gab es in der französischen Monarchie Beispiele einer engen Zusammenarbeit des Königs mit seiner Schwester, prominent um 1500 bei Anne de France und Charles VIII. oder bei Marguerite de Navarre und François I. Häufiger jedoch war die in der Forschung oft beschriebene Rolle von Frauen als Mediatorinnen zwischen ihrer Heiratsfamilie und ihrer Herkunftsfamilie.[18] Zwei Töchter von Catherine de Médicis und Schwestern von Henri III. und François, Elisabeth und Marguerite, sind Beispiele, die unterschiedliche Handlungsspielräume von Schwestern aufzeigen: Elisabeth war die älteste Tochter, und auch im Fall von Töchtern/Schwestern spielte die Geburtenfolge eine Rolle. Selbst in Monarchien mit strikt männlicher Primogenitur wie der französischen waren sie die begehrtesten Ehepartnerinnen und hatten oft eine herausgehobene Position, in der sie ihren jüngeren Brüdern gegenüber beispielsweise beratend auftreten konnten. Elisabeth heiratete den spanischen König Philipp II. und spielte als Schwester des französischen Königs bis zu ihrem frühen Tod 1568 eine wichtige Rolle als Vermittlerin zu den spanischen Habsburgern. Hinzu kam, dass sie selbst Mutter wurde, was ihre Bedeutung innerhalb des Verwandtschaftsnetzes der Valois und Habsburger stärkte – die Mutterposition war letztlich diejenige, die Frauen am meisten Autorität bringen konnte. Noch 1592 betonte Philipp II. Elisabeths Position als älteste Tochter des Königs und als Mutter, um vor den französischen Generalständen (erfolglos) zu argumentieren, dass die Tochter Elisabeths, Isabella, die rechtmäßige Thronfolgerin Frankreichs sei. In Instruktionen an seine Gesandten schrieb er, Isabella sei „fille de la reine Elisabeth, sœur aînée dudit roi Henri, et […], représentant la personne de sa mère, elle se trouve au degré le plus proche du dernier

---

17 Theresa Earenfight, Two Bodies, One Spirit. Isabel and Fernando's Construction of Monarchical Partnership, in: Barbara F. Weissberger (Hg.), Queen Isabel I of Castile. Power, Patronage, Persona, Woodbridge 2008, 3–18, 5.
18 Vgl. Giulia Calvi u. Isabelle Chabot (Hg.), Moving Elites. Women and Cultural Transfers in the European Court System, Florenz 2010.

possesseur [...]. Donc, si l'on considère le sang et la légitimité de la succession, personne ne peut, à juste titre, régner en France que la dame infante."[19]

Marguerite, die jüngste Königstochter, hatte im Vergleich weniger Handlungsspielraum: Durch ihre Ehe mit dem Protestanten Henri de Navarre und ihre Kinderlosigkeit ohnehin in einer schwierigen Lage, wurde von ihr erwartet, in den religiösen Auseinandersetzungen zu vermitteln. Sie selbst äußerte 1580 in einem Brief an Henri III., dass das Balancieren zwischen ihren Relationen als Ehefrau und Schwester sie zerreiße.[20] Marguerite lebte schließlich ab 1585 getrennt von ihrem Ehemann und hielt offenbar auch kaum noch Kontakt zu ihrem Bruder und ihrer Mutter, entzog sich also letztlich beiden Relationen; sie war gewissermaßen nur noch Marguerite und weniger die ‚Schwester von' oder ‚Ehefrau von'. Beide Beispiele zeigen so die unterschiedlichen Handlungsspielräume von Schwestern und deren enge Verknüpfung mit anderen Relationen wie dem Muttersein und insbesondere der Ehe – sie waren sozusagen die Garantinnen bilateraler Beziehungen in patrilinearen Verwandtschaftsordnungen. Zugleich zeigen die Fälle die Bedeutung einer sorgfältigen Kontextualisierung, denn Geschlecht, Ehe und Geburtenfolge erklären diese Handlungsspielräume nicht ausreichend.

Die Mehrfachrelationalität von Geschlecht ist in der Geschlechtergeschichte schon häufig betont worden und ermöglicht einen differenzierteren Blick auf die Bedeutung von Geschlecht in der Vormoderne.[21] Mit meinen Ausführungen möchte ich dafür plädieren, Verwandtsein als wichtige Facette dieser Mehrfachrelationalität zu verstehen. Und das bedeutet zuallererst, Verwandtsein konsequent zu historisieren – Sohn, Mutter oder Schwester zu sein, ist nicht einfach ein biologischer Fakt, sondern es muss je nach Situation gefragt werden, was ein Sohn, eine Mutter oder eine Schwester sein konnten. Man kann die spezifischen Diskurse und Praktiken der französischen Monarchie nicht auf andere Fälle übertragen. Für eine Untersuchung von Herrschaft

---

19 Isabella sei „die Tochter der Königin Elisabeth, der ältesten Schwester des genannten Königs Henri, und [...], da sie die Person ihrer Mutter repräsentiert, befindet sie sich im nächsten [verwandtschaftlichen] Grad des letzten Inhabers [des Throns] [...]. Deshalb kann, wenn man das Blut und die Legitimität der Sukzession berücksichtigt, niemand mit Recht in Frankreich regieren außer der Infantin." „Le but de Sa Majesté dans les affaires de France, et ce qu'elle a ordonné et veut qu'on tache d'obtenir des Etats Généraux" (25. 1. 1592), in: Lettres de Philippe II à ses filles les infantes Isabelle et Catherine, écrites pendant son voyage en Portugal (1581–1583) [...], hg. von M. Gachard, Paris 1884, 75.
20 „d'un côté, je balance l'honneur et le respect que je vous porte avec ce que je désire, comme je dois, votre repos et l'heureuse conservation de votre Etat; [et] j'ai d'autre part, comme je dois aussi, l'amour et l'affection que je porte au roi mon mari, à quoi mon honneur et réputation me rendent obligée". Marguerite an Henri III., [April 1580], in: Marguerite de Valois, Correspondance, 1569–1614, hg. v. Éliane Viennot, Paris/Genf 1998, 137.
21 Vgl. v. a. Claudia Opitz, Staatsräson kennt kein Geschlecht. Zur Debatte um die weibliche Regierungsgewalt im 16. Jahrhundert und ihrer Bedeutung für die Konzipierung frühneuzeitlicher Staatlichkeit, in: Feministische Studien, 2 (2005), 228–241; Lutter, Herrschaft und Geschlecht, wie Anm. 7.

und Geschlecht in der Vormoderne ist es sinnvoll, sich damit auseinanderzusetzen, wie in spezifischen Fällen Verwandtsein gedacht und praktiziert wurde: Das umfasst Sukzessionsordnungen und Besitztransfers genauso wie Vorstellungen von Leib und Körper, Liebe und Verbundenheit. Dann zeigt sich, dass Verwandtschaft je nach Kontext eine politische Ressource sein konnte für Mütter, Söhne und Schwestern, manchmal aber auch ein Hindernis, und oft beides zugleich. Wenn wir diesen Fokus in die Frage nach geschlechtsspezifischen Handlungsspielräumen und Herrschaft integrieren, sehen wir zum Beispiel, dass Königinmütter wie Catherine de Médicis ihre Herrschaftsposition auf eine zentrale leibliche Relation zurückführen konnten – nämlich die zu ihren Nachkommen – und dabei von einem Wandel hin zu patrilinearen Verwandtschaftsordnungen profitierten. Die Primogenitur brachte für Königssöhne unterschiedliche Herrschaftschancen; sie alle konnten trotz ihrer Männlichkeit in fragilen Positionen sein. Schwestern hatten zentrale Rollen als Mediatorinnen, Ehefrauen und damit als Garantinnen bilateraler Verwandtschaftsbeziehungen, mussten aber auch schwierige Mehrfachloyalitäten balancieren. Diese Perspektiven vermögen die Bedeutung von Geschlecht zu relativieren. Damit möchte ich nicht negieren, dass Herrschaftslegitimation für Frauen meist schwieriger war als für Männer. Das zeigen die zahlreichen misogynen Schriften gelehrter Männer der Zeit. Aber der relationale Blick auf Verwandtschaftsfiguren und vormoderne Politik hilft vorschnelle Zuschreibungen von (männlicher) formeller Herrschaft und (weiblicher) informeller Macht zu vermeiden. Er kann stattdessen zeigen, dass ‚Weiblichkeit' und ‚Männlichkeit' Herrschaftshandeln in spezifischen Kontexten bestimmte und dass Geschlecht manchmal hinter der verwandtschaftlichen Position zurücktreten konnte – oder, um es pointiert mit Louise de Savoie zu sagen: Die *Lex Salica* betrifft Frauen, nicht jedoch Mütter.

Christina Antenhofer

Medieval and Early Modern Gendered Power Politics from the Perspective of Material Culture

A growing number of material culture studies have opened up fruitful avenues for reconsidering mobile objects as powerful agents in social networks. This article presents findings based on extensive research into inventories of bridal trousseaus from Italian and German princely marriages of the fourteenth and fifteenth centuries to explore the relevance of marital goods for women's agency.[1] Using the examples of the Visconti and Sforza princesses, who married German princes, the article explores the central question: how did women's economic resources affect their agency, and what role did objects play as mediators of power? The first section outlines the importance of the bridal trousseau as resource for women's agency. Mobile objects will be further studied as a means of representation for women's visibility and the visual codification of spaces. The second section investigates the role of objects as agents of networking. The article concludes with a methodological questionnaire for the study of networks based on material culture.

1. The material base of marriage: dowries, bridal trousseaus and gendered spheres of action

Marriages are primary instances of alliances in all social strata. Claude Lévi-Strauss already pointed out that weddings are moments of extensive gift exchange.[2] Jack Goody provided one of the first in-depth studies of how the system of marital goods developed in Europe under the influence of Christianity in the context of family systems and the transmission of property.[3] Christiane Klapisch-Zuber opened up the important path of

---

1 For an extensive analysis of the mentioned examples, see Christina Antenhofer, Die Familienkiste. Mensch-Objekt-Beziehungen im Mittelalter und in der Renaissance, Ostfildern 2022. See also the review of this book by Christof Muigg in this issue.
2 Cf. Claudie Lévi-Strauss, Les Structures élémentaires de la parenté, Paris 1949.
3 Cf. Jack Goody, The Development of the Family and Marriage in Europe, Cambridge 1994.

studying marital goods within the system of the house from a gender perspective.[4] For the medieval German context, Karl-Heinz Spieß systematically examined the monetary value of dowries for the higher nobility *(Herrenstand)*. He was able to show how the size of the dowry reflected the status of the bride, her family of origin and her new family. In the German, and sometimes international, context, the dowry had to be balanced by a counter-dowry *(Widerlage, contrados, dower)* of the same amount. The money was usually secured by various properties, for example castles or towns, from which annual rents were paid.[5] However, this well-balanced system was open to a wide range of variations, especially at the international level. While researchers have paid close attention to the monetary value of dowries and the ways in which dowries were linked to property in the context of medieval European noble families, they have rarely taken an interest in the material objects that were exchanged in the form of the bridal trousseau. There has also been a lack of comparative studies of how princely women from the Italian and German contexts could use the monetary and material goods of their dowry, including their bridal trousseau and the morning gift *(Morgengabe)* they received from their husbands after the first night.[6] The handling of marital gifts is very complex, and different terminologies for the individual parts, as well as cultural differences, have contributed to misunderstandings even among contemporaries.[7] From a gender perspective, on the one hand, the availability of goods determined the structure of women's agency in relation to their control over resources in the form of rents and precious objects. On the other hand, these material resources, especially the morning gift and the bridal trousseau, opened up avenues for individual agency.

The case of the fourteenth-century Visconti sisters, who married German princes, reveals the many facets of the management of marital property in the context of these transnational marriages. The Visconti are examples of the new Italian nobility associated with the transformation of the northern Italian city-states into *signorie*.[8] Verde, Antonia, Taddea, Maddalena and Elisabetta Visconti were all daughters of the Milanese couple Bernabò Visconti and Beatrice Regina della Scala. According to dynastic logic, the sisters were married in the order of their birth and all received impressive dowries,

---

4 Cf. Christiane Klapisch-Zuber, La maison et le nom. Stratégies et rituels dans l'Italie de la Renaissance, Paris 1990; see in this line, L'Homme. Europäische Zeitschrift für Feministische Geschichtswissenschaft (L'Homme. Z. F. G.), 22, 1 (2011): Mitgift, ed. by Karin Gottschalk and Margareth Lanzinger.
5 Cf. Karl-Heinz Spieß, Familie und Verwandtschaft im deutschen Hochadel des Spätmittelalters, Stuttgart 1993.
6 On rural examples, see Martine Segalen, Gender and Inheritance Patterns in Rural Europe: Women as Wives, Widows, Daughters and Sisters, in: History and Anthropology, 32, 2 (2021): Kinship and Gender. Comparative Reassessments between the 8th and 19th Centuries CE, ed. by Andre Gingrich and Christina Lutter, 171–187.
7 Cf. Christina Antenhofer, Antiquated Meets Modern. Conflicting Rules in Late Medieval Chancery Practices. The Example of the Gorizian Chancery, in: eadem and Mark Mersiowsky (eds.), The Roles of Medieval Chanceries. Negotiating Rules of Political Communication, Turnhout 2021, 137–162.
8 Cf. Andrea Gamberini and Isabella Lazzarini (eds.), The Italian Renaissance State, Cambridge 2012.

which were intended to elevate the lower status of these new Italian *signori* to the princely nobility of the Holy Roman Empire through prestigious marriages.⁹ This aspiration was reflected in the amount of roughly 100,000 florins each daughter received on marriage. Earlier historiographical research assumed that the German princes married these women primarily for the financial impact of these dowries, but ignored the fact that in the context of marital goods, the dowry was part of the woman's possession, even though it was administered by the husband.¹⁰ Above all, the annual rents were intended to provide the means for the women's court and to ensure their maintenance in the event of widowhood. The dowry and the trousseau constituted the women's share of their family's inheritance. Should no children result from the marriages, the dowries were to be repaid to the wife's family of origin according to the marriage contracts, which regulated the interests of both parties and were negotiated and confirmed by both heads of families.¹¹ Recent historiographical research has rightly asked whether these enormous dowries had to be secured by the German princes and what this meant for their economic capacity.¹² For each of the sisters, different documents survive that allow an insight into the transactions (table 1).¹³

Visconti Princess	Dowry	Counter-dowry (dower)	Morning gift	Annual rents	Trousseau
Verde	100,000 fl.	100,000 fl. (promised)	unclear	10,000 fl. (as widow)	unclear
Taddea	unclear	unclear	unclear	unclear	yes
Antonia	70,000 fl.	unclear	Bietigheim (963 fl. annual rents)?	7,042,5 fl.	yes
Maddalena	unclear	unclear	10,000 fl. (?)	unclear	yes
Elisabetta	75,000 fl.	assurances of dowry and morning gift	10,000 fl.	7,500 fl.	yes, worth 12,880 fl.

Table 1: Marital goods given to Visconti daughters married to German princes

---

9 Cf. Peter Rückert and Sönke Lorenz (eds.), Die Visconti und der deutsche Südwesten. Kulturtransfer im Spätmittelalter, Ostfildern 2008.
10 Cf. Ulrich Schludi, Mailänder Stolz und schwäbische Sparsamkeit – die Heiratsverhandlungen für Antonia Visconti und Eberhard III. von Württemberg in den Jahren 1379/80, in: Rückert/Lorenz, Die Visconti, see note 9, 131–152.
11 Cf. Antenhofer, Familienkiste, see note 1, 456–468. *Dowry* refers to the matrimonial property given to the bride by her family of origin; *counter-dowry (dower)* designates the property given by the husband to compensate for the dowry; *morning gift* refers to the goods donated explicitly to the bride by her husband after the wedding night; *trousseau* stands for mobile goods given to the bride by her family of origin.
12 Cf. Schludi, Mailänder Stolz, see note 10.
13 Cf. Antenhofer, Familienkiste, see note 1, 456–468.

In all five cases, we see similar arrangement, with the greatest difference between the oldest, Verde, and the youngest sister, Elisabetta. Verde, who in 1365 married Leopold III of Habsburg, received the full amount of 100,000 fl., which reflects her status as the oldest daughter and the prestige of the Habsburg marriage, given the alliance with Leopold's aspiring brother Rudolf IV. Rudolf had promised to balance the dowry in his brother's stead. However, this was only a promise for the future in the event of her widowhood, when she was to receive annual rents of 10,000 fl. In fact, Verde was widowed early on with Leopold's death in 1386, but she had to take legal action through her son to claim the payments.[14] An inventory of her documents, found after her death in her house in Ljubljana, where she had her widow's seat, shows that Verde was actively involved in many economic transactions with a plethora of citizens there. Verde invested money by pawning, buying and selling houses, farms, mills and agricultural plots. Like other noble women, she used her marital goods to invest and increase her income, thus opening up her own field of agency.[15]

For the youngest of the sisters, Elisabetta, many other charters have survived that allow her economic transactions to be traced based on her marital goods. As she died before her husband, her case is a telling example of how princesses could act with economic independence even during their husbands' lifetimes. As in Verde's case, documents often show her together with her son, Albrecht III of Wittelsbach. For instance, in 1402 her husband Ernst and his brother Wilhelm confirmed that they had borrowed jewels worth 3,940 fl. from Elisabetta to pay off their debts.[16] In 1431 Ernst confirmed that he had borrowed 100 fl. from Elisabetta's maintenance rents *(Leibgeding)* and that he would pay this debt to their daughters should she die before he could return the money.[17] This example documents that women could dispose of the annual rents from the properties assigned to them as a morning gift even during their husbands' lifetimes, and that the husbands could not freely use this money. Women had the liberty to dispose of the goods in the bridal trousseaus, which served as a resource for gift-giving and pawns. However, power structures within dynasties could easily alter this picture.

If we look at the example of Bianca Maria Sforza, who married Maximilian I of Habsburg in 1493, we see a highly distorted situation from the perspective of marital goods. Bianca Maria received an exorbitant dowry of 400,000 ducats (see figure 1). Maximilian, however, used this money primarily for his own needs. Negotiations on how to secure the goods lasted for some time, and were finally based on the arrange-

---

14 Cf. Antenhofer, Familienkiste, see note 1, 457.
15 Cf. Klaus Brandstätter, Die Tiroler Landesfürstinnen im 15. Jahrhundert, in: Julia Hörmann-Thurn und Taxis (ed.), Margarete "Maultasch". Zur Lebenswelt einer Landesfürstin und anderer Tiroler Frauen des Mittelalters, Innsbruck 2007, 175–217. On the importance of economic resources, see Lazzarini in this volume.
16 Cf. Antenhofer, Familienkiste, see note 1, 407.
17 Cf. Antenhofer, Familienkiste, see note 1, 408.

ments made for his mother.¹⁸ These agreements would have included a morning gift of 10,000 fl. However, there is no surviving deed to prove that Maximilian ever granted Bianca Maria this gift, nor did he give the Sforza a guarantee to repay the dowry in the event of a childless marriage. Bianca Maria's annual rents were constantly reduced, restricting her agency and that of her entourage to the point that in 1505 she was unable to meet French ambassadors for lack of decent clothing.¹⁹

Fig. 1: Bridal Portrait of Bianca Maria Sforza, Giovanni Ambrogio de Predis, National Gallery of Art, Widener Collection. Source: Wikimedia Commons / public domain (for detailed picture credits see footnote 18)

This example points to the importance of material culture for women's agency in terms of their visibility and power at court. Beyond its mere monetary value, the bridal

---

18 Cf. Antenhofer, Familienkiste, see note 1, 474–479. Detailed picture credits to figure 1: Bridal Portrait of Bianca Maria Sforza, Giovanni Ambrogio de Predis, National Gallery of Art, Widener Collection. Source: Wikimedia Commons / public domain, online accessible at: https://commons.wikimedia.org/wiki/File:Ambrogio_de_Predis_-_Bianca_Maria_Sforza_-_Google_Art_Project.jpg.
19 Cf. Antenhofer, Familienkiste, see note 1, 479.

trousseau was essential to women's power in terms of agency and representation. The trousseau provided them with objects to display their status on their bodies through the clothes they wore, as well as in terms of spaces they could adorn with furnishings and thus materially bring into their possession. Particularly revealing are elements on objects that would associate them with the bride and her native family. These could be coats of arms (see figure 2) or more personalised *imprese*, but also colours attributed to the bride and her family, or symbolic elements on clothes and objects. Many objects in the bridal trousseau were decorated with an alliance coat of arms, which referred to the marriage and the objects associated with the two families involved. The Visconti sisters, for instance Taddea and Antonia, had many such decorated items in their trousseaus.[20] Interestingly, such objects are completely absent from Bianca Maria Sforza's treasure. Her bridal inventory only mentions *imprese* of the Sforza context, as well as symbolic elements, such as draperies of covers and fringes in the Sforza style: "Coperte cinque de panno rosso per le ceste de le done cum le franze ala Sforzesca".[21] These examples show how the Sforza used the bridal trousseau to appropriate spaces at court, in this case to symbolically frame the riding gear of the court ladies.

This strategic play with the material coding of areas becomes even more evident in the case of female clothing. Here again, we see differences in the examples studied: Taddea Visconti had several dresses in her trousseau decorated with "Bavarian ruffles", addressed to her new Bavarian court, when she married Stephan III of Wittelsbach in 1367.[22] The dominant colours in her material culture, violet and green, personalise her objects beyond the dynastic level.[23] Her sister Antonia did not have any dresses with references to her new court in Württemberg when she married there in 1380, while her belongings also display a personalised colour, an azure blue.[24] Above all, mobile decorations such as tapestries allowed the women to flexibly appropriate spaces and give them individualised or dynastic significance.[25] Bridal trousseaus are divided into different groups of objects that refer to spaces of agency. An overview of these categories of objects associated with spaces provides an insight into the expected agency of the consorts (table 2).

---

20 Antonia had for instance many silverware objects for the table decorated with the Visconti-Württemberg alliance coat of arms: e. g. two large gold-plated silver basins *(bacilia)*, two large silver, gold-plated ceremonial goblets, a gilded ship decorated with enamel, a silver gilded *confeteria*, as well as eight tapestries, cf. Antenhofer, Familienkiste, see note 1, 327.
21 Haus-, Hof- und Staatsarchiv (HHStA) Vienna UR FUK 828 fol. 10v.
22 Cf. Antenhofer, Familienkiste, see note 1, 581.
23 Cf. Antenhofer, Familienkiste, see note 1, 380.
24 Cf. Antenhofer, Familienkiste, see note 1, 370.
25 Cf. Bart Lambert and Katherine Anne Wilson (eds.), Europe's Rich Fabric. The Consumption, Commercialisation, and Production of Luxury Textiles in Italy, the Low Countries and Neighbouring Territories (Fourteenth–Sixteenth Centuries), Farnham/Burlington, VT 2016.

Fig. 2: Seal of Antonia Visconti with her coat of arms, Hauptstaatsarchiv Stuttgart A 502 U 450.
© Original and photograph: Hauptstaatsarchiv Stuttgart

Categories of objects	Number of entries in the bridal inventories		
	Taddea 1367	Antonia 1380	Bianca Maria 1493
Silverware	73	33	20
Jewellery	22	48	13
Books	2	2	3
Girdles, buckles	4	6	7
Bags	–	2	–
Linens	88	50	42
Utensils (body care, handiwork)	9	7	13
Underwear	2	16	9
Personal items (devotion, play)	7	9	1
Chests and containers	7	13	2
Saddles, covers and mattresses	–	–	17
Fabrics and clothing	5	25	–
Dresses	44	71	34
Tapestries	1	3	4
Chairs	–	–	3

(Continued)

Categories of objects	Number of entries in the bridal inventories		
	Taddea 1367	Antonia 1380	Bianca Maria 1493
Paraments for the bed (with pillows and covers)	16	11	19
Ribbons, yarns, threads	6	6	6
Gloves and stockings	2	2	1
Collars and bonnets	–	–	25
Shoes and slippers	–	–	2
Decoration for the altar	13	21	23

Table 2: Overview of object categories of bridal trousseaus from the Visconti and Sforza background[26]

A comparison of the groups of objects in the Visconti and Sforza trousseaus shows the dominance of silverware and jewellery for display, both in the spaces of the court, such as the table and the chapel, and on the female body. Equally significant were paraments for the women's apartment, textiles and clothes, and the decoration of the altar. As future queen, Bianca Maria even had riding gear for herself and her ladies-in-waiting, who served as multipliers of her persona.[27]

2. Objects for networking: gift exchange and gendered objects

In some cases, inventories of bridal trousseaus allow us to study the extensive exchange of gifts that took place on the occasion of the marriages. Antonia Visconti and Bianca Maria Sforza can serve as examples. Antonia's inventory of 1380[28] lists the gifts she received and the items she gave to whom. Rings appear here as the most common gift, some of which were immediately presented by Antonia to others, illustrating the power of social networking through rings (see figure 3).[29] More prestigious, however, were precious pieces of jewellery *(zoyellus)* and luxury textiles. Some wedding presents bore

---

26 Cf. Antenhofer, Familienkiste, see note 1, 498–499.
27 On the role of the court ladies, see Jan Hirschbiegel and Werner Paravicini (eds.), Das Frauenzimmer. Die Frau bei Hofe in Spätmittelalter und früher Neuzeit, Stuttgart 2000; Michail A. Bojcov, Zum Frauenzimmer am Innsbrucker Hof Erzherzog Sigmunds, in: Heinz Noflatscher and Jan Paul Niederkorn (eds.), Der Innsbrucker Hof. Residenz und höfische Gesellschaft in Tirol vom 15. bis 19. Jahrhundert, Wien 2005, 195–211.
28 Cf. Hauptstaatsarchiv (HStA) Stuttgart A 602 Nr. 32 = WR 32.
29 Cf. Gabriela Signori, Ringomania. Ring Production and Consumption in Late Medieval Constance, in: Gerhard Jaritz and Ingrid Matschinegg (eds.), My Favourite Things. Object Preferences in Medieval and Early Modern Material Culture, Wien 2019, 57–73. For Antonia's gifts, see Antenhofer, Familienkiste, see note 1, 326–343.

the coat of arms of the donors, for instance that of her cousin Gian Galeazzo. Through his coat of arms, Gian Galeazzo ensured that he was visible at the Württemberg court when precious gifts were displayed at court.[30] The gift exchange is symmetrical, with Antonia receiving 32 gifts and donating 31 items from her trousseau. She donated these items to members of different social groups. All rings were given exclusively to Italian nobles. For her new in-laws, she chose precious gold fabrics. Her other gifts were more varied: two Italian nobles each received a paternoster. Furthermore, she gave three of her coats, two to men and one to a woman. Interestingly, these gifts of clothing were not gender-specific. Of the seven bonnets she donated, one was given to a man in her entourage. Some gifts stand out in this symmetric exchange involving her entourage and her new relatives: Antonia donated one of her bonnets *(Kapuze)* to a girl who had come to the tournament. This could be seen as an act of generosity towards the local spectators. Finally, two very personalised gifts were dedicated to her husband Eberhard: the first is not explicitly mentioned, but can be reconstructed from entries in the inventory. Here we read that Antonia presented Eberhard with 12 grains from one of her coral paternosters, together with a silver cross and 12 gold buttons. This could be a devotional item she had made from parts of her own religious objects. The second gift consisted of two silver bells, which she gave him from her stock of 52 such items. These bells were probably exquisite objects, as they do not appear in any other bridal inventory of the period I have studied. Both qualities, the personal attachment to Antonia, as the gifts were made from parts of her own items, and the exclusivity associated with the rarity of the silver bells, gave these two gifts a special semantic value. They stood out among the symmetrical and traditional forms of wedding gift exchange that stabilised hierarchies and forged networks among her entourage and relatives.[31]

In the case of Bianca Maria Sforza, the bridal inventory does not provide such insights. However, the inventory of her wardrobe, which covers the entire period after the wedding until her death, allows us to reconstruct what gifts she made from her clothes and textiles. While Antonia's inventory only documents the immediate time of the wedding, Bianca Maria's register covers a wider period and shows how she continued to give away items from her trousseau over the years. Most of the objects were donated within the first year (1494) of the marriage (17), while the last one was donated six years later, in 1500.[32] Along the timeline, different places are associated with these

---

30 Cf. Ute Kümmel, Fürsten im Wettstreit? Das Tafelgeschirr im Schatz der spätmittelalterlichen Reichsfürsten, in: Anna Paulina Orlowska, Werner Paravicini and Jörg Wettlaufer (eds.), Atelier Vorbild, Austausch, Konkurrenz. Höfe und Residenzen in der gegenseitigen Wahrnehmung, Kiel 2009, 83–94.
31 On gift exchanges, see Jan Hirschbiegel, Étrennes. Untersuchungen zum höfischen Geschenkverkehr im spätmittelalterlichen Frankreich der Zeit König Karls VI. (1380–1422), München 2003; Gadi Algazi, Valentin Groebner and Bernhard Jussen (eds.), Negotiating the Gift. Pre-Modern Figurations of Exchange, Göttingen 2003; Natalie Zemon Davis, The Gift in Sixteenth-Century France, Oxford 2000.
32 On her gifts, see Antenhofer, Familienkiste, see note 1, 521–532.

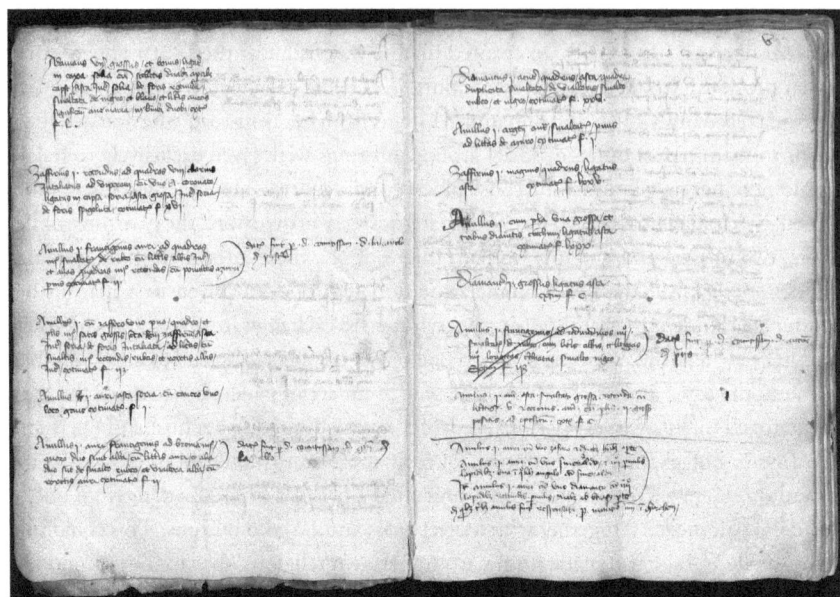

Fig. 3: Inventory of the bridal trousseau of Antonia Visconti, Liber iocalium, HStA Stuttgart A 602 no. 32 = WR 32: fol. 4v–5r. Entries on rings with addenda on rings given on the occasion of the wedding 1380. © Original and photograph: Hauptstaatsarchiv Stuttgart

gift exchanges, allowing for the reconstruction of a gift itinerary. Almost all the gifts were given to her entourage, with the exception of the unspecified nuns and Church of Santa Maria,[33] her brother Ermes and the ambassador Erasmo Brascha. This may also have to do with the particular semantics of clothes, which were usually not neutral objects, especially if they had already been worn. Once worn, clothes could not be presented as gifts to people of the same rank, unless they were family members.[34] Clothes were mainly donated to members of the entourage and family, who would often inherit clothes, again demonstrating their role as multipliers of the princely persona. When looking for indicators of emotional attachment to particular members of the court, it is helpful to consider not only whether they received gifts but also what kind of gifts they received and how often, which in turn gives them a special semantic (table 3).

---

33 "le monage da / Santa Marya […] la giessa de Sa(n)ta / Marya", Tiroler Landesarchiv (TLA) Inventare A1.2 fol. 2r. Possibly the church of St. Maria Himmelskron in Worms, in the immediate vicinity of the Liebenau Dominican convent, cf. Antenhofer, Familienkiste, see note 1, 524.
34 Cf. Jan Keupp, Die Wahl des Gewandes. Mode, Macht und Möglichkeitssinn in Gesellschaft und Politik des Mittelalters, Ostfildern 2010. On clothes as wedding gifts by Mary of Burgundy to Maximilian, see Lutter and Muigg in this volume.

Parameters for the studying of gifts	Persons/ gender	Objects	Occasions/ frequency	Place/ spaces	Affordance/ actions/ practices
Gift exchanges throughout the lifecycle	Are there ritualised gift exchanges along the female lifecycle? Gifts for weddings? Birth gifts (childbed)? Other gifts linked to family and lifecycle? Goods bequeathed in last wills?				
Annual gift exchanges	Gift exchanges not linked to family and lifecycle? Do some gifts recur annually (New Year's gifts? Name days?)				
Situational gift exchanges	Are there non-recurring gift exchanges? What are the occasions (e. g. travel)? Are there gifts with no clear occasions?				
Personalised gifts	Are gifts handmade? Made of recycled parts? Have donors been involved in procuring the gifts? Are the objects particularly rare or otherwise exceptional?				
Standardised gifts	Can patterns of gift-giving be detected (e. g. rings, jewels?) What hierarchies are displayed through these exchanges?				

Table 3: Questionnaire for studying material culture linked with gift exchange. The horizontal heading refers to parameters connected with gift exchange, the vertical heading refines gift types

In terms of gendered objects, it is noticeable that most items could be offered to both men and women. To find clearer traces of gendered object groups, it is helpful to study marriage contracts, which also deal with the question of what kind of objects could be used by women arriving at the castles they received as collateral for their dowries. These contracts again show a great variety of arrangements, but they are clear on one point: women were not to have anything to do with the armour stored in the castles.[35] Another special arrangement in many marriage contracts concerns the question of whether the women were allowed to keep their gifts. Interestingly, certain dynasties, including the Habsburgs, reserved presents from husbands as temporary for the lifetime of the consort. After their deaths, these gifts were returned to the family treasure and added to the stock of objects used commonly by different women at court.

3. Conclusion

Women's agency depended to a large extent on the economic resources they derived from their marital property. These resources had a major influence on how they could shape power structures at court and beyond. Of paramount importance was their annual income, often derived from the goods of their morning gift. Similarly, the objects in their bridal trousseaus functioned as a money reserve and a fund for gift-giving. These objects also served as markers for materially appropriating spaces at court

---

35 "[…] was wir pfärd, harnasch, püchsen und ander wére groß oder klain, so dann zue slossern und were gehöret, hinder uns liessen, darauss / sol ir nichts volgen und sol auch darein nichts ze reden noch ze sprechen haben ungeverlich", cit. following Antenhofer, Familienkiste, see note 1, 786. With reference to the warrior/hunter image, see Lutter and Muigg in this volume.

and participating in the politics of representation and visibility. Studying material culture throughout the lifecycle of princesses and all other people of different social strata associated with the court opens up fruitful avenues for implementing new approaches to a cultural history of politics with a focus on agency, spaces, representation and networks as the backbone of power politics.

Carina Siegl

Geschlecht und Herrschaftshandeln im Spiegel der Quellen der Hofstaaten von Maria von Habsburg und Anna Jagiełło (1515–1520)[1]

Im Jahr 1514 traf die neunjährige Habsburgerin Maria in Wien ein. Sie war von ihrem Großvater, Kaiser Maximilian I., aus dem niederländischen Mechelen gerufen worden, wo sie am Hof ihrer Tante Margarethe, der Tochter Maximilians, aufgewachsen war. Doch nun sollte sie gemäß seinen dynastischen Plänen eine neue Rolle erfüllen. Wenig später erreichte auch die zwölfjährige Anna Jagiełło, die Tochter des böhmisch-ungarischen Königs Vladislav II., die Stadt. Maria war Annas Bruder Ludwig versprochen; Anna sollte einen der Enkel Maximilians heiraten – ob Karl oder Ferdinand, wurde erst 1516, und damit erst einige Monate nach der Hochzeitszeremonie im Wiener Stephansdom, entschieden, bei der zunächst der Kaiser als Stellvertreter die junge Jagiellonin ehelichte. Die endgültigen Hochzeiten sollten zwar aufgrund des Kindesalters aller Beteiligten erst 1521 beziehungsweise 1522 stattfinden; die sogenannte „Wiener Doppelhochzeit" 1515 war dennoch ein dynastisches Großereignis und ein Meilenstein in der Hausmachtpolitik von Habsburgern und Jagiellonen. Zudem diente sie maßgeblich der Verteidigung gegenüber dem expandierenden Osmanischen Reich.[2]

Für die beiden neuen Schwägerinnen Maria und Anna war Wien die erste Station einer längeren gemeinsamen Reise. Von Wien führte sie der Weg über Steyr und Salzburg schließlich nach Innsbruck. Nach der „Doppelhochzeit" wurden ihre Hofstaaten zusammengeführt; diese Gemeinschaft bestand bis zum Jahr 1521, als Anna aufbrach, um Maximilians Enkel Ferdinand, auf den die Wahl als Bräutigam letztlich gefallen war, in Linz zu treffen. Diese liminale Phase im Leben der jungen Fürstinnen, beginnend mit dem Aufbruch aus ihren gewohnten Umgebungen bis zum Antritt ihrer Rollen als verheiratete Fürstinnen, war von Ausbildung und der Vorbereitung auf ihre künftigen Herrschaftsaufgaben geprägt. Begleitet wurden sie von vielen Männern und Frauen unterschiedlichen Alters, unterschiedlicher Herkunft und Interessen. Der

---

1 Die im Text vorgestellte Forschung wird ermöglicht durch den SFB 92 *Managing Maximilian (1493–1519) – Persona, Politics, and Personnel through the Lens of Digital Prosopography* (Sprecher A. Zajic), Projekt *Gendering Maximilian – Gendered Dimensions of Court Organisation and Representation* (PI C. Lutter), gefördert durch den FWF, 2023–2026.
2 Vgl. zuletzt Bogusław Dybás u. István Tringli (Hg.), Das Wiener Fürstentreffen von 1515. Beiträge zur Geschichte der Habsburgisch-Jagiellonischen Doppelvermählung, Budapest 2019.

Forschungsgegenstand des Dissertationsprojektes, in dessen Zusammenhang dieser Beitrag entstanden ist, ist also von ständigem Wandel geprägt. Diese Komplexität dokumentiert das Material „aus den Archiven".

Als Ausgangspunkte für das genannte Projekt dienen die frühen Hofstaaten der Fürstinnen, die eine dichte Überlieferung hinterlassen haben, welche noch nicht systematisch untersucht wurde.[3] Das Archivmaterial im Haus-, Hof- und Staatsarchiv in Wien sowie im Tiroler Landesarchiv in Innsbruck weist verschiedene Schwerpunkte auf:

(1) Aus Hofordnungen erfahren wir über Regeln, die von Maximilian I. und ab 1519 von Karl V. erlassen wurden. Bestimmt wurde über Personen, ihre Funktionen und ihr Verhalten, über Tagesabläufe und den Umgang mit Gegenständen, insbesondere den Verzehr von Lebensmitteln.

(2) Hofamtslisten informieren über Namen und Funktionen der Mitglieder der Hofstaaten. Sie stammen aus unterschiedlichen Jahren und können systematisch verglichen werden – auch mit jenen vor 1515 und nach 1521, um zu untersuchen, welche Personen die Fürstinnen längerfristig begleiteten.[4]

(3) Darüber hinaus entstanden vielfältige Dokumente der Hofverwaltung, etwa Verzeichnisse von Gästen, Besoldung, Gewändern, konsumiertem Wein, Brot und Essig sowie Berichte über Konflikte am Hof.

Dieses Kernkorpus der Überlieferung wird zusammen mit anderen Quellentypen analysiert. Korrespondenzen dokumentieren den Austausch zwischen Angehörigen der Herrscherhäuser untereinander, aber auch mit Vertrauten. Gesandte im Dienst von Fürst*innen sowie anderer politisch Handelnder berichteten aus verschiedenen Perspektiven. Panegyrik und Erziehungstraktate bilden Rollenmodelle und Herrschaftsideale ab.

Herrschaftsorganisation und -repräsentation beruhten auf dem Handeln und Verhandeln vieler Menschen. Wie auch in Ulrike Marlows Beitrag in diesem Themenheft deutlich wird, eignet sich das Material aus höfischem Kontext in besonderer Weise dazu, die Karrieren von adeligen und nicht adeligen Frauen zu untersuchen und in Bezug zu Fragen der Herrschaftspraxis zu setzen. Anhand der folgenden zwei Beispiele möchte ich zeigen, welche Einblicke das von mir untersuchte Archivmaterial aus

---

3 Die wichtigsten Studien sind: Gernot Heiß, Königin Maria von Ungarn und Böhmen. Ihr Leben und ihre wirtschaftlichen Interessen in Österreich, Ungarn und Böhmen (1505–1558), Bd. 1 und 2, unveröff. Dissertation, Universität Wien, 1971; Orsolya Réthelyi, Mary of Hungary in Court Context 1521–1531, unveröff. Dissertation, CEU Budapest, 2010; Jacqueline Kerkhoff, Die Hofhaltung Marias von Ungarn, in: Martina Fuchs u. Orsolya Réthelyi (Hg.), Maria von Ungarn (1505–1558). Eine Renaissancefürstin, Münster 2007.

4 Es besteht jedoch ein Ungleichgewicht zwischen Maria und Anna, da die spätere Lebenszeit Marias genau untersucht wurde (siehe Anm. 3 sowie die Referenzen im Beitrag von Elodie Lecuppre-Desjardin zu dieser *Special Issue*, Anm. 3), Studien zu Anna aber fehlen.

den Hofstaaten der Fürstinnen in die Lebenswege und Handlungsspielräume von Frauen und Männern unterschiedlichen Ranges bietet.

Ausgangspunkt für das erste Beispiel ist ein Brief, den Marias Tante Margarethe, Statthalterin der habsburgischen Niederlande, 1513 an ihren Vater schrieb. Sie bat ihn, Marias „bercheresse", also ihre Kinderfrau, Marguerite de Poitiers und deren Kinder mit Maria nach Österreich reisen zu lassen.[5] Maria war in der Obhut ihrer Tante in Mechelen aufgewachsen und es war Margarethes Aufgabe, deren Reise nach Österreich vorzubereiten und den Hofstaat ihrer Nichte zusammenzustellen. Margarethe war als Tochter Maximilians und als Statthalterin der Niederlande eine einflussreiche Politikerin und Beraterin ihres Vaters. Durch das Gegenlesen mehrerer Hofordnungen und Hofamtslisten aus Marias Zeit in Steyr und Innsbruck lässt sich vermuten, dass es sich bei zwei häufig genannten Personen – Madame Marguerite de Poitiers, der „Peseresserin", und Madame de Bailleul – um dieselbe Person handelt. Sie dürfte seit Marias Abreise von Innsbruck bis zur deren endgültigen Verheiratung mit Ludwig in Ungarn und darüber hinaus bis 1524 auch Marias Hofmeisterin gewesen sein.[6] Erschwert wird die eindeutige Identifikation dadurch, dass auch ihre Tochter Marguerite (Margarethe) hieß und ebenfalls Mitglied des Frauenzimmers war. Verfolgt man die Familie weiter, findet man Charles de Bailleul, wahrscheinlich Ehemann Marguerites (der Älteren), der 1524 im Hofamtsverzeichnis von Buda genannt wird.[7] Er dürfte ebenfalls Marias Vertrauen genossen haben, da sie ihn 1525 mit einer Nachricht zu ihrem Bruder Ferdinand sandte.[8] Als viertes Familienmitglied scheint Philippe de Bailleul, der Sohn von Marguerite (der Älteren) und Charles de Bailleul, als Mundschenk im Innsbrucker Frauenzimmer auf.[9] Er folgte Maria 1521 nach Buda, 1531 in die habsburgischen Niederlande und blieb bis mindestens 1543 in ihrem Dienst.[10]

Auch dem zweiten Beispiel, das ich hier anführen möchte, liegt ein Briefwechsel (1519–1520) zugrunde, in dem Karl V. mit dem Innsbrucker Regiment über die Finanzierung des Hofstaates Marias und Annas verhandelte.[11] Durch die Entlassung mehrerer Personen sollten Einsparungen erfolgen. Da das Ende des geteilten Hofstaates in Innsbruck nahte und die nächsten Lebensabschnitte der Fürstinnen bereits

---

5 André Joseph Ghislain Le Glay (Hg.), Correspondance de l'empereur Maximilien Ier et de Marguerite d'Autriche, sa fille, gouvernante des Pays-Bas, de 1507 à 1519, Bd. 2., New York 1966, 126.
6 Vgl. Réthelyi, Mary of Hungary, wie Anm. 3, 91.
7 Vgl. András Kubinyi, The Court of Mary of Hungary and Politics between 1521 and 1526, in: Orsolya Réthelyi, Beatrix Romhányi, Enikő Spekner u. András Végh (Hg.), Mary of Hungary, Widow of Mohács. The Queen and her Court 1521–1531. Exhibition catalogue, Budapest 2010, 13–25, 16.
8 Vgl. Réthelyi, Mary of Hungary, wie Anm. 3, 101.
9 Vgl. „Hofstaat und Ordnung von Königin Maria mit Namen, Besoldung", 1520, Österreichisches Staatsarchiv/Archiv der Republik (ÖStA/AdR), Haus-, Hof- und Staatsarchiv, Reichskanzlei, Maximiliana 45-5-1, fol. 14.
10 Vgl. Réthelyi, Mary of Hungary, wie Anm. 3, 102.
11 Belegt ist die Korrespondenz in den Copialbüchern, Missiven 1519–21, im Tiroler Landesarchiv.

vorbereitet wurden, war der Verbleib von vertrauten Bediensteten wohl besonders wichtig. Maria und Anna wehrten sich gegen die Entlassung zweier Kämmerer, Christoph und Philippe, denen „Unschicklichkeiten" im Frauenzimmer vorgeworfen wurden.[12] Zu berücksichtigen ist, dass – sofern den Hofordnungen Folge geleistet wurde – nur wenige Männer mit besonderen Ämtern Zugang zu den Räumlichkeiten der Fürstinnen hatten. Dass zumindest einer der beiden Kämmerer, Philippe de Feure, Marias Vertrauen genoss, ist plausibel, da er mit ihr aus den Niederlanden nach Österreich gereist war und sie später von Innsbruck nach Ungarn begleitete.[13] Dies lässt auf ein Naheverhältnis zwischen ihm und den Fürstinnen schließen und weist darüber hinaus auf die Handlungsspielräume der Fürstinnen in der Gestaltung ihres personalen Umfelds hin. Beide Beispiele dokumentieren die besondere Bedeutung personaler Beziehungen, die auf Vertrauen beruhten, an neuen, ‚fremden' Orten der Herrschaftsausübung.

Neben der systematischen prosopographischen Analyse der Hofstaaten bezieht meine Studie auch Objekte mit ein, die ebenfalls Auskunft über Beziehungskulturen und das Leben bei Hof geben können.[14] Von Bedeutung sind etwa Listen der verzehrten Lebensmittel, die mit Verzeichnissen der speisenden Personen einhergehen und beispielsweise dokumentieren, dass auch die Tochter des polnischen Königs Sigismund I. und Cousine Annas, Katharina, am Hof unterhalten wurde.[15] Ebenso sind Gewänder interessant – von Annas Kleid „deutschen Schnitts", das sie am Wiener Fürstentag trug,[16] bis hin zur Ausstattung des Frauenzimmers, die auf Wetterbedingungen und Tätigkeiten wie die Jagd schließen lässt.[17] Dabei ist eine geschlechtergeschichtliche Perspektive wichtig, die geschlechtsspezifische Rollenmodelle ebenso miteinbezieht wie kontextspezifische Handlungsweisen von Personen beiderlei Geschlechts.

Weitere Fragen an das Archivmaterial gelten der Vorbereitung von Reiserouten und Entourage, in denen Personen verschiedener Herkunft zusammenkamen, der Verteilung ihrer Rollen und der materiellen Vorbereitung solcher großen Unternehmun-

---

12 „Karl an das Regiment in Innsbruck", 1521, Landesarchiv Innsbruck, Copialbücher, Missiven 1519–22, fol. 47f. (zit. nach: Heiß, Königin Maria, Bd. 2, wie Anm. 3, 425.)
13 Vgl. Heiß, Königin Maria, Bd. 2, wie Anm. 3, 425; Réthelyi, Mary of Hungary, wie Anm. 3, 78.
14 Zur Bedeutung von Objekten in der Gestaltung personaler Beziehungen vgl. Christina Antenhofer, Die Familienkiste. Mensch-Objekt-Beziehungen im Mittelalter und in der Renaissance, 2 Bde., Ostfildern 2022. Siehe auch die Rezension von Christof Muigg zum genannten Werk in diesem Heft.
15 Sie wird mehrmals in den Innsbrucker Quellen genannt, zum Beispiel: „Bericht des Küchenschreibers über jene Personen, die im Juli in Innsbruck gespeist haben", 1519, ÖStA/AdR, HHStA, RK, Maximiliana 38-3-32, fol. 4.
16 Beschreibung von Riccardo Bartolini, zit. nach: József Fógel, II. Ulászló Udvártartása 1490–1516, Budapest 1913, 41.
17 Vgl. „Bericht über die Weinlieferung in die Küche von Kaiserin und Königin [in Innsbruck]", 1519, ÖStA/AdR, HHStA, RK, Maximiliana 38-3-27, fol. 3.

gen.¹⁸ Zu klären ist weiters, wann und in welchem Umfang die Zusammenlegung der Hofstaaten der beiden Schwägerinnen vollzogen wurde. Tatsächlich weisen einige Quellen auf Differenzierungen hin, was zweckmäßig scheint, da die Planung für die getrennten Reisen der Fürstinnen zu ihren neuen Residenzen eine lange Vorlaufzeit erfordert haben muss.¹⁹ In all diesen Fällen zeichnet sich ab, dass die gelebte Praxis des höfischen Alltags oft von den rigiden Vorgaben der Hofordnungen abwich, wie dies auch von anderen zeitgenössischen Höfen bekannt ist.

Da die prosopographischen Daten aus dem skizzierten Quellenkorpus systematisch in der gemeinsamen Datenbank des Spezialforschungsbereiches *Managing Maximilian (1493–1519) (ManMAX)*²⁰ erfasst werden, im Rahmen dessen meine Dissertation entsteht, wird so auch dem von Ulrike Marlow in diesem Heft thematisierten Problem des „Gender-Data-Gap" Rechnung getragen. Die Untersuchung von Lebensläufen am preußischen Hof im 19. Jahrhundert zeige, so Marlow, dass vor allem nach Heiraten eine solche geschlechterbedingte Informationslücke entstehe, da Karrieren an dieser Stelle oft abbrachen. Eine Projektzusammenarbeit wie der *SFB ManMAX*, bei dem kollaborativ zehntausende Daten zu Personen beiderlei Geschlechts erfasst werden, bietet neue Chancen, diese Lücke zu schließen: So können Hofämter, die zunächst wie ein letztlich bescheidenes „Maximum an Karriere"²¹ für Frauen wirken mögen, zu Knoten in einem Netz an Personen-Nennungen in unterschiedlichen Quellentypen werden. Ihre strukturierte Sammlung und Analyse erlauben es also, Lebenswege auch über das letzte Hofamt vor einer Eheschließung hinweg weiterzuverfolgen und so mit der Einbindung der betroffenen Frauen und Männer in deutlich größere Personenverbände ein vollständigeres Bild ihrer Handlungsspielräume zu erhalten.

---

18 Detailliert dokumentiert etwa im Bericht der Helene Kottannerin drei Generationen früher: Christina Lutter und Julia Burkhardt (Hg.), Ich, Helene Kottanerin. Die Kammerfrau, die Ungarns Krone stahl, Darmstadt 2023.
19 Zum Beispiel im genannten Fall der Entlassung der Kammerdiener, bei der einer Anna und einer Maria zugewiesen wird, vgl. Heiß, Königin Maria, Bd. 2, wie Anm. 3, 425–426.
20 Siehe Anm. 1.
21 Ulrike Marlow, „Die gute Tante war der ganzen Familie ein so reger geistiger Mittelpunkt …" Zur mangelnden Sichtbarkeit weiblicher adliger Lebensläufe am preußischen Hof im 19. Jahrhundert, in: L'Homme. Europäische Zeitschrift für Feministische Geschichtswissenschaft (L'Homme. Z. F. G.), 36, 1 (2025), 141–146.

Ulrike Marlow

„Die gute Tante war der ganzen Familie ein so reger geistiger Mittelpunkt ..."[1] Zur mangelnden Sichtbarkeit weiblicher adliger Lebensläufe am preußischen Hof im 19. Jahrhundert

Das Titelzitat macht auf ein bekanntes Phänomen in der Frauen- und Geschlechtergeschichte aufmerksam: Das Leben der Gräfin Amélie von Dönhoff (1808–1871), Hofdame der preußischen Königin Elisabeth, ist in Zeugnissen ihrer weiblichen Verwandten nachvollziehbar, jedoch kaum über Quellen ihres Arbeitgebers, des preußischen Hofes. Ausgehend davon geht es im Folgenden um den sogenannten Gender-Data-Gap in den Archiven und die Vermeidung eines solchen beziehungsweise das Problembewusstsein für dessen Reproduktion im digitalen Bereich. Abschließend wird Amélie von Dönhoffs Lebenslauf exemplarisch vorgestellt, um die Bedeutung von adligen Frauen innerhalb des Familiennetzwerkes bei der Karriereplanung zu zeigen.

Die britische Journalistin und Frauenrechtlerin Caroline Criado-Perez schärfte mit ihrem Bestseller „Unsichtbare Frauen"[2] das Problembewusstsein für den Gender-Data-Gap:[3]

> „Der Großteil der Menschheitsgeschichte ist eine einzige Datenlücke. [...] männliche Lebensläufe [gelten] als repräsentativ für alle Menschen. Über das Leben der anderen Hälfte der Menschheit wurde und wird oft einfach nur geschwiegen. [...] Diese Leerstelle hat eine dezidiert weibliche Form. Es ist eine geschlechtsbezogene Lücke in den wissenschaftlichen Daten, eine Gender Data Gap."[4]

---

1 Geheimes Staatsarchiv Preußischer Kulturbesitz (GStA PK), VI. HA, FA Below, v., Nr. 38, 11.11. 1871 Clara von Below an Cäcilie von Below über den Tod der preußischen Hofdame Gräfin Amélie von Dönhoff.
2 Caroline Criado-Perez, Unsichtbare Frauen. Wie eine von Daten beherrschte Welt die Hälfte der Bevölkerung ignoriert, München 2020⁴.
3 Zur Rezeption des Gender-Data-Gaps und zur Problematik von binären Daten zu Gender vgl. Sara Juen, Feminismus, Algorithmen, Gender-Data-Gap und was das alles mit Bibliotheks- und Informationswissenschaft zu tun hat, in: LIBREAS. Library Ideas, 39 (2021), unter: https://libreas.eu/ausgabe39/juen/, Zugriff: 7.11.2023; Catherine D'Ignazio u. Lauren Klein, „What Gets Counted Counts." in: Data Feminism (2020), unter: https://data-feminism.mitpress.mit.edu/pub/h1w0nbqp, Zugriff: 14.9.2023.
4 Criado-Perez, Unsichtbare Frauen, wie Anm. 2, 11.

Auf diesen Gender-Data-Gap stoßen wir als Mitarbeiter*innen des Akademievorhabens „Anpassungsstrategien der späten mitteleuropäischen Monarchie am preußischen Beispiel 1786–1918" an der Berlin-Brandenburgischen Akademie der Wissenschaften täglich. Wir erforschen die preußische Monarchie des 19. Jahrhunderts aus der Perspektive der Kulturgeschichte des Politischen und fragen nach ihren Legitimationsstrategien und Integrationspotenzialen. Das dazugehörige Online-Forschungsportal „Praktiken der Monarchie"[5] bietet einen strukturellen (Organigramme), räumlich-sozialen (Wohntopografie) und prosopografischen (Biogramme) Zugang zu den recherchierten Daten.

Die Biogramme liefern über die stichpunktartigen Angaben im Personenregister hinausgehende biografische Informationen zu Personen, die im Untersuchungszeitraum entweder preußische Hofämter innehatten oder in den Zivil- und Militärkabinetten und im Umfeld von Monarch oder Monarchengattin wirkten. Ziel dabei ist es, prosopografisches Datenmaterial zu den Lebens- und Karriereverläufen dieser Personen für die weitere Forschung zur Verfügung zu stellen. Ein Schwerpunkt liegt auf den Verwandtschaftsbeziehungen, die Rückschlüsse auf soziale Beziehungen, Netzwerke sowie adlige Karriere- und Familienstrategien ermöglichen.[6] Die Biogramme lassen sich nach der Kategorie Geschlecht filtern und gliedern sich derzeit (Juli 2024) in 76 Prozent Männer und 24 Prozent Frauen.[7] Auch hier zeigt sich der Gender-Data-Gap.

Doch die geschlechtsbezogene Datenlücke beginnt in den genutzten gedruckten Quellen,[8] in der Forschungsliteratur[9] und im Archiv bereits in der Überlieferung zu

---

5 Vgl. Berlin-brandenburgische Akademie der Wissenschaften, Praktiken der Monarchie, unter: https://actaborussica.bbaw.de/, Zugriff: 21.2.2024.
6 Zu sozialen Netzwerken und Hoffamilien am preußischen Hof vgl. Anja Bittner u. Bärbel Holtz (Bearb.), Der preußische Hof von 1786 bis 1918. Ämter, Akteure und Akteurinnen, 100–105; zu weiblicher Verwandtschaft vgl. Michaela Hohkamp, Tanten: vom Nutzen einer verwandtschaftlichen Figur für die Erforschung familiärer Ökonomien in der Frühen Neuzeit, in: Werkstatt Geschichte, 46 (2007), 5–12; dies., Leibliche Schwestern und Schwägerinnen in der frühneuzeitlichen Fürstengesellschaft des Heiligen Römischen Reiches (15. bis 19. Jahrhundert), in: L'Homme. Europäische Zeitschrift für Feministische Geschichtswissenschaft (L'Homme. Z. F. G.), 28, 2 (2017), 15–33; Stefani Engelstein, Geschwister und Geschwisterlichkeit in der Epistemologie der Moderne, in: ebd., 49–68.
7 Auf der Website https://actaborussica.bbaw.de/ sind 261 Biogramme abrufbar, die nach Geschlecht gefiltert werden können. 198 dieser Biogramme entfallen auf Männer und 63 auf Frauen. Ein ähnliches Verhältnis zeigt sich vermutlich in den Einträgen des Personenregisters, das über 11.000 Personen verzeichnet. Seit 2023 wird im Register den Einträgen die Kategorie Geschlecht maschinenlesbar zugewiesen, um das Geschlechterverhältnis der Personen mit Beziehungen zum preußischen Hof zukünftig ermitteln zu können. Für die Einträge unter „A" ergibt sich ein vorläufiges Verhältnis von 20 Prozent Frauen zu 80 Prozent Männern.
8 Während die Gothaischen genealogischen Taschenbücher weibliche wie männliche Mitglieder der Adelsfamilien mit ihrem Sozialstatus auflisten, bleiben weibliche Verwandte in den Memoiren oder biografischen Darstellungen von Männern oft nur eine Randbemerkung.

Lebens- und Karrierewegen von Frauen am preußischen Hof. Die Akten aus dem Geheimen Staatsarchiv Preußischer Kulturbesitz (GStA PK) von Ministerien und Hofbehörden, die wir in großem Umfang einsehen und analysieren, wurden fast ausnahmslos von Männern verfasst oder bearbeitet und im 19. Jahrhundert von männlichen Archivaren in die Überlieferung gebracht. Diese Quellen sind nicht neutral; sie dokumentieren eine männliche Sichtweise auf eine männliche Welt, in der Frauen nur an bestimmten Punkten schriftlich erwähnt wurden.[10] Die Ehefrauen von ranghohen und einflussreichen Männern, wie Monarchengattinnen, Prinzessinnen oder adlige Amtsträgerinnen, werden in diesen Akten nur punktuell erwähnt. Je niedriger die Stellung eines Mannes in der Sozialhierarchie war, desto schwieriger sind Hinweise auf seine Ehefrau oder Tochter zu finden. Zudem haben wir es in der Geschichtswissenschaft stets mit Verlusten von einst vorhandenen Daten zu tun, verursacht durch Kriegseinwirkungen oder Skartierungen bei der Annahme von Archivgut.

Die Personalakten des preußischen Hofes sind im GStA PK nicht mehr vorhanden, aber es hat sie für Männer und Frauen gegeben.[11] Dafür sprechen einzelne Hinweise in verschiedenen Beständen.[12] In den Akten findet sich dennoch Material über die an den Parallelhöfen[13] beschäftigten adligen wie nichtadligen Personen.[14] Gehaltsbücher verzeichnen Männer und Frauen sowie die Lohnlücke (Gender-Pay-Gap) zwischen den Geschlechtern.[15]

---

9 Zur Unsichtbarkeit von Frauen vgl. Carl van Schaik u. Kai Michel, Die Wahrheit über Eva. Die Erfindung der Ungleichheit von Frauen und Männern, Hamburg 2022; Marylène Patou-Mathis, Weibliche Unsichtbarkeit. Wie alles begann, München 2021; Emmanuel Todd, Où en sont-elles? Une esquisse de l'histoire des femmes, Paris 2022.
10 Regina Wecker zeigt, wie das Ranke'sche Verständnis von Geschichtswissenschaft Frauen als wissenschaftlichen Gegenstand ausschloss und damit geschlechterspezifische Machtstrukturen aus Rankes Gegenwart festschrieb und legitimierte. Vgl. Regina Wecker, Vom Nutzen und Nachteil der Frauen- und Geschlechtergeschichte für die Gender Theorie. Oder: Warum Geschichte wichtig ist, in: L'Homme. Z. F. G., 18, 2 (2007), 27–52. Zur ‚männlichen' Geschichtswissenschaft und Historiografie vgl. den Überblick von Claudia Opitz-Belakhal, Geschlechtergeschichte, Frankfurt am Main 2010, 148–177.
11 Darauf deuten vereinzelte Angaben in den Findbüchern bzw. Altfindmitteln hin.
12 Vgl. GStA PK, I. HA Rep. 133, Nr. 707, Anstellung der Silberwäscherin Charlotte Sophie Sichter 1818 und des Silberburschen Palmig 1825 und die Angelegenheiten der Silberwäscherin Schmidt, geb. Ebers; GStA PK, BPH, Rep. 53, Nr. 995, Personalakte der Weißzeugaufseherin Schultze; GStA PK, BPH, Rep. 53, Nr. 994, Personalakte der Kammerjungfer Schindler.
13 Unter Parallelhöfen versteht man all jene Hofstaaten, die neben dem großen Hofstaat des Monarchen bestanden. Dazu zählen etwa die Hofstaaten von Königin, Königinwitwe, Prinzen und Prinzessinnen.
14 Vgl. GStA PK, I. HA Rep. 89, Nr. 3318, Einzelne Angelegenheiten des Personals des Hofstaats und der Hofdienerschaft des Königs und der Königin, Bd. 11; GStA PK, I. HA Rep. 100, Nr. 775–794 (Hofdamen); GStA PK, BPH, Rep. 58III, Nr. 45, Verlobung, Ehevertrag, Vermählung, Etat und Hofstaat von Prinz Wilhelm von Preußen und Prinzessin Maria Anna von Hessen-Homburg.
15 Vgl. GStA PK, BPH, Rep. 58 Ic, Nr. 3 und 4; GStA PK, BPH, Rep. 58 Ib, Nr. 11 und 12.

Vor diesem Hintergrund stößt das Bemühen, jene Frauen sichtbar zu machen, die am preußischen Hof in unterschiedlichen Sozialpositionen lebten, an Grenzen. Die Quellen selbst sind limitiert und aus einer Perspektive verfasst, die diese Frauen verdeckt. Insofern stehen wir vor dem Problem, auch im Digitalen ungewollt den Gender-Data-Gap zu reproduzieren. Die Auswertung der Register nach Geschlechtern sowie die Ausrichtung der Biogramme auf Verwandtschaftsbeziehungen und mögliche Netzwerke sollen zur Überwindung dieser Datenlücke beitragen.

Das Raster, das die Biogramme strukturiert, ist aber nur scheinbar objektiv.[16] Es sortiert recherchierte Informationen zu biografischen Kerndaten (Namen, Lebensdaten, Konfession, Grundbesitz), zum höfischen und außerhöfischen Karriereverlauf, zu Auszeichnungen und zum gesellschaftlichen Wirken. Für Frauen lassen sich meist nur Karriereschritte am Hof festmachen. Verglichen mit manchen berühmten Männern mag dies dürftig erscheinen, ist aber darauf zurückzuführen, dass Frauen aufgrund ihres Geschlechts andere Karriereorte in den Bereichen Politik, Verwaltung und Militär verwehrt waren.

Das gesellschaftliche Engagement wird im Frageraster nach sozial-karitativem, kirchlichem und kulturellem Engagement, dem Unterhalten von Salons, der Mitgliedschaft in Vereinen oder in Freimaurerlogen aufgeschlüsselt. In diesen Rubriken können wir für Frauen ebenfalls kaum Daten eintragen. Einerseits, weil es ihnen grundsätzlich erschwert war, in diesen Feldern aktiv zu sein, andererseits, weil sich meist keine Hinweise auf ein mögliches Wirken in den genutzten Quellen finden.

Beim Vergleich der Biogramme von weiblichen und männlichen Hofamtsträgern entsteht der Eindruck, dass Frauen weniger geleistet hätten als Männer. Das nur scheinbar objektive Frageraster verdeckt, dass Frauen und Männer mit grundverschiedenen Voraussetzungen und Erwartungshaltungen an ihr Geschlecht und die damit verbundene gesellschaftliche Rolle konfrontiert waren.[17] Dies entspricht jedoch Darstellungskonventionen bei Lebensbeschreibungen.[18] Da Frauen aller Stände ihr Lebensziel als Ehefrau und Mutter im häuslichen Bereich zu suchen hatten und nicht in der Öffentlichkeit, war ein Hofamt als Kammerfrau, Hofdame oder Oberhofmeisterin schon das Maximum an Karriere, das eine adlige Frau erreichen konnte.[19] In

---

16 Vgl. Criado-Perez, Unsichtbare Frauen, wie Anm. 2, 11, 29, 35–43; Wecker, Vom Nutzen und Nachteil, wie Anm. 10, 27–52.
17 Vgl. Criado-Perez, Unsichtbare Frauen, wie Anm. 2, 29, 35–43.
18 Vgl. den Aufbau entsprechender Artikel in Personenlexika wie Allgemeine Deutsche Biographie, Neue Deutsche Biographie, Biographisches Lexikon des Kaiserthums Österreich oder auch bei Wikipedia. Betätigung in der Familie sind nicht Gegenstand, aber ein markantes Merkmal weiblicher Leben.
19 Vgl. Christa Diemel, Adelige Frauen im bürgerlichen Jahrhundert. Hofdamen, Stiftsdamen, Salondamen 1800–1870, Frankfurt am Main 1998; Nadine Hüttinger, „Ein glänzendes Elend?" Adelige Hofdamen im 19. Jahrhundert, in: Markus Raasch (Hg.), Adeligkeit, Katholizismus, Mythos: neue Perspektiven auf die Adelsgeschichte der Moderne, München 2014, 153–170; Bittner, Ämter, wie Anm. 6, 74–100.

der Regel endete die Karriere dieser Frauen mit deren Verheiratung. Dennoch kam ihnen als Bindeglied in Familiennetzwerken ein wichtiger Part zu. Über die angezeigten Verwandtschaftsbeziehungen in den Biogrammen werden diese Frauen sichtbar(er).

Welches Potenzial der Blick auf weibliche Lebensläufe birgt, zeigt das Biogramm der Amélie von Dönhoff (1808–1871) besonders deutlich. Die Gräfin war zwischen 1831 und 1842 Hofdame bei Prinzessin Marie von Preußen (1808–1877), bevor sie ab 1843 dasselbe Amt im Hofstaat der preußischen Kronprinzessin und späteren Königin Elisabeth versah. Ihre männlichen Verwandten bekleideten ebenfalls Ämter am Hof oder im Staat. Ihr Vater war Flügeladjutant von König Friedrich Wilhelm III., ihre vier Brüder verfolgten Karrieren im Staatsdienst sowie im Militär und am Hof. Die beiden Schwestern waren mit einem Staatsbeamten beziehungsweise einem Grundherren verheiratet.[20] Amélie von Dönhoff konnte ihr Amt in den 1860ern aus gesundheitlichen Gründen nicht mehr ausüben.[21] Wahrscheinlich war sie deshalb ab 1864 Stiftsdame des adligen Damenstifts Rietschütz in Schlesien, von dem sie eine Präbende[22] bezogen haben dürfte. Sie lebte aber bis zu ihrem Tod in den Wohnorten ihrer Dienstherrin in der Berlin-Potsdamer Residenzlandschaft. Ihre Neffen und eine Nichte konnten in der nachfolgenden Generation hohe Ämter in prinzlichen Hofstaaten besetzen. An der sich über mehrere Jahre hinziehenden Karriereplanung ihrer Nichte Emmy von Below (1842–1899)[23] zur Hofdame war Amélie von Dönhoff aktiv beteiligt. Sie besprach in den Briefen an ihre Schwester Cäcilie von Below in den 1860er Jahren immer wieder das Für und Wider einer Hofdamenkarriere.[24] Auch August von Eulenburg (1838–1921), kronprinzlicher Hofmarschall, freute sich 1870 persönlich darüber, seine Cousine womöglich bald als Hofdame am Kronprinzenhof zu wissen.[25] Zwar standen die Below-Eltern einer Hofkarriere ihrer jüngsten Tochter, wohl wegen ihrer angeschlagenen Gesundheit, verhalten gegenüber, doch verwies Eulenburg auf den familiären Anschluss für Emmy „in ihrem außerdienstlichen Leben" im „Wrangelsche[n] Haus, [bei] Tante Amélie, Gerdt's und mir".[26]

Das über die Biogramme sichtbar gemachte Verwandtschaftsnetzwerk lädt dazu ein, nach Zeugnissen zu suchen, welche die Karriereplanung am preußischen Hof nicht nur als eine individuelle Entscheidung, sondern als ein gemeinsames Unternehmen einer Adelsfamilie aufzeigen. Forschungen zu Frauen am preußischen Hof im 19. Jahr-

---

20 Vgl. das Biogramm unter: https://actaborussica.bbaw.de/biogramme/detail.xql?id=P6414747, Zugriff: 21.3.2024.
21 Vgl. GStA PK, VI. HA, FA Below, v. Nr. 45, Brief vom 2.6.1862, 12.7.1864.
22 Damenstifte vergaben neben dem symbolischen Kapital für ihre Stiftsdamen auch eine finanzielle Versorgung (Präbende).
23 Vgl. das Biogramm unter: https://actaborussica.bbaw.de/biogramme/detail.xql?id=P6452762, Zugriff: 21.3.2024.
24 Vgl. GStA PK, VI. HA, FA Below, v., Nr. 44; GStA PK, VI. HA, FA Below, v., Nr. 45; GStA PK, VI. HA, FA Below, v., Nr. 46.
25 Vgl. Bundesarchiv, N 2015/1, Bl. 139r–142, 11.2.1870 August von Eulenburg an Karl von Below.
26 Bundesarchiv, N 2015/1, Bl. 140v, 11.2.1870 August von Eulenburg an Karl von Below.

hundert sind unter anderem wichtig, um den bestehenden Gender-Data-Gap zu minimieren. Dies gilt insbesondere für rangniedere Frauen, die völlig unbekannt sind. Ungewollt wird dieser Gender-Data-Gap durch Datenstrukturen, die nach männlichen Lebensläufen modelliert wurden, im Digitalen reproduziert, zumal konventionelle, scheinbar objektive Kriterien weibliche Handlungsräume verdecken. Das Beispiel der Amélie von Dönhoff zeigt jedoch das Vorhandensein solcher Räume und veranschaulicht, wie adlige Frauen sich an der Karriereplanung ihrer Verwandten beteiligten.

Andrea Griesebner u. Evdoxios Doxiadis (eds.), **Gender and Divorce in Europe: 1600–1900. A Praxeological Perspective**, London/New York: Routledge 2024, 249 p., ca. EUR 54,– (paperback), ISBN 978-1032369341.

Over the past three decades, family history in its broader sense has flourished and broadened considerably in scope. Part of the significance of this renewal has been the shift in attention from stable structures such as marriage and the household to broader, more diverse and dynamic social networks and relationships. Today, there is a growing emphasis on delving more deeply into areas that may at first appear to be outside the family framework, such as loneliness or the lives of single and non-marital individuals. In this sense, and probably since Lawrence Stone's pioneering study *Broken Lives*, the end of the formal family, separation and divorce have attracted growing attention from researchers across a range of disciplines.

Against this backdrop, *Gender and Divorce in Europe: 1600–1900. A Praxeological Perspective* is an important contribution to the historical study of the family, proposing a broad comparison between different regions, contexts and periods. The editors' introduction sets the scene and offers different keys to interpretations, emphasising four dimensions that are found in the chapters of the book: the different definitions and terminologies of "divorce from marriage", "the regulation of the consequences of divorce", "making a living" and the question of the "well-being" of divorced women and men. The book insists strongly on the economic and material conditions of the spouses involved in divorce proceedings, while at the same time pointing out some of the limitations imposed by the sources and the state of research.

The list of historical contributions to this interesting volume opens with a crosssectional article by the Swedish historian Maria Agren on "Women and Work" (pp. 16–30). The main thesis of the article is not difficult to sum up: despite ideological notions about divergent gender roles in the family, almost all early modern "households must have been based on a two-supporters model according to which both spouses were expected to contribute to the common economy" (p. 27). This model presupposed that both husband and wife could take on a wide variety of tasks and had to have some authority to administer and govern their households. This is important because women, who in most of the cases sought separation or divorce from their husbands, had to see themselves as capable of leading an economically independent life. As the editors point out in the introduction, economic rules and arrangements prove crucial in order to understanding the chances and limits of divorce litigation and the material conditions of married life or, especially for women, of an independent existence.

Agren's work is a frequently cited reference in the chapters that follow, probably because of the book's emphasis on economic matters. However, the relevance of Agren's conclusions for the different countries and cultures considered in the volume is not self-evident: can the Scandinavian case studies be seen as representative for Europe – for example for the southern Catholic countries – and for the Ottoman Empire? A contextualisation by the editors would certainly have been useful, all the more so as they strongly underline in their introduction the huge degree of regional, cultural and religious variation associated with separation and divorce.

The following contributions to the volume are divided into two main parts: Part I deals with "Divorce from bed and board", Part II with "Divorce with dissolution of the marriage". This structure confronts the reader with a terminological and conceptual problem, which is discussed in the introduction to the volume and recurs in several contributions: it is indeed questionable whether a separation of wife and husband without dissolution of the marriage can be assimilated to a divorce. In the Catholic tradition, this is basically seen as a temporary separation – separation from bed and board – although in practice the break can last for the rest of the spouses' existence. Since the separation does not allow husband and wife to remarry, it is not a true divorce. The editors of the volume point out that this fundamental difference is often not so clear in practice. This is certainly true. But it represents an important doctrinal and legal distinction between different confessions concerning the very nature of marriage.

Nevertheless, reading the different chapters provides many interesting elements for understanding the variety of forms of separation. As some chapters in part I demonstrate, the theoretical subordination of wives to their husbands was not absolute: in several cases women could achieve a certain degree of economic autonomy, running their own estates and businesses. In this field, social variation is indeed astonishing.

A number of contributions focus on the laws governing the material conditions of separated spouses and on the practical arrangements which might be made between spouses in a national or regional context – (Andrea Griesebner and Susanne Hehenberger, Habsburg Monarchy; Krista Kesselring and Tim Stretton, England; Nere Jone Intxaustegi Jauregi, Bilbao; Claire Châtelain, France; Zuzana Pavelková Čevelová and Jessica Reich, Bishoprics of Prague and Trent, Birgit Dober, Lower Austria).

Marie Malherbe's contribution to the volume stands out for its micro-historical analysis of a single case: the "divortio" trial between Marianna Valmarana and her husband Sebastiano Mocenigo in Venice in 1785 (pp. 97–109). As in other regions, the number of "divorzii" increased significantly between 1775 and 1800, and in most cases it was the women who demanded separation: separation from bed and board in this case meant the separation from property. In the aristocratic Republic of Venice, divorce was perceived as a threat to the order of state and society. Despite this conservative tendency, the intertwined ecclesiastical and civil processes left families some room for manoeuvre. In particular, the ecclesiastical courts were accused of being too tolerant towards Venitian women who wished to separate from their husbands. In fact the ecclesiastical courts were often a safeguard against domestic abuse, a feature that Intxaustegi Jauregi observes in Bilbao (pp. 70–83).

Malherbe's micro-historical approach shows that Marianna was supported by her brother and probably by a broader kin group. This aspect underlines the importance of a favourable social network – especially since the *publica vox et fama* was decisive for women at court. The availability or lack of a solid kin network proves to be a crucial factor, especially for women. This partly nuances the book's emphasis on the individual material backgrounds of the spouses. Even though Marianna won the civil case, she had to live apart from her children and suffered a social burden: the dimension of "well-being" of divorced women and men was not only a material issue.

The merit of the second part of the volume is that it brings together examples from various regional and religious cultures: the focus is not only on Catholic or Protestant Western European couples, but examples from the Ottoman Empire, Habsburg Bosnia and Herzegovina and Jewish couples under the Austrian Civil Code are also described and analysed. The contributions (by Iris Fleßenkämper on the County of Lippe; Evdoxios Doxiadis on Greece; Ninja Bumann on Bosnia and Herzegovina; Ellinor Forster on Jewish couples in Austria) focus in particular on the different options for arrangements and economic solutions for separated or divorced men and women, highlighting the bewildering variety of legal frameworks, social conditions and actual situations.

Gamze Yavuzer's essay on "The Indistinct Line between Marriage and Divorce. The Ambiguous Nature of Marital Status in the 17th-Century Ottoman Empire" may be of particular interest to Western readers, as it allows comparison with a different political and religious context. The author emphasises the strong reliance on orality in the Ottoman Islamic world: in this legally "obscure atmosphere", marriage was often an ambiguous and precarious status, especially for women, which could be terminated by the husband with a simple sentence. All the more so as different forms of divorce were available: "Talâk" could be decided unilaterally by the husband, but he had to respect formal financial obligations towards the divorced wife. "Hul", on the other hand, could also be requested by the wife, but required the consent of the husband. "Feish", a third form of divorce, required the formal intervention of the courts, but could only be granted in special cases, such as impotence or apostasy. The complex and ambiguous definitions of divorce opened up wide spaces for negotiation and manipulation by both spouses, especially if they could rely on favourable witnesses to support their case. In this context, the written legal document is only the final formalisation of an essentially oral process.

In conclusion, Griesebner and Doxiadis's volume is an original and important contribution to the comparative study of marriage and divorce. Its strong focus on economic aspects fills a gap in family history studies – although recent research cited in the volume has already paved the way for a renewal – and opens up new avenues of investigation that will certainly prove fruitful in the years to come. Such a book remains an ambitious undertaking: it is in part a difficult book, considering a wide range of cases and situations, involving different confessions and religions – Catholic and Orthodox, Protestant and Anglican, Jewish and Muslim – in various geographical regions and therefore often different legal frameworks, as well as covering a wide period of time, from around 1600 to the First World War. As the subject is not simple and depends on many institutional, legal, religious and cultural variables, the comparison remains a challenge. In this respect, *Gender and Divorce in Europe* is a courageous undertaking.

Sandro Guzzi-Heeb, Lausanne

Theresa Earenfight, **Catherine of Aragon. Infanta of Spain, Queen of England**, Pennsylvania: The Pennsylvania State University Press 2021, 251 S., ca. EUR 35,–, ISBN 978-0271091648.

Wie verfasst man heutzutage die Biographie einer Person, die derartig im Rampenlicht ihrer Zeit sowie im Zentrum zahlreicher Kontroversen der Nationalgeschichte stand, wie Katharina von Aragon: spanische Prinzessin, politische Botschafterin, Ehefrau von zwei englischen Königen, Regentin und Heerführerin von England und – last but not least – für den scheidungswilligen Tudorkönig Heinrich VIII. Ursache (wenn auch nicht Auslöserin!) des religiösen Schismas und der Entstehung der anglikanischen Kirche? Und wer wäre für diese Aufgabe besser geeignet als Theresa Earenfight, die einen Großteil ihrer universitären Karriere dem vormodernen spanischen Königinnentum gewidmet hat? Der Ansatz, den Earenfight als Biographin wählt ist dreifach: Erstens handelt es sich um einen resolut feministischen Ansatz, der hauptsächlich die weiblichen Protagonistinnen in den Blick nimmt und die männlichen Personen nur wo nötig in die Geschichte einbringt. Die persönlichen wie auch politischen Beziehungen zu Katharinas Ehemännern Arthur und Heinrich VIII., zu Politikern wie Thomas Cromwell oder zu ihrem Vater Fernando werden nur dort relevant, wo sie Katharina direkt betreffen. Hier seien beispielsweise neueste medizinhistorische Analysen zu einer möglichen Erbkrankheit Heinrichs VIII., dem McLeod-Syndrom, erwähnt, das eventuell die Ursache für die zahlreichen Fehlgeburten, die Katharina erlitt, gewesen sein könnte (S. 117). Earenfights Ansatz ist zweitens auch dadurch gekennzeichnet, dass er Katharinas Persönlichkeit und ihre Handlungen von ihrer spanischen Herkunft ableitet: Insbesondere ihre Mutter Isabella I., Königin von Kastilien und Léon aus eigenem Recht und damit Vorbild und Lehrerin Katharinas, ihre enge Verbindung zu ihren spanischen Hofdamen und Familienmitgliedern sowie vor allem ihre lebenslang am englischen Hofe hochgehaltene „Hispanität" in Verhalten, Mode und den sie umgebenden Personen bilden ein Erklärungsraster, um Katharinas Person und Positionen zu verstehen. Drittens fokussiert die Autorin in der vorliegenden Biographie auf eine materielle Ebene, indem sie Bildzeugnisse wie Portraits, aber auch Architektur oder Widmungs-Handschriften, Rechnungsbücher sowie erhaltene Stoffe, Objekte und Kleidung für ihre Analyse heranzieht. Orte, an denen Katharina verweilte, sowie Materialien, die ihr oder Zeitgenossinnen gehört hatten, werden so als Quellen stark gewichtet, mit dem erklärten Ziel, so nah wie möglich an das Forschungsobjekt heranzukommen.

Die Studie geht in fünf straffen und fokussierten Kapiteln vor, die den maßgeblichen Etappen in Katharinas Leben folgen: ihre Kindheit am wandernden kastilischen Hof und die Beobachtung ihrer Mutter bei der Regierungsausübung; ihre Reise nach und Akkulturation in England im Kontext ihrer ersten Hochzeit mit Arthur Tudor und die mehrjährige „Limbo-Phase" ihrer Witwenschaft; der Lebensabschnitt der zweiten Ehe mit Heinrich VIII., in dem sie die Rolle einer politisch aktiven Königin einnahm; gefolgt von einer Phase geprägt von zahlreichen Schwangerschaften und Fehlgeburten, während gleichzeitig der Aufstieg männlicher Berater sie von der politischen Bühne entfernte; und schließlich das Kapitel zu ihrer Entfremdung von Heinrich VIII. sowie ihr Widerstand gegen dessen Ränke und Prozesse, und letztendlich ihr einsamer Tod im Alter von 50 Jahren.

In der Biographie stehen sowohl die regierungspolitischen Handlungen Katharinas im Vordergrund als auch die kulturellen Bezüge zu Kastilien. Hier werden vor allem die engen Beziehungen zur weiblichen, im weitesten Sinne spanischen Verwandtschaft betont: Frauen wie Königin Isabella I., aber auch Margarethe von Österreich oder ihre Schwester Juana übten ihrem hohen Rang entsprechend angemessene Regierungspositionen aus. Die durchaus ebenfalls mächtigen Frauen (wie Margaret von Beaufort), die der Tudordynastie im Rosenkrieg den Thron sicherten, bleiben in Earenfights Erzählung hingegen eher im Schatten. Möglicherweise ging die Autorin davon aus, dass dem englischsprachigen Publikum ihres Buches die Geschichte der Tudors ohnehin bekannt sei und somit nur der kastilische Hintergrund Katharinas einer intensiveren Hervorhebung bedürfe.

Die Entscheidung Earenfights, Katharina ausgehend von ihrer spanischen Prägung zu kontextualisieren, spiegelt sich auch im materialgeschichtlichen Ansatz der Autorin wider. Zahlreiche Ausführungen und Abbildungen geben den Lesenden Einblick ins materielle Umfeld der Königin: mehrere Portraits und Embleme samt Interpretation oder die spanischen Stoffe, Schuhe und Mode, denen Katharina lebenslang treu blieb. Dementsprechend lesen sich einige Absätze des Buches wie ein Kriminalroman in der englischen Provinz auf der Suche nach verschollenen Stoffen aus Katharinas Haushalt, in dem erzählerisch die Distanz zwischen verfassender Autorin, historischem Forschungsobjekt und aktiver Feldforschung aufgehoben wird (paradigmatisch der Stoff-Fund in Ludlow, der dreimal erwähnt wird, S. x, S. 23f. sowie S. 78f.). Solche Brüche lockern die Erzählung auf und führen vor allem vor Augen, dass selbst bei einer solch bekannten Figur aus der englischen Nationalgeschichte die Forschung von Zufällen geprägt ist. Diese Fokussierung auf Schuhe, Stoffe, Gebäude, um „ihre Welt mit ihren Augen zu sehen" (S. 21) wirkt hier schon fast wie eine Erweiterung von Arlette Farges „Goût de l'archive": Materielle Kultur erlaubt es, ein Schlaglicht auf das Erleben einer historischen Person zu werfen, gleichzeitig bergen Archivalien das Potenzial, die Forschenden zu begeistern. Tritt dieser Fall ein, rückt neben dem historischen Objekt vor allem die forschende Person in den Vordergrund. Diese Offenlegung der Passion der forschenden Person, die sich etwa darin äußerte, Katharinas Lebensorte zu bereisen und dort zu wohnen (S. 23) ist per se durchaus sinnvoll. Immerhin entsteht in historischen Studien häufig, und das zeigt der Ansatz der Autorin, eine Spannung zwischen emotional aufgeladenem Material, wissenschaftlicher Analyse und der Suche nach dem richtigen Ton beim Schreiben für die jeweilige Zielgruppe. Welcher Stellenwert diesen unterschiedlichen Aspekten beigemessen wird, ist vor allem dem subjektiven Ermessen der Forschenden geschuldet.

Die von Earenfight vorgelegte Biographie diskutiert insbesondere im Epilog (S. 200 ff.), wie im Umfeld von Katharina von Aragon um 1500 „Politik gemacht" und „Macht verhandelt" wurde – um auf das Thema und die Einleitung der vorliegenden „L'Homme"-Ausgabe Bezug zu nehmen. Katharina war keine Herrscherin, die aus eigenem Recht regierte (wie ihre Mutter). Ihre Macht rührte aus mehreren, sich wandelnden Rollen her, die sie im Laufe ihres Lebens einnahm und für die sie Herrschaftsansprüche geltend machen konnte. So war sie Königstochter einer einflussreichen Dynastie, temporäre Regentin, aber stets auch diplomatische Agentin für sich und ihr spanisches Umfeld. Die Grenzen ihrer Macht waren dabei klar durch ihr Geschlecht und die ihr zugeschriebenen Rollen begrenzt: Während ihrer Zeit als Prinzessin entschieden andere über mögliche Ehekandidaten; als *Queen consort* in England stand ihr nur ein Bruchteil der royalen Macht zu; später konnte sie als Mutter das erklärte dynastische Ziel ihres Ehemannes, einen männlichen Nachfolger zu liefern, nicht erfüllen. Als Frau, insbesondere während der ständigen Schwangerschaften, wurde sie von Männern aus den Regierungsgeschäften verdrängt. Nichtsdestotrotz blieben ihr, wie finanzielle und personelle Entscheidungen in ihrem Umfeld deutlich machen, auch in solchen Situationen gewisse Handlungsspielräume, etwa die kulturelle und religiöse Patronage für ihre engsten Vertrauten oder die Erziehung ihrer Tochter. Es ist also eine stets temporäre und instabile Macht, die Katharina strategisch je nach ihrer aktuellen Rolle neu zu verhandeln und einzusetzen wusste (S. 201). Neben ihrer Persönlichkeit, die Earenfight hier vor allem in Szene setzt, illustriert sie damit aber eben auch die strukturellen und kulturellen Kriterien, die Katharinas Leben bestimmten. Die Ironie, dass Heinrich VIII. seine Ehe mit Katharina von Aragon und die kirchenpolitische Stabilität aufgrund fehlender überlebender männlicher Erben aufgab, die Tudor-Dynastie ihren Fortbestand aber vor allem mehreren Töchtern von Heinrich VIII., darunter Mary I. aus der Ehe mit Katharina, verdankte, unterstreicht noch einmal mehr die Bedeutung der Auseinandersetzung mit vormodernen Königinnen und ihrer Macht, jenseits von Männerbiographien oder weiblichen „Ausnahmefiguren" aus einer eindimensionalen patriarchalen Perspektive.

Als besonders hilfreich erweisen sich die Zeittafeln am Ende jedes Kapitels, der ausführliche Index, die zahlreichen Karten und (Farb-)Bilder, die ein auch rein visuell ansprechendes und qualitativ hochwertiges Buch abrunden. Insbesondere die präzise Einleitung und der kurze Schlussteil, die den fünf Hauptkapiteln einen Rahmen geben, veranschaulichen die Erzählkunst der Autorin. Mit dem vorliegenden Buch hat sie eine kompakte und gut lesbare Biographie abgeliefert, die Katharina von Aragon, ihre Beziehungen und ihre Welt packend zum Leben erweckt.

Vanina Kopp, Erfurt

Christina Antenhofer, **Die Familienkiste. Mensch-Objekt-Beziehungen im Mittelalter und in der Renaissance** (= Mittelalter-Forschungen, Bd. 67), 2 Bde., Ostfildern: Jan Thorbecke Verlag 2022, 1376 S., ca. EUR 112,–, ISBN 978-3799543743.

Christina Antenhofer präsentiert mit „Die Familienkiste", der überarbeiteten Fassung ihrer 2014 an der Universität Innsbruck vorgelegten Habilitationsschrift, eine umfassende Studie zur Aussagekraft von Mensch-Objekt-Beziehungen für Lebensentwürfe und Handlungsspielräume von Fürstinnen und Fürsten. Diese werden anhand von dynastischen Eheprojekten der Familien Gonzaga, Visconti, Sforza und Görz-Tirol sowie Habsburg, Wittelsbach und Württemberg im 14. und 15. Jahrhundert untersucht. Die Autorin interessiert besonders, inwiefern sich über die Erforschung der Beziehungen zwischen Menschen und Dingen Fragen nach Lebenspraxis, Emotionalität und Geschlechterverhältnissen beantworten lassen. Sie geht von der These aus, dass Praktiken des Besitzens, Verwaltens und Verwahrens, des Verschenkens, aber auch des Erhaltens von Objekten für die Gestaltung fürstlicher Lebens- und Selbstentwürfe eine tragende Rolle zukam. In ihrer methodischen Herangehensweise folgt Antenhofer Ansätzen der „Material culture studies" (S. 6) und der Geschlechtergeschichte, um Fragen nach der *agency* von Dingen und solche nach der *agency* von Fürstinnen und Fürsten miteinander zu verschränken. Die Leitbegriffe der Studie, „Fetisch" und „Familienkiste", rekurrieren auf ideengeschichtliche Traditionen, die versuchen, die komplexen Beziehungen zwischen Menschen und Dingen zu erfassen, allerdings auf unterschiedliche Weise und mit unterschiedlichen Schwerpunkten. So hat der Fetischbegriff eine bis ins 15. Jahrhundert zurückreichende Geschichte und wurde spätestens in der Moderne in seinen Adaptionen durch Karl Marx, Sigmund Freud und den Strukturalismus zu einem zentralen Begriff der Kulturtheorie, den Antenhofer übernimmt, um die Beziehung zwischen Menschen und Einzeldingen zu analysieren. Ihr Begriff der „Familienkiste", den sie unter Rückgriff auf die Theorie der Gabe von Marcel Mauss entwickelt, dient Antenhofer zur Analyse der Beziehung von Menschen mit „Ensembles von Objekten" (S. 48).

Diese Mensch-Objekt-Beziehungen spürt Antenhofer in Brautschatzinventaren, Testamenten und Eheverträgen auf, schriftlichen und personenbezogenen Quellen also, die mehr oder weniger detaillierte Verzeichnisse von Dingen enthalten. Über diese Objekte wurden soziale Beziehungen gestiftet, was im von Antenhofer untersuchten Kontext der dynastischen Eheschließungen besonders anschaulich zu Tage tritt: Ein Beispiel sind Eheringe und repräsentatives Tafelgeschirr mit Allianzwappen, das zur

Aufstellung am Hof der Ehepartner bestimmt war. Alle Objekte mit Allianzwappen sollten die Gegenwart der Dynastie der Braut wie auch das durch die Ehe geschlossene Bündnis kommunizieren, etwa im Fall der Ehe von Taddea Visconti mit Stephan III. von Bayern oder der Ehe von Antonia Visconti mit Eberhard von Württemberg (S. 305 u. 327). Die Quellenauswahl sowie die sachliche, räumliche und zeitliche Eingrenzung ihres Untersuchungsgegenstandes begründet die Verfasserin mit der im Untersuchungszeitraum stetig dichter werdenden Überlieferung und mit der Möglichkeit, die Verbindungen zwischen bislang von der Forschung eher getrennt untersuchten geografischen Räumen (Norditalien, Süddeutschland) und historischen Epochen (Spätmittelalter, Renaissance) zu erforschen. Es ist ihre erklärte Intention, traditionelle Grenzziehungen anhand sachlicher, epochaler oder geografischer Kategorien (Menschen / Dinge, Mittelalter / Renaissance, Italien / Deutschland) gezielt zu dekonstruieren, um raum- und epochenübergreifende Gemeinsamkeiten besser herausarbeiten zu können.

Entgegen der verbreiteten Praxis, Inventare und Verzeichnisse als ‚objektive' Quellen zu verstehen, verfolgt Antenhofer im Einklang mit Gerhard Jaritz den Ansatz, die narrative Konstruktion der Inventare in den Vordergrund zu rücken. Sie betont, dass in diesen Quellen eben nicht nur über Dinge als solche geschrieben wird, sondern über „Handlungen, Gedanken, Leidenschaften von Individuen und Gruppen sowie über die Interaktion zwischen Menschen und Dingen" (S. 172). Es gelte, den Kontext, in dem die Inventare geschrieben wurden, stärker zu berücksichtigen, „um die vielfältigen Ebenen von Objektbesitz und -bindungen, die sich anhand unterschiedlicher Quellengattungen – wie Geschenklisten, Inventare, Testamente, Eheverträge – erschließen lassen", in den Blick zu bekommen (S. 42). Daran anschließend liefert die Verfasserin eine instruktive Besprechung „zentraler Paradigmen, die für die Erfassung der materiellen Kultur des Mittelalters und der Renaissance" (S. 113) in der Forschung Verwendung finden – hier sind schlagwortartig zu nennen: Reliquien und ihre Verehrung, Relikte, Schätze, Sammlungen, Gaben, Geschenke, Memoria, museale Objekte und Spuren.

Aufschlussreich für die Frage nach geschlechtsspezifischen Markierungen von Dingen ist Kap. III/6 („Frauengut – Männergut"), das sich den Unterschieden und Gemeinsamkeiten zwischen „Männergut" und „Frauengut" (S. 196) widmet. Antenhofer vergleicht Brautschatz- und Ausstattungsinventare von Fürstinnen mit Nachlassinventaren von Fürsten, um die geschlechtliche Markierung von Dingen zu diskutieren. Erwartungen hinsichtlich der geschlechtsspezifischen Zuordnung von bestimmten Objektgruppen werden gelegentlich bestätigt, manchmal jedoch auch nicht; vor allem aber werden sie systematisch analysiert und differenziert eingeordnet. Auf diesem Weg belegt ausgerechnet der direkte Vergleich der Inventare von Männern und Frauen, dass eine eindeutige Zuordnung von Objektgruppen entlang der Kategorie Geschlecht der Komplexität historischer Verhältnisse kaum gerecht wird.

Zwar verdeutlicht der systematische Vergleich, dass bestimmte Dinge wie Stoffe, Textilien und Betten, aber auch Wägen offenbar Handlungsräume von Frauen markierten, während Jagdutensilien, Trinkpokale sowie Waffen und Rüstungen wiederum in Inventaren von Männern signifikant öfter verzeichnet wurden, was begründete Rückschlüsse über die männliche Markierung dieser Handlungsbereiche zulässt. Doch gelingt es Antenhofer zu zeigen, dass die geschlechtsspezifische Markierung von Dingen, Räumen, Handlungsfeldern und selbst von Menschen mit vielschichtigen und komplexen sozialen Prozessen der Sinnstiftung und Bedeutungszuschreibung seitens der Akteure und Akteurinnen zusammenhing. Am Beispiel eines Schachtisches im Ausstattungsinventar der Taddea Visconti kann die Verfasserin etwa veranschaulichen, dass im Frauenzimmer nicht nur Handarbeit und Devotion, sondern auch intellektuelle Tätigkeiten wie das Schach- oder das Kartenspiel zum Alltag gehörten. Andererseits kennzeichneten Objekte wie Nähnadeln oder ein erlesener Kokosnusspokal Praktiken, die als ‚weiblich' gelesen wurden, was wiederum diesen Objekten selbst eine „deutlich weibliche Konnotation" (S. 386) verlieh.

Anhand der Inventare lässt sich aber nicht nur die geschlechtliche Markierung unterschiedlicher Praktiken bewerten und gewichten, sondern auch die politische und soziale *agency* von Fürstinnen – und Fürsten – differenziert darstellen. Ein Vergleich zwischen dem Inventar der Paula Gonzaga und der Bianca Maria Sforza unterstreicht vordergründig die unterschiedlichen Lebensentwürfe der beiden Fürstinnen. Paula Gonzaga erscheint aufgrund von Schreibutensilien und Büchern als gebildete, umsichtige und politische Aktivitäten ausübende Fürstin, während sich für Bianca Maria Sforza das verzerrte Bild einer Fürstin ergibt, die nahezu ausschließlich an Selbstrepräsentation interessiert war und sich ihrer „Putzsucht" hingegeben habe. Die Verfasserin kann diese stereotypen Befunde aber mithilfe weiterer Quellen umsichtig differenzieren: So zeigt sich, dass Paula Gonzaga trotz des Stellenwerts von Schreibmaterial in ihrem Inventar selbst nicht gerne schrieb. Allerdings war sie sehr wohl eine geschickte diplomatische Akteurin, die beispielsweise ihre nicht ausbezahlte Mitgift mit Nachdruck und Erfolg einforderte. Bianca Maria Sforza hingegen besaß Bücher, die sie mit großer Wahrscheinlichkeit auch gelesen hat. Zudem entfaltete sie eine rege Korrespondenz mit ihrem Onkel, dem Herzog von Mailand, in der Versuche einer politischen Einflussnahme nachweisbar sind. Viele ihrer Kleider reichte sie als Geschenke weiter, womit sie soziale Beziehungen stärken konnte.

So kann Christina Antenhofer in ihrer umfassenden und detailreichen Studie, für die sie 2024 den Österreichischen Staatspreis für Geschichtswissenschaften erhielt, zeigen, dass die Untersuchung von Mensch-Objekt-Relationen einen entscheidenden Beitrag dazu leisten kann, die weitreichenden sozialen und politischen Gestaltungs- und Handlungsmöglichkeiten von Fürstinnen nachzuzeichnen. Für die Frauen- und Geschlechtergeschichte liefert die Studie daher wertvolle Impulse und Anleitungen nicht nur für Forschungen zu Spätmittelalter und Renaissance, sondern auch für

Forschungen auf der Basis von Nachlässen aus späteren Jahrhunderten sowie zu Frauen und Männern, die nicht den sozialen Eliten angehörten.

Christof Muigg, Wien

Ruth Mazo Karras, **Thou Art the Man. The Masculinity of David in the Christian and Jewish Middle Ages**, Philadelphia: University of Pennsylvania Press 2021, 30 S., ca. EUR 66,–, ISBN 978-0812253023.

Ruth Mazo Karras, seit langem einschlägig ausgewiesene Expertin der mittelalterlichen Geschichte der Geschlechter und Sexualitäten, hat mit „Thou Art the Man" eine Fallstudie zu Vorstellungen von Männlichkeit im Mittelalter vorgelegt. Gegenstand, wenngleich nicht Akteur (S. 3: „David was not performing anything in the Middle Ages") ihres Buches ist der biblische König David. Das Quellenkorpus bilden christliche und jüdische Deutungen dieser Figur, die Aufschluss darüber geben, ob und vor allem in welchem Sinne David als ‚männlich' angesehen wurde.

König David ist für eine solche Fallstudie sicher eine gute Wahl. Nicht nur ist er prominent genug, so dass vergleichsweise reichlich Quellen vorhanden sind, vor allem ist der biblische David eine ambivalente Figur, die immer wieder der Deutung bedurfte. Ambivalent ist er schon in moralischer Hinsicht, als Sünder, der trotzdem vor Gott Gnade fand; ambivalent sind viele der in der Bibel nur knapp erzählten Episoden über ihn, deutungsbedürftig war schließlich auch, wie sich diese zueinander verhielten. David der Hirtenjunge, David der weise König, David der Ehebrecher, David der Prophet. Wie Karras deutlich macht, haben unterschiedliche Darstellungen Davids hier immer wieder neue Akzente gesetzt und dabei reichhaltiges Material produziert, das veranschaulicht, wie unterschiedlich „Männlichkeit" verstanden werden konnte und verstanden wurde.

Konsequenterweise ist das Buch daher auch nicht chronologisch, sondern thematisch gegliedert. Die Einleitung skizziert das Vorgehen und adressiert explizit auch Leser*innen ohne nähere Vorkenntnisse (insbesondere ohne Bibelkenntnis). Den Hauptteil des Buches bilden fünf thematische Kapitel, die David als fähigen Krieger und gottesfürchtigen Herrscher darstellen (S. 23–63), seine Beziehung zu seinem Freund und Schwager Jonathan beleuchten (S. 64–100), David als Sünder und Büßer (S. 101–135), als Propheten, Harfenspieler und ekstatischen Tänzer (S. 136–164) und schließlich als Gründer einer Dynastie untersuchen (S. 165–204). Ein sehr knappes Schlusskapitel (S. 205–208) wird gefolgt von den leider als Endnoten präsentierten Anmerkungen, dem Literaturverzeichnis und einem nützlichen Index.

Der Schwerpunkt des Buches liegt auf der Vielfalt, einerseits seitens der Rezeption (jüdische und christliche Quellen werden immer wieder im Vergleich angeführt, was oft sehr gewinnbringend ist) und andererseits hinsichtlich der vielen Formen von

Männlichkeit, die David repräsentierte und die oft selbst paradoxe Elemente aufweisen. Dazu gehört die scheinbar einfache Dichotomie von ‚männlicher Aktivität' und ‚weiblicher Passivität'. Der biblische Bericht lässt zum Beispiel keine Zweifel daran aufkommen, dass David in der Beziehung zu Batseba der Handelnde war: Er ließ Batseba zu sich holen, er schlief mit ihr, er sorgte dafür, dass ihr Mann Urija im Kampf umkam (letzteres wird in der Bibel noch deutlicher David zugeschrieben, wenn der Prophet Natan von David sagt, dieser habe „Urija mit dem Schwert erschlagen"). Spätere Traditionen hielt dies nicht davon ab, die Schuld für Davids Ehebruch bei Batseba zu suchen, was für Karras' Buch vor allem deshalb interessant ist, weil hier die Grenzen von ‚männlicher Aktivität' deutlich werden: ‚Männlich' war einerseits der selbstbestimmt handelnde, potente Mann, was durch Sündhaftigkeit, Reue und Buße nicht in Frage gestellt werden musste; andererseits aber reichte der Anblick einer Frau offenbar, um auch starke, mächtige und weise Männer jede Kontrolle über das eigene Tun verlieren zu lassen. Auch diese Deutungen haben ihre Geschichte, wie Karras deutlich macht: Im Hochmittelalter überwog eindeutig das Interesse an David als Büßer, während im Spätmittelalter und in der Frühen Neuzeit Batseba als Verführerin in den Vordergrund rückte, was sich nicht zuletzt in bis heute bekannten Bildtraditionen („Batseba im Bade") niederschlug.

Prominenter als diese moralische Ambivalenz des Sünders und Büßers David war in der Forschung des 20. Jahrhunderts die Ambivalenz seiner Beziehung zu Jonathan, einer Liebe „wundersamer als Frauenliebe" (2. Samuel 1, 26). Viel ist geschrieben worden über Freundschaft, Homoerotik, Homosexualität und andere Konzepte, die dabei helfen sollten, diese Liebe zu verstehen. Es mag daher überraschen, wie knapp und unaufgeregt Karras diese Beziehung darstellt, die sie etwas leger, aber inhaltlich überzeugend als *bromance* tituliert. Man kann das die Verfügbarkeit neuer Deutungskategorien nennen, vor allem aber spricht es für die Reife des Fachs, wenn weniger Aufregung um möglicherweise positive Konnotationen homosexueller Handlungen herrscht und mehr systematische Untersuchung von „Männlichkeit" geboten wird als das jeweils in der älteren Literatur der 1970er und 1980er Jahre der Fall war. Fast ein halbes Jahrhundert nach dem Erscheinen von John Boswells wirkmächtigem Werk „Social Tolerance", in dem die mittelalterliche Rezeption von David und Jonathan ohne viel Federlesens als Beleg für die Akzeptanz männlicher Homosexualität gedeutet wurde,[1] ist die Forschung ganz offensichtlich weitergekommen. Dazu gehört, dass Karras in ihrer Untersuchung nicht nur dem jungen Krieger, dem mächtigen König, dem potenten Ehemann (und Ehebrecher) und dem mäßig erfolgreichen Vater Raum gibt, sondern auch dem Dichter und Sänger David. Anders als in der Gegenwart war im

---

[1] John Boswell, Christianity, Social Tolerance, and Homosexuality. Gay People in Western Europe from the Beginning of the Christian Era to the Fourteenth Century, Chicago, Ill. 1980, 238: „Increased familiarity with and tolerance of gay people and their feelings by persons who were not themselves gay is nowhere more poignantly illustrated than in the use of the theme of David and Jonathan by Peter Abelard."

Mittelalter vermutlich das Harfespiel das prominenteste Bild, das Leser*innen mit dem Namen David verbanden. Gleichzeitig waren Musizieren und Tanzen (anders als das Komponieren) Tätigkeiten, die weder mit Männlichkeit noch mit hohem sozialen Status verbunden waren. Die exegetische Tradition konnte diesen Aktivitäten zwar positive Seiten abgewinnen (Demut), aber wie Karras herausarbeitet, ist in den Quellen ein gewisses Unbehagen erkennbar, dass König David Tätigkeiten ausübte, die man eher mit Sklavinnen und Chorknaben assoziierte. Das Kapitel belegt damit einerseits, dass vormoderne Männlichkeit nicht monolithisch war, andererseits aber auch, dass es deutliche Konstanten gab, wenn über Jahrhunderte Autoren ganz unterschiedlicher Herkunft immer wieder das Musizieren und Tanzen in ähnlicher Weise als Problem ansahen.

Gleiches lässt sich als Fazit festhalten: Karras' Buch besticht vor allem durch die kenntnisreiche Darstellung sowohl christlicher als auch jüdischer Zugänge zur Figur des biblischen David und belegt, dass „Männlichkeit" durchaus sehr Verschiedenes meinen konnte; zugleich zeigt sich aber auch, dass im gesamten Untersuchungszeitraum gewisse Grundvorstellungen einer kriegerischen Männlichkeit in vielen Milieus geteilt wurden.

„Thou Art the Man" ist ein gelungenes Werk, dem man viele Leser*innen wünscht. Kritikpunkte lassen sich trotzdem finden: Im Einzelfall hätte man sich oft eine ausführlichere Diskussion gewünscht, insgesamt ist das aber als Kompliment an die Darstellung zu verstehen, die Lust auf mehr macht. Das Literaturverzeichnis ist ganz überwiegend englischsprachig, aber die Quellen weisen eine beeindruckende Vielfalt an Sprachen, Medien und Kontexten auf. Jüdische Exegese und christliche Buchmalerei, mittelfranzösische Dichtungen und lateinische Predigten werden in teils dichter Folge zitiert. Gerade angesichts der erfreulichen Berücksichtigung bildlicher Quellen wären gute Abbildungen (farbig, hochaufgelöst und urheberrechtsfrei) wünschenswert gewesen. Die Druckkosten allein können nicht der Grund für die Mängel in diesem Bereich – die wohl in der Verantwortung des Verlags liegen – gewesen sein, denn auch die Bebilderung der digitalen Version ist schwarz-weiß gehalten. In mehreren Legenden wird zudem, was sicher nicht Karras anzulasten ist, *copyfraud* reproduziert, das heißt irrige Behauptungen von Urheberrecht unter Missachtung der geltenden Gesetze. Immerhin sind die Quellennachweise präzise, so dass man in vielen Fällen bessere Abbildungen im Internet finden kann. Schöner wäre aber eine angemessene Bebilderung des Buches selbst gewesen. Diese Kritikpunkte schmälern aber nicht den positiven Gesamteindruck: Karras hat eine innovative und gut lesbar gehaltene Fallstudie vorgelegt, die einen facettenreichen Eindruck vormoderner Männlichkeit vermittelt.

Christof Rolker, Bamberg

Gabriela Signori u. Claudia Zey (Hg.), **Regentinnen und andere Stellvertreterfiguren. Vom 10. bis zum 15. Jahrhundert** (= Schriften des Historischen Kollegs, Kolloquien 111), Berlin/Boston: De Gruyter Oldenbourg 2023, 210 S., EUR 64,95, ISBN 978-3-11-099216-8.

Der aus einer Tagung im Herbst 2021 hervorgegangene Band ist der Frage gewidmet, wie Frauen im Hoch- und Spätmittelalter stellvertretend Herrschaft für ihre königlichen beziehungsweise fürstlichen Söhne oder Ehemänner ausüben konnten. Das Phänomen weiblicher Regentschaft und anderer Vertretungstypen wird in neun Beiträgen (zuzüglich einer Einführung) und mit Blick auf Beispiele aus ganz Europa untersucht. Der geografische Fokus reicht von der iberischen Halbinsel und Süditalien über Frankreich, England und das römisch-deutsche Reich bis nach Osteuropa; als Vergleichsfolie wird mehrfach das Königreich Jerusalem herangezogen. Der Band schließt damit gezielt eine Forschungslücke und schafft Ansätze für weitere Untersuchungen, da die mehrfach vergleichende Perspektive, das heißt der überzeitliche und überregionale Blick auf unterschiedliche Typen stellvertretender Herrschaft, bislang noch nicht angewandt wurde.

Wie die Einführung der Herausgeberinnen Gabriela Signori und Claudia Zey zeigt, wurden für den Band mehrere prägnante Leitfragen konzipiert: Konkret wird gefragt, welche verschiedenen Typen von Regentschaft erkennbar sind, unter welchen Umständen sie jeweils eingerichtet wurden und welche Kräfte auf die Entscheidung für eine solche Stellvertreterschaft einwirkten. Ferner geht es darum, wie eine Regentschaft im Hinblick auf andere „Formen reginaler Herrschaft" eingeordnet werden kann und ob die herrschenden Frauen eventuell sogar überzeitliche dynastische Interessen im Blick hatten. Eine weitere Frage betrifft die Kategorie „Geschlecht" und ihre Relevanz in den verschiedenen Regentschaftstypen (S. 7).

Das Panorama exemplarischer Analysen wird von Anne Foerster eröffnet, die sich mit Herrscherwitwen und „dem Risiko eines fremden Herrschers" (S. 11) befasst. Anhand von hochmittelalterlichen Beispielen aus dem römisch-deutschen Reich, England und Frankreich untermauert sie die These, dass die zeitgenössische „Skepsis gegenüber verwitweten Stellvertreterinnen" nicht zuletzt darin begründet gewesen sei, dass das Fehlen eines Königs „ein Einfallstor für Außenstehende" (S. 11), etwa über eine erneute Ehe oder über Affären der Regentin, geboten habe. Zum Vergleich wird das Königreich Jerusalem mit der 1212 begonnenen Regentschaft Johanns von Brienne für seine Tochter Isabella herangezogen. Im Mittelpunkt von Linda Dohmens Aufsatz stehen Judith, die Witwe des 955 verstorbenen Herzogs Heinrich I. von Bayern, und ihr Wirken zugunsten ihres Sohnes Heinrich II. Zuerst wird eruiert, welche Kenntnisse zu Judith überhaupt vorliegen und wie sie als Regentin in der Überlieferung bezeichnet wird. Darüber hinaus geht es um drei weitere Frauen und Zeitgenossinnen Judiths sowie um ihre Rollen als verwitwete Mütter minderjähriger Herrschaftsnachfolger, wobei herausgestellt wird, dass die Verwendung des Titels *dux* auch für Frauen in jener

Zeit nicht unüblich war (S. 47). Marianne Wenzel legt ein Augenmerk auf Sachsen und befasst sich mit Kaiserin Richenza, die eine Regentschaft für ihren Ehemann Lothar III. ausübte, sowie mit deren Tochter Gertrud, die nach dem Tod Herzog Heinrichs des Stolzen als Regentin für den gemeinsamen Sohn Heinrich den Löwen auftrat. Beleuchtet werden die Ausgangslagen für die Stellvertreterfunktionen, die konkrete Ausgestaltung dieser Positionen und mögliche Vorbilder, wobei deutlich wird, dass Mutter und Tochter in ganz verschiedenen Situationen Regentschaftsverantwortung übernahmen und entsprechend über unterschiedliche Handlungsspielräume verfügten.

Im Mittelpunkt von Julia Beckers Aufsatz steht die auf die Jahre 1101 bis 1112 zu datierende Regentschaft der Gräfin Adelasia von Kalabrien und Sizilien für ihre Söhne Simon und schließlich Roger II. Die Quellenlage vermittelt den Eindruck einer „weitreichenden sozialen Akzeptanz" der Regentschaft der Witwe (S. 82), was in ähnlicher Form auch das Wirken anderer Frauen in der Region auszeichnete. Auch wenn Konflikte nicht ausblieben, lässt sich Adelasias Handeln insgesamt als das „einer politisch aktiven Regentin" umschreiben, die „eigenverantwortlich" agierte und nicht nur versuchte, die Rechte des unmündigen Sohns zu wahren (S. 79). Cristina Andenna befasst sich mit dem Königreich Sizilien-Neapel und der dortigen Rolle der Vikarin, die den angevinischen königlichen Ehefrauen ab dem Ende des 13. und Beginn des 14. Jahrhunderts zukam. Nach einem Blick auf die Genese des Generalvikariats in der Region werden die Königinnen Maria von Ungarn und Sancia von Majorca thematisiert. An diesen Beispielen zeigt sich, dass die verschiedenen Aspekte, die im Handeln der beiden Königinnen erkennbar sind, „weit über die traditionelle Auffassung der *consors*" hinausgingen (S. 108) und die Frauen nötigenfalls auch stellvertretend Herrschaftsaufgaben übernahmen. Ebenfalls auf den Mittelmeerraum konzentriert sich Sebastian Roebert mit seinem Aufsatz zur Krone Aragón und der Frage, ob die dort übliche „weibliche Stellvertretung" als „Modellfall" angesehen werden könne (S. 111). Analysiert werden die Statthalterschaften von Frauen vom 13. bis zum 15. Jahrhundert anhand der sie begründenden Ernennungen und ihrer „diplomatische[n] Charakteristika", der „verwendete[n] Terminologie und Registrierung" sowie der den Frauen „verliehenen Kompetenzen" (S. 120). Auch wenn dies noch keine sicheren Aussagen zum tatsächlichen Handeln der Königinnen ermöglicht, bieten die umfangreichen, die Ernennungen präzise umreißenden Quellen die Chance, die Verhältnisse in der Krone Aragón detailliert zu beschreiben und die Tür für Vergleiche mit anderen Regionen zu öffnen.

Unter dem Titel „Lenken im Hintergrund" (S. 137) steht ein Sonderfall, der sich gerade nicht mit rechtshistorischen Termini fassen lässt (S. 152), im Zentrum von Eric Böhmes Beitrag. Agnes von Courtenay konnte nicht offiziell das Amt einer Regentin für ihren Sohn, König Balduin IV. von Jerusalem, übernehmen, wohl aber in seinem engen Umfeld gemeinsam mit ihrem Bruder Joscelin III. von Courtenay Einfluss ausüben. Nachgezeichnet werden Agnes' Verbindung mit König Amalrich, ihr Engagement am Hof des an einer chronischen Krankheit leidenden Balduin und die Bemühungen darum, die Thronfolge für die eigenen Nachkommen zu sichern. Auch wenn Agnes keine rechtlich begründete Stellung einnahm und ihre Bedeutung am Hof auf ihrer Position als Balduins Mutter sowie auf personellen Kontakten beruhte, wird deutlich, dass sie sich behaupten und ihren Nachkommen Herrschaftsrechte sichern konnte.

Dem „Selbstverständnis" und der „Herrschaftspraxis schlesischer Regentinnen im 13. Jahrhundert" (S. 157) widmet sich Julia Burkhardt. Auf einleitende Überlegungen zu Analyseansätzen sowie zum Umgang mit den unterschiedlichen Quellenarten folgt ein Überblick zur Gestaltung der dynastischen Sukzession in der polnischen Geschichte zu Beginn des 13. Jahrhunderts, ehe zwei Beispiele näher behandelt werden: Viola von Oppeln-Ratibor, die als Witwe Herzog Kasimirs I. eine Regentschaft für die gemeinsamen Söhne ausübte, und Anna von Böhmen, die Witwe Herzog Heinrichs II. und Mutter von fünf Söhnen, die den Inhalten der chronikalischen Überlieferung zufolge als „Mediatorin und integrative Kraft" (S. 174) angesehen werden kann. Den Abschluss des Bandes bildet Maike Sachs Beitrag zur Großfürstin Sofija Vitovtovna von Moskau, die ab dem Tod ihres Mannes 1425 die Regentschaft für ihren Sohn Vasilij II. übernahm. Hier zeigen sich die Bedeutung unterschiedlicher Sukzessionsregelungen, das heißt des Seniorats und der Primogenitur, sowie der großfürstlichen Testamente, die Einfluss auf die Gestaltung der Herrschaft haben konnten. Eine Regentin musste sich gegenüber den übrigen Dynastiemitgliedern behaupten, eigene Kontakte etablieren und den Status des Sohnes absichern. Auch nach der Volljährigkeit des Herrschaftsnachfolgers blieb die Mutter am Hof eine feste und familienpolitisch relevante Größe.

Der Sammelband bietet somit einen thematisch äußerst umfangreichen und vielschichtigen Einblick in das Phänomen der Stellvertreterschaft von Frauen in unterschiedlichen Regionen des mittelalterlichen Europas. Das breite Panorama zeigt, wie wichtig es ist, die Rollen von Frauen am Hof und im Kontext der stellvertretenden Herrschaft in vergleichender, zeitlich wie räumlich übergreifender Perspektive zu beleuchten. Dies leistet der Band in vorbildlicher Weise und bietet zugleich Anknüpfungspunkte für weitere Forschungen. Ein Register hätte die Erschließung des Bandes nach Personen noch etwas vereinfacht; die englischen Abstracts sowie die umfangreichen Abbildungen runden die Beiträge aber sehr gut ab und erleichtern – wie etwa die als besonders übersichtlich hervorzuhebenden Stammtafeln – das Verständnis der allesamt äußerst lesenswerten Aufsätze.

Frederieke Maria Schnack, Würzburg

Andrea Stieldorf, Linda Dohmen, Irina Dumitrescu u. Ludwig D. Morenz (Hg.), **Geschlecht macht Herrschaft – Interdisziplinäre Studien zu vormoderner Macht und Herrschaft** (= Macht und Herrschaft, Bd. 15), V&R unipress, Göttingen u. a. 2021, 380 S., 28 Abb., EUR 62,–, ISBN 978-3-8471-1343-0.

Der hier rezensierte Sammelband geht auf die internationale Tagung „Geschlecht macht Herrschaft. Gender Power Sovereignity" zurück, die vom 30. September 2019 bis zum 2. Oktober 2019 im Rahmen des Sonderforschungsbereichs (SFB) 1167 „Macht und Herrschaft. Vormoderne Konfigurationen in transkultureller Perspektive" in Bonn stattfand. Zeitlich und räumlich umfasst der Band ein weites Spektrum: Die Beiträge reichen vom Alten Ägypten (5. Jahrtausend vor Christus) bis ins europäische 17. Jahrhundert; auch die chinesische Geschichte wird einbezogen. Nach der Einleitung des Herausgeber*innenteams, die sich vornehmlich mit definitorischen Fragen der Schlüsselbegriffe „Geschlecht", „Macht" und „Herrschaft" befasst, die Relevanz des Themas begründet sowie die einzelnen Beiträge vorstellt und kontextualisiert, setzt sich der Aufsatz von Doris Gutsmiedl-Schümann mit „Gender Archaeology – zwischen archäologischem Befund und (re)konstruiertem Lebensbild" auseinander. Die Autorin stellt fest, dass die in ihrem Beitrag vorgestellten Beispiele sich mit den Kategorien „Geschlecht", „Macht" und „Herrschaft" und, wenn auch in Abstufungen, mit den archäologischen Befunden verbinden ließen. Am schwierigsten sei dies bei der Kategorie „Herrschaft". Hier sei definitiv ein Zusammenspiel mit schriftlichen Quellen nötig, um die archäologischen Quellen zum Sprechen zu bringen.

Katharina Gahbler zeigt in ihrem Aufsatz „ ,…wenn weibliche Schwäche siegt und männliche Kraft schändlich unterliegt'. Bourdieus ,Männliche Herrschaft' und die jungfräulichen Märtyrerinnen bei Hrotsvit von Gandersheim", dass Hrotsvit zwar als Hagiographin durchaus nachhaltig und ,mächtig' habe agieren können. Sie weist aber andererseits auch darauf hin, dass diese das christliche Weltbild, das als göttliche Heilsordnung und Herrschaftssystem mit einem allmächtigen göttlichen Vater stark männlich und patristisch geprägt gewesen sei, dabei nicht hätte überwinden können. Somit habe Hrotsvit ihren Leserinnen und Lesern keine „story of overpowerment" geboten, sondern sei den Denkstrukturen dieses Weltbildes verbunden geblieben.

Regina Toepfer („Fertilität und Macht. Die Reproduktionspflicht mittelalterlicher Herrscherinnen und Herrscher") untersucht Fertilität bei männlichen und weiblichen Herrschenden. Wer nie die Gelegenheit hatte, Toepfers beeindruckendes Werk über „Kinderlosigkeit. Ersehnte, verweigerte und bereute Elternschaft im Mittelalter" (Stuttgart 2000) zu lesen, sollte sich den hier zu besprechenden Band allein wegen dieses Beitrags besorgen. Fertilität, so Toepfer, sei eine Frage der Macht; sie versteht die Fähigkeit, Kinder zu bekommen, nicht als eine natürliche Anlage, einen biologischen Drang oder eine anthropologische Konstante und auch nicht als eine persönliche Entscheidung, sondern als eine soziale und politische Angelegenheit. Im Einzelnen untersucht Toepfer anhand von hoch- und spätmittelalterlichem Quellenmaterial (1) die Macht der Gesetze, (2) die Macht der Religion, (3) die Macht der Medizin und (4) die Macht des Erzählens, um den Faktor der Fertilität in der mittelalterlichen Gesellschaft zu ermessen. Dabei kommt sie keineswegs zu dem erwartbaren Ergebnis (Kinderlosigkeit als Gottesstrafe), sondern durchaus auch zu überraschenden Einsichten. Michel Foucault, so Toepfer am Ende ihres Beitrags zusammenfassend, habe auf die vielfältigen Effekte, Instrumente und Einflüsse der Macht hingewiesen; eine entscheidende Bedeutung habe er dabei stets jenen Diskursen zugeschrieben, die vorgegeben hätten, auf welche Weise über Sexualität gedacht, gesprochen und mit ihr umgegangen werde. Laut Toepfer sei Fertilität wie Sexualität ein „politisches Dispositiv" (S. 195), bei dem sich biologische und kulturelle Aspekte untrennbar miteinander verschränkt hätten. Sprache und Sprachgebrauch versteht die Autorin dabei weniger als ein Instrument patriarchaler Herrschaft. Vielmehr betrachtet sie das Reden über Unfruchtbarkeit als ein Instrument, durch das Reproduktion für Herrscherinnen und Herrscher zur Pflicht erklärt werde und Kinderlose dazu angeleitet würden, Passionsgefühle auszubilden. Dass es im Mittelalter allerdings nicht nur das ‚feudalpolitische', das heißt radikal auf die Bewahrung der Herrschaft innerhalb einer Dynastie ausgerichtete Paradigma, sondern auch konkurrierende Diskurse über Unfruchtbarkeit gegeben habe, belege die Legende von Kaiser Heinrich II. und Kaiserin Kunigunde exemplarisch. Ob das Leben kinderloser Paare als Diskriminierungs-, Krankheits-, Erlösungs- oder Erwählungsgeschichte erzählt werde, hinge von übergeordneten Deutungs-, Erzähl- und Gattungsschemata ab.

Ganz besonders wichtig, da ebenfalls viele grundsätzliche, über den einzelnen Fall hinausweisende Sachverhalte klärend, ist ferner der Beitrag der viel zu früh verstorbenen Alheydis Plassmann (1969–2022): „Weibliche Erbfolge. Möglichkeiten und Grenzen weiblicher Herrschaftsausübung bei fehlenden männlichen Nachfolgern im Hochmittelalter". Plassmanns Aufsatz widmet sich vorrangig der englischen Geschichte. Sie befasst sich etwa mit der berühmten Empress Matilda (†1167), der Erbtochter des 1135 verstorbenen Königs Heinrich I. von England (gerade die gegen sie vorgenommene Königserhebung Stephans von Blois zeige die Bedeutung der weiblichen Linie, denn seine Abstammung von Wilhelm dem Eroberer habe in der Argumentation eine große Rolle gespielt, S. 305). Darüber hinaus geht es in Plassmanns Studie auch um Eleonore von Aquitanien, bei der die Autorin auch auf die Möglichkeiten eigener Herrschaftsübung in der Witwenzeit eingeht (S. 304). Plassmann kommt insgesamt zu einem ausgewogenen Gesamtbild. Sie meint, dass die größere Handlungsfähigkeit der Erbtochter – in diesem Fall Eleonores von Aquitanien – sicher etwas sei, das sich durch politische Entwicklungen habe ergeben können, dass dieses Phänomen aber nicht unbedingt angestrebt worden sei. Ziel sei vielmehr die Kontrolle über die fragliche Herrschaft gewesen. Seitens des regionalen Adels und der Familie selbst hieß dies, den Erhalt der Eigenständigkeit sicherzustellen. Die uneindeutige Situation, das heißt, die Frage, wer genau eigentlich die Herrschaft innehatte, habe den Erbtöchtern durchaus ‚Handlungsspielräume' eröffnet, dennoch seien sie der Logik des Ausbalancierens zwischen zentralen und regionalen Interessen und dem Zwang zum Erhalt der vorhandenen Institution unterworfen geblieben.

In einem weiteren Beitrag des Bandes beschäftigt sich Elizabeth Robertson („Pity would be no more. Compassion for Lucrece in Augustine's ‚City of God', Gower's ‚Confessio Amantis' and Chaucers's ‚Legend of Good Women'") mit dem Konzept der Frau in Geoffrey Chaucers „Legend of Good Woman", das sie vor allem im Hinblick auf Chaucers explizite Betonung des weiblichen Urteilsvermögens würdigt; das deutlich wahrnehmbare Konzept stehe sehr im Gegensatz zur Rolle der Frau in Chaucers berühmten „Canterbury Tales", in denen bei aller Bandbreite der Charaktere das Bild der Frau wesentlich unklarer erscheine.

Uroš Matić („He is looking at Bowmen like women. Gender as a Frame of War in New Kingdom Egypt", ca. 1539–1077 BC) untersucht die Feminisierung von Feindbildern in Texten und Bildern im Alten Ägypten zur Zeit des Neuen Reiches (1550 bis 1070 v.Chr., 18. bis 20. Dynastie). Dabei arbeitet er heraus, dass das ‚framing' des Feindes als ‚weiblich' diesen in der öffentlichen Wahrnehmung im Vergleich mit dem ägyptischen König, dessen Männlichkeit als „Hyper-Männlichkeit" schlechthin galt, in eine untergeordnete Position bringen sollte.

Jennifer D. Thibodeaux plädiert in ihrem Aufsatz „Pierre de la Roque. An Exemplar of Crisis Masculinity in Fifteenth-Century Normandy" dafür, insbesondere Herrschaftswechsel als lohnende zukünftige Forschungsfelder der Geschlechtergeschichte anzusehen, da diese – wie von ihr anhand der durch England im Hundertjährigen Krieg eroberten Normandie gezeigt – häufig auch eine große soziale Dynamik erzeugten und auf den verschiedensten Ebenen Frauen in Machtpositionen bringen konnten, die ihnen ansonsten in einem männerdominierten Umfeld versagt geblieben wären. Unter dem Titel „Von pointierter Maskulinität im Ägypten des späten dritten Jahrtausends v.Chr. Zur funerären Inszenierung des Potentaten Anchtifi als übermenschlichem ‚Manns-Kerl'" analysiert Ludwig D. Morenz die funeräre Inszenierung des Mannes im Ägypten des dritten Jahrtausends vor Christus. Anchtifis Vision seiner Männlichkeit, so Morenz, als der seiner irdischen Entsprechung zum Sonnen- und Schöpfergott hebe auf eine herausragende, geradezu einmalig übermenschliche, sogar mythologisch inszenierte Männlichkeit ab. Im sozio-kulturellen Rahmen seiner Grabinschrift, die vom Autor genau untersucht wird, ziele die so überragende Männlichkeit dieses „Manns-Kerl[s] ohne seines gleichen" nicht etwa auf Sex, sondern auf Gender.

Anne Behnke Kinney („Empress Lü. China's First Female Ruler") arbeitet anhand des Lebens und des politischen Wirkens der chinesischen Kaiserin Lü (ca. 241–180 v.Chr.) heraus, wie im China dieser Zeit eine Herrscherin durchaus dazu in der Lage war, Macht auszuüben, wenn diese dazu diente, den politischen *status quo* wiederherzustellen.

Alex McAuley „Daughters, Princesses, and Agents of Empire, Royal Women as Transcultural Agents in Seleucid Empire" stellt in Bezug auf das seleukidische Königtum fest, dass die Konzepte „Königtum" und „Legitimität" Aspekte sowohl des männlichen wie des weiblichen Geschlechts aufweise und dass beide Elemente vorhanden sein müssten, damit ‚das' Königtum als komplett betrachtet werden könne. Konsequenterweise schlägt MacAuley vor, dass es nicht heißen sollte „Geschlecht macht Herrschaft", sondern „Geschlechter machen Herrschaft" (S. 238).

Wichtig ist auch der literaturwissenschaftliche Beitrag von Andrea Sieber: „Zwischen Macht und Ohnmacht. Überlegungen zu den Königinnen Kriemhild und Brünhild im ‚Nibelungenlied'". Die Autorin kommt zu dem überzeugenden Schluss, dass die im Nibelungenlied auftretenden Königinnen ohne zum Schwert zu greifen, allein dadurch, dass sie es gewagt hätten, ihre eigentlich legitimen Machtansprüche unter sich auszuhandeln, eine in der damaligen Männerwelt sensible Grenze überschritten hätten. Sie hätten damit die ihnen auferlegten patriarchalen Strukturen an einem ganz besonders neuralgischen Punkt – der normsetzenden Instanz des männlichen Überlegenheitsdiskurses – auf bedrohliche Weise in Frage gestellt.

Birgit Ulrike Münch („Idealmutter für ‚Hofzwerge' und Volk – Witwe im Habit der Macht. Rollenmodelle und Agitationsräume Isabella Clara Eugenias, 1566–1633") untersucht die Agitationsräume der Statthalterin der Niederlande Isabella Clara Eugenias und die (selbstverantwortete wie ihr zugeteilte) weibliche Inszenierung von Macht und stellt fest, dass Isabella ganz verschiedene Rollen einnahm (kinderlose Herrscherin, aber auch Idealmutter des Volkes; die Nonne; die umsichtige Regentin der friedvollen Regierung etc.). In der Rolle als Monstranzträgerin auf einem Bild von Peter Paul Rubens (S. 291, Abb. 6) zeige sie sich gar in einer Rolle, die über den Tod hinausweise.

Elena Woodacre („Obstacles and Opportunities for Female Power and Sovereignity") beschäftigt sich – hauptsächlich anhand von Beispielen aus dem kastilischen und aragonesischen Hoch- und Spätmittelalter – mit der faszinierenden Frage weiblicher Thronfolge und regierender Königinnen. Sie veranschaulicht, dass es situationsbedingte Faktoren gewesen seien, die für die Übernahme der Königsherrschaft durch eine Frau verantwortlich zu machen seien. Als der klassische „Plan B" („second choice successor") habe es so vieler unterstützender Faktoren wie möglich bedurft, um eine Nachfolge zu ermöglichen.

Von zentraler Bedeutung ist auch der Beitrag von Anne Foerster über die Thematisierung von Genderfragen in der mittelalterlichen Geschichtsschreibung („Gender and Authority. The Entanglement of Two Concepts in High Medieval Historiography"). Foerster konzentriert sich in ihrer Auswertung vor allem auf die Historiographen William of Malmesbury, Roger of Wendover und Matthew Paris aus dem 12. und 13. Jahrhundert. Sie kommt dabei zu der überzeugenden Einsicht, dass in den Werken der von ihr untersuchten Autoren die Ausübung von Herrschaft eindeutig als Vorrecht männlicher Herrscher konzeptionalisiert werde. Das historiographische Konzept der „Weiblichkeit" (*femininity*) habe sich bei den von ihr untersuchten Geschichtsschreibern mit dem Konzept „herrscherlicher Autorität" nicht gedeckt.

Die meisten Beiträge des Bandes, der vor allem durch seine große zeitliche und thematische Bandbreite besticht, zeigen auf eindrucksvolle Weise, dass in der Vormoderne Konzepte wie „Macht" und „Herrschaft" eindeutig ‚männlich' konnotiert gewesen sind. Der ‚ideale Herrscher' ist stets ‚männlich' gedacht worden; ‚weibliche' Elemente oder Akteurinnen hingegen sind im Rahmen vormoderner Theoretisierungen zwar vorhanden – zum Teil sogar auffällig stark –, sind aber der Herrschaft eher ‚sekundär' zugeordnet worden. Dabei erscheint der ‚männliche' Standard in der Regel nicht eindeutig markiert worden zu sein. Dennoch haben auch unter diesen eher ungünstigen Voraussetzungen einzelne Frauen umfangreiche ‚Handlungsspielräume' erlangen können, die von mehreren Faktoren abhängig gewesen sind. Überaus hilfreich ist das Personenregister, das ein schnelles Auffinden der Akteurinnen und Akteure des Bandes ermöglicht.

Jörg Schwarz, Innsbruck

Abstracts

Isabella Lazzarini, "Two Bodies and One Soul". Power Games between Spouses in Northern Italian Principalities (Fifteenth Century)

The Italian peninsula in the late Middle Ages and early modern period consisted of a wide range of different political entities. The result was a rather distinctive political environment, in which several principalities, mainly arising from communal cities, played a crucial role. Their authority was built on the initiative of both men and women, in sometimes different but equally crucial ways. A careful study of the role of the princesses in late medieval Italy reveals the traits and mechanisms of what was born and structured as a shared authority, due to its only partially legitimate origin (these were dynasties without any legitimate title to rule over the cities from which they emerged) and its inchoate nature (these were political systems far removed from the solidity and awareness of monarchical or imperial models). The article focuses on a range of case studies covering the fifteenth century over three generations (from the early fifteenth century to the years of the Italian Wars) and considers the principalities of the Po plain and their allies, from Milan to Savoy, from Mantua or Ferrara to Pesaro or Urbino. Culture, power, devotion, wealth, age, luck or misfortune all played a role in the lives and successes (or difficulties) of the couples we examine.

Julia Burkhardt, Power Couples in Central Europe around 1500

In premodern Europe, the political and cultural influence of royal couples was considerable. However, previous studies have focused on the role and impact of individual kings or queens. This article thus analyses the forms of joint and competitive rule in the context of contemporary reflections and representations of royal "power couples". The article presents examples from Poland and Hungary, which are particularly suitable for comparison in terms of similarities (for example the longevity of the rulers) and striking differences (for example marriage and later family constellations): the Polish rulers Elisabeth of Habsburg (1436–1505) and Casimir IV (1427–1492), and the Hungarian rulers Beatrice of Aragon (1457–1508) and Matthias "Corvinus" Hunyadi (1443–1490). Despite the existence of conflicts and competition, these couples were not only able to exert outstanding political, social and/or cultural influence; they also used mutual influences between the possibilities of joint rule and premodern concepts of gender and gendered role models. The article argues that approaching "power couples" helps avoid the construction of political gender dichotomies and stimulates further discussion on the dynamics of gender and power in premodern Europe.

Elodie Lecuppre-Desjardin, Foreign Princesses in the Service of the Great Principality of Burgundy: Delegations of Power in Favour of Duchesses in the Fifteenth Century

In the territories that made up the ancient Burgundian Low Countries, even before the arrival of the dukes of Valois, who gradually built up the Great Principality of Burgundy, marriages negotiated with *suo jure* princes and princesses were the origin of numerous international alliances. The arrival of these men and women from more or less distant lands does not seem to have disrupted the exercise of power and was part of a common diplomatic logic. If the local populations preferred native sovereigns capable of becoming their "natural and feared lord" (*naturel et redouté seigneur*), assimilation nevertheless took place. The aim of this study is to take a comparative approach to the delegation of power entrusted to foreign princesses such as Margaret of Bavaria (1372–1424), wife of John the Fearless, Isabella of Portugal (1397–1471), wife of Philip the Good, and Margaret of York (1446–1503), wife of Charles the Bold. Despite their rather strong personalities, the education of these women, their entourage and the need for the prince to entrust them with responsibilities within a "composite principality", tended to give rise to the model of princesses whose activities had to be considered as an important factor within the princely couples' rule. By integrating the political agency of these Burgundian princesses into the norms and structures of their time, the study reveals a more subtle but nonetheless firm assertion of their authority.

Christina Lutter and Christof Muigg, Gendered Power Politics in a Nascent Empire. The Case of Maximilian of Habsburg (1459–1519) and Mary of Burgundy (1457–1482)

Around 1500 Europe's political landscape saw major territorial changes brought about by long-term conflicts and dynastic politics. In the heart of the continent, the reign of Maximilian I of Habsburg is a case in point. As acting king (from 1493) and emperor (from 1508) of the Holy Roman Empire, he greatly enhanced his family's dynastic position. His own two marriages, to Mary of Burgundy (arranged by their parents) and to Bianca Maria Sforza of Milan, bear witness to this, as do the far-reaching dynastic projects involving the Spanish and Bohemian progeny. Dynastic politics was a family affair. Kin of both sexes – spouses, sons and daughters, aunts and nieces – were key partners in the common dynastic agenda. In addition, both male and female rulers were legitimised and accompanied by formal councils and supported by officials and advisors, courtiers and staff of both sexes. Likewise, each ruler's political agency was enabled and constrained by cultural traditions and educational norms that were deeply gendered. This contribution focuses on the impact of gendered representations on the early reign of Maximilian himself and his first wife Mary. It argues that gender as an analytical category not only helps to systematically compare representations of female and male rulers within complex power relations: as a relational category, it also allows us to open up gendered binaries to the practical dimensions of premodern rule, which was always shared by various individuals and representative bodies.

Oliver Auge and Laura Potzuweit, Gendered Celibacy and Rulership. Three Examples from the Late Medieval Baltic Rim

Given the importance of marriage as a stabilising factor in securing succession, this article examines the significance of celibacy in the late medieval Baltic Sea region through three ruler figures: Waldemar IV of Denmark, Margaret I of Denmark and Henry V of Mecklenburg. The Danish king Waldemar remained unmarried after the death of his wife, which caused concern in political circles all the way to the emperor, as his lack of male heirs led to an uncertainty that affected the entire region. His daughter Margarethe, on the other hand, who remained unmarried and childless after the death of her husband and son, used her widowhood to consolidate her power in the three Scandinavian kingdoms, in particular as the architect of the Kalmar Union. Duke Henry V of Mecklenburg refrained from a third marriage for decades to avoid jeopardising the succession of his two sons, but married again in old age after the death of his eldest and the mental illness of his youngest heir. In view of this, the article argues that celibacy was not necessarily a sign of weakness, but could also be used as a strategy to maintain or even increase power. For women in particular, it opened up new room for manoeuvre, especially if they already held a strong dynastic position.

Sabine Veits-Falk, Official Female Doctors in Bosnia and Herzegovina (1892–1918). Politics, Medicine, Culture and Gender

Between 1891 and 1918, the Austro-Hungarian Empire implemented the concept of public health officers in the occupied and then annexed provinces of Bosnia and Herzegovina – not least for imperialist political purposes. As Muslim women refused to be examined by male doctors for religious and cultural reasons, the Austrian authorities decided to employ female Austro-Hungarian graduates from Swiss universities as official female doctors. The category of gender, which had been a criterion for excluding women from academic medicine in their own country, was used here as a factor in targeted recruitment and labour migration. The primary aim was to combat disease, improve medical care and promote the health of women, especially the Muslim female population. In addition, the state charged the female doctors with an 'Austrian cultural' mission as a further field of action.

Anschriften der Autor*innen

Christina Antenhofer, Paris Lodron Universität Salzburg, Fachbereich Geschichte, Rudolfskai 42, 5020 Salzburg, Österreich – christina.antenhofer@plus.ac.at

Oliver Auge, Christian-Albrechts-Universität zu Kiel, Historisches Seminar, Abteilung für Regionalgeschichte, Leibnizstraße 8, 24118 Kiel, Deutschland – oauge@email.uni-kiel.de

Julia Burkhardt, Ludwig-Maximilians-Universität München, Historisches Seminar, Mittelalterliche Geschichte, Geschwister-Scholl-Platz 1, 80539 München, Deutschland – julia.burkhardt@lmu.de

Sandro Guzzi-Heeb, Departement of History, Bâtiment Anthropole, Office 5176, 1015 Lausanne, Suisse – sandro.guzzi-heeb@unil.ch

Julia Heinemann, University of Antwerp, Department of History, City Campus – S. J. 007, Sint-Jacobsmarkt 9–13, 2000 Antwerpen, Belgium – Julia.Heinemann@uantwerpen.be

Vanina Kopp, Universität Erfurt (Campus), Historisches Seminar, Nordhäuser Str. 63, 99089 Erfurt, Deutschland – vanina.kopp@uni-erfurt.de

Isabella Lazzarini, University of Turin, Department of Historical Studies, Via S. Ottavio 20, 20124 Turin, Italy – isabella.lazzarini@unito.it

Elodie Lecuppre-Desjardin, Université de Lille, IRHiS (UMR 8529), Domaine universitaire du Pont-de-Bois, 59650 Villeneuve d'Ascq, France – elodie.lecuppre@univ-lille.fr

Christina Lutter, Universität Wien, Institut für Geschichte, Universitätsring 1, 1010 Wien, Österreich – christina.lutter@univie.ac.at

Ulrike Marlow, Berlin-Brandenburgische Akademie der Wissenschaften, Akademienvorhaben „Anpassungsstrategien der späten mitteleuropäischen Monarchie am preußischen Beispiel 1786–1918", Jägerstraße 22/23, 10117 Berlin – ulrike.marlow@bbaw.de

Christof Muigg, Universität Wien, Institut für Geschichte, Universitätsring 1, 1010 Wien, Österreich – christof.muigg@univie.ac.at

Laura Viktoria Potzuweit, Christian-Albrechts-Universität zu Kiel, Historisches Seminar, Abteilung für Regionalgeschichte, Leibnizstraße 8, 24118 Kiel, Deutschland – potzuweit@histosem.uni-kiel.de

Christof Rolker, Universität Bamberg, Historische Grundwissenschaften, Am Kranen 12, 96047 Bamberg, Deutschland – christof.rolker@uni-bamberg.de

Frederieke Maria Schnack, Julius-Maximilians-Universität Würzburg, Institut für Geschichte, Am Hubland, 97074 Würzburg, Deutschland – frederieke.schnack@uni-wuerzburg.de

Jörg Schwarz, Universität Innsbruck, Institut für Geschichtswissenschaften und Europäische Ethnologie, Innrain 52 d, 6020 Innsbruck, Österreich – joerg.schwarz@uibk.ac.at

Carina Siegl, Universität Wien, Institut für Geschichte, Universitätsring 1, 1010 Wien, Österreich – carina.siegl@univie.ac.at

Sabine Veits-Falk, Stadtarchiv Salzburg, Glockengasse 8, 5020 Salzburg, Österreich – Sabine.Veits-Falk@stadt-salzburg.at

Weitere Hefte von „L'Homme. Europäische Zeitschrift für Feministische Geschichtswissenschaft"

35. Jg., Heft 2 (2024)
vor Gericht
hg. von Maria Fritsche
und Ulrike Krampl

176 Seiten, kartoniert
€ 25,– D / € 26,– A
ISBN 978-3-8471-1738-4
eBook: € 23,–
ISBN 978-3-8470-1738-7

35. Jg., Heft 1 (2024)
Ukraïne
hg. von Dietlind Hüchtker
und Claudia Kraft

175 Seiten, kartoniert
€ 25,– D / € 26,– A
ISBN 978-3-8471-1677-6
eBook: € 23,–
ISBN 978-3-8470-1677-9

Vorschau:

36. Jg., Heft 2 (2025)
Migration
hg. von Ulrike Krampl,
Kristina Schulz
und Xenia von Tippelskirch

Erscheint im Herbst 2025

37. Jg., Heft 1 (2026)
Dis-Ability
hg. von Anelia Kassabova
und Claudia Opitz-Belakhal

Erscheint im Frühjahr 2026

L'Homme Schriften

Bd. 29: Maximiliane Berger /
Mirjam Hähnle / Anna Leyrer (Hg.)

Männer über sich
Wissenschaft – Biografie – Geschlecht
2024. 166 Seiten mit einer Abbildung, gebunden
€ 45,– D / € 47,– A
ISBN 978-3-8471-1688-2
Open Access
ISBN 978-3-7370-1688-9

Bd. 28: Veronika Helfert

Frauen, wacht auf!
Eine Frauen- und Geschlechtergeschichte von
Revolution und Rätebewegung in Österreich,
1916–1924
2021. 399 Seiten mit 15 Abbildungen, gebunden
€ 50,– D / € 52,– A
ISBN 978-3-8471-1184-9
eBook: € 50,– D
ISBN 978-3-8470-1184-2

Vandenhoeck & Ruprecht Verlage

www.vandenhoeck-ruprecht-verlage.com

Ältere Ausgaben von „L'Homme. Z. F. G." (1990 bis 2015) sind im Böhlau Verlag erschienen und über die Redaktion erhältlich: https://lhomme.univie.ac.at/ und lhomme.geschichte@univie.ac.at

Heft 26, 2 (2015)
Maria Fritsche, Anelia Kassabova (Hg.)
Visuelle Kulturen

Heft 26, 1 (2015)
Ulrike Krampl, Xenia
von Tippelskirch (Hg.)
mit Sprachen

Heft 25, 2 (2014)
Gabriella Hauch, Monika Mommertz,
Claudia Opitz-Belakhal (Hg.)
Zeitenschwellen

Heft 25, 1 (2014)
Margareth Lanzinger, Annemarie
Steidl (Hg.)
Heiraten nach Übersee

Heft 24, 2 (2013)
Claudia Ulbrich, Gabriele Jancke,
Mineke Bosch (Hg.)
Auto/Biographie

Heft 24, 1 (2013)
Ingrid Bauer, Christa Hämmerle (Hg.)
Romantische Liebe

Heft 23, 2 (2012)
Almut Höfert, Claudia Opitz-Belakhal,
Claudia Ulbrich (Hg.)
Geschlechtergeschichte global

Heft 23, 1 (2012)
Mineke Bosch, Hanna Hacker, Ulrike
Krampl (Hg.)
Spektakel

Heft 22, 2 (2011)
Sandra Maß, Kirsten Bönker, Hana
Havelková (Hg.)
Geld-Subjekte

Heft 22, 1 (2011)
Karin Gottschalk, Margareth
Lanzinger (Hg.)
Mitgift

Heft 21, 2 (2010)
Caroline Arni, Edith Saurer (Hg.)
**Blut, Milch und DNA. Zur Geschichte
generativer Substanzen**

Heft 21, 1 (2010)
Bożena Chołuj, Ute Gerhard, Regina
Schulte (Hg.)
Prostitution

Heft 20, 2 (2009)
Ingrid Bauer, Hana Havelková (Hg.)
Gender & 1968

Heft 20, 1 (2009)
Ulrike Krampl, Gabriela Signori (Hg.)
Namen

Heft 19, 2 (2008)
Christa Hämmerle,
Claudia Opitz-Belakhal (Hg.)
Krise(n) der Männlichkeit?

Heft 19, 1 (2008)
Ute Gerhard, Karin Hausen (Hg.)
Sich Sorgen – Care

Heft 18, 2 (2007)
Caroline Arni, Susanna Burghartz (Hg.)
Geschlechtergeschichte, gegenwärtig

Heft 18, 1 (2007)
Gunda Barth-Scalmani,
Regina Schulte (Hg.)
Dienstbotinnen

Heft 17, 2 (2006)
Margareth Lanzinger, Edith
Saurer (Hg.)
Mediterrane Märkte

Heft 17, 1 (2006)
Ingrid Bauer, Christa Hämmerle (Hg.)
Alter(n)

Heft 16, 2 (2005)
Mineke Bosch, Hanna Hacker (Hg.)
Whiteness

Heft 16, 1 (2005)
Ute Gerhard, Krassimira
Daskalova (Hg.)
Übergänge. Ost-West-Feminismen

Heft 15, 2 (2004)
Erna Appelt, Waltraud Heindl (Hg.)
Auf der Flucht

Heft 15, 1 (2004)
Caroline Arni, Gunda Barth-Scalmani,
Ingrid Bauer, Christa Hämmerle, Margareth Lanzinger, Edith Saurer (Hg.)
Post/Kommunismen

Heft 14, 2 (2003)
Susanna Burghartz, Brigitte
Schnegg (Hg.)
Leben texten

Heft 14, 1 (2003)
Gunda Barth-Scalmani, Brigitte Mazohl-Wallnig, Edith Saurer (Hg.)
Ehe-Geschichten

Heft 13, 2 (2002)
Mineke Bosch, Francisca de Haan, Claudia Ulbrich (Hg.)
Geschlechterdebatten

Heft 13, 1 (2002)
Karin Hausen, Regina Schulte (Hg.)
Die Liebe der Geschwister

Heft 12, 2 (2001)
Waltraud Heindl, Claudia Ulbrich (Hg.)
HeldInnen?

Heft 12, 1 (2001)
Susanna Burghartz, Christa Hämmerle (Hg.)
Soldaten

Heft 11, 2 (2000)
Ute Gerhard, Edith Saurer (Hg.)
Das Geschlecht der Europa

Heft 11, 1 (2000)
Christa Hämmerle, Karin Hausen, Edith Saurer (Hg.)
Normale Arbeitstage

Heft 10, 2 (1999)
Hanna Hacker, Herta Nagl-Docekal, Gudrun Wolfgruber (Hg.)
Glück

Heft 10, 1 (1999)
Erna Appelt (Hg.)
Citizenship

Heft 9, 2 (1998)
Christa Hämmerle, Karin Hausen (Hg.)
Heimarbeit

Heft 9, 1 (1998)
Susanna Burghartz, Edith Saurer (Hg.)
Unzucht

Heft 8, 2 (1997)
Waltraud Heindl, Regina Schulte (Hg.)
Höfische Welt

Heft 8, 1 (1997)
Hg. vom Herausgeberinnen-Gremium der L'Homme. Z. F. G.
Vorstellungen

Heft 7, 2 (1996)
Andrea Griesebner, Claudia Ulbrich (Hg.)
Gewalt

Heft 7, 1 (1996)
Gunda Barth-Scalmani, Ingrid Bauer, Christa Hämmerle, Gabriella Hauch, Waltraud Heindl, Brigitte Mazohl-Wallnig, Brigitte Rath (Hg.)
Tausendundeine Geschichten aus Österreich

Heft 6, 2 (1995)
Gudrun-Axeli Knapp, Edith Saurer (Hg.)
Interdisziplinarität

Heft 6, 1 (1995)
Erna Appelt, Verena Pawlowsky (Hg.)
Handel

Heft 5, 2 (1994)
Susan Zimmermann, Birgit Bolognese-Leuchtenmüller (Hg.)
Fürsorge

Heft 5, 1 (1994)
Herta Nagl-Docekal (Hg.)
Körper

Heft 4, 2 (1993)
Christa Hämmerle, Bärbel Kuhn (Hg.)
Offenes Heft

Heft 4, 1 (1993)
Hanna Hacker (Hg.)
Der Freundin?

Heft 3, 2 (1992)
Waltraud Heindl, Jana Starek (Hg.)
Minderheiten

Heft 3, 1 (1992)
Hg. vom Herausgeberinnen-Gremium der L'Homme. Z. F. G.
Krieg

Heft 2, 2 (1991)
Brigitte Mazohl-Wallnig, Herta Nagl-Docekal (Hg.)
Intellektuelle

Heft 2, 1 (1991)
Erna Appelt, Edith Saurer (Hg.)
Ernährung

Heft 1, 1 (1990)
Christa Hämmerle, Edith Saurer (Hg.)
Religion

Diese Hefte sind Open Access unter https://lhomme-archiv.univie.ac.at abrufbar.